WALKER PERCY'S VOICES

WALKER PERCY'S VOICES

Michael Kobre

THE UNIVERSITY OF GEORGIA PRESS

ATHENS AND LONDON

© 2000 by the University of Georgia Press
Athens, Georgia 30602
All rights reserved
Designed by Betty Palmer McDaniel
Set in 10.5 on 13 Bembo by Betty Palmer McDaniel
Printed and bound by Maple-Vail Book Group
The paper in this book meets the guidelines for
permanence and durability of the Committee on
Production Guidelines for Book Longevity of the
Council on Library Resources.

Printed in the United States of America
04 03 02 01 00   C   5 4 3 2 1

Library of Congress Cataloging-in-Publication Data
Kobre, Michael, 1957–
   Walker Percy's voices / Michael Kobre.
      p.   cm.
   Includes bibliographical references (p.   ) and index.
   ISBN 0-8203-2140-0 (alk. paper)
   1. Percy, Walker, 1916–   —Criticism and interpretation.
2. Bakhtin, M. M. (Mikhail Mikhaĭlovich), 1895–1975—Contributions
in criticism. 3. Psychological fiction, American—History and criticism.
4. Interpersonal relations in literature. 5. Dialectic in literature. I. Title.
PS3566.E6912Z737   2000
813'.54—dc21   99-31362

British Library Cataloging-in-Publication Data available

for Suz-Anne,
whose voice echoes
in my heart and mind,

and

for Hannah,
whose voice
is just emerging.

Contents

Acknowledgments

No one can complete a project like this without the help of many others. I am indebted, first, to all those other writers whose books and essays on Walker Percy I have drawn on in my own work. Even when I disagreed with their conclusions, they helped define the territory that I knew I must explore, and I felt privileged to enter into a critical dialogue with them. Perhaps most of all, my greatest scholarly debt is to Dr. Dean McWilliams of Ohio University, who showed me the enormous potential of Mikhail Bakhtin's critical theory. That discovery opened a new world of possibilities and allowed me to find my own place in the critical dialogue on Percy's writings.

I am also thankful to all of those who helped with the preparation of this book. At the University of Georgia Press, Malcolm L. Call guided me through the long process of editorial consideration with patience and good humor. I am particularly grateful to Robert H. Brinkmeyer Jr. and John F. Desmond, who read this book in manuscript for the press; their comments helped me to see clearly both the potential of this book and the ways it might be strengthened. I also thank Ellen D. Goldlust-Gingrich for her sharp-eyed and sensitive copyediting, which saved me from any number of embarrassing mistakes. As a neophyte in the arcane ways of computers, I am indebted to my friends Colleen Beale and Beth Arundell for their crucial last-minute technical support; they found the solutions when I didn't even know the right questions.

I am grateful, too, for the friendship and support of my colleagues at Queens College, who provided both the gift of time—a leave of absence near the end of this project—and a grant from the Professional Development Committee. I am also grateful—in ways that are difficult to define precisely—to the students in my literature classes at Queens. Their insights, their questions, and their enthusiasm have continually reminded me of the real power and beauty of literature. I particularly acknowledge my students over the years in English 460, "Studies in Literature and Criticism," who have kept me honest and reminded me of the importance of clarity and grace in critical writing.

Of course, I am also immensely grateful to Dr. Percy himself, whose works moved and inspired and intrigued me. Studying his work so closely for so long has been, without doubt, the greatest intellectual experience of my life.

On a personal level, I am grateful to my parents for their long years of patience and support. You see, Mom and Dad, *at last*, this book is finished.

Finally, my greatest debt is to Suz-Anne Kinney, who every day shared both the exhilaration and the despair of writing this work. In the truest sense, I wrote this work both for and with her.

Abbreviations

Con. Lewis A. Lawson and Victor A. Kramer, eds. *Conversations with Walker Percy.* Jackson: UP of Mississippi, 1985.

LC Walker Percy. *Lost in the Cosmos: The Last Self-Help Book.* New York: Farrar, Straus, and Giroux, 1983.

Ll Walker Percy. *Lancelot.* New York: Farrar, Straus, and Giroux, 1977.

LG Walker Percy. *The Last Gentleman.* New York: Farrar, Straus, and Giroux, 1966.

LR Walker Percy. *Love in the Ruins: The Adventures of a Bad Catholic at a Time Near the End of the World.* New York: Farrar, Straus, and Giroux, 1971.

MB Walker Percy. *The Message in the Bottle: How Queer Man Is, How Queer Language Is, and What One Has to Do with the Other.* 1975. New York: Farrar, Straus, and Giroux, 1980.

MG Walker Percy. *The Moviegoer.* New York: Knopf, 1961.

More Con. Lewis A. Lawson and Victor A. Kramer, eds. *More Conversations with Walker Percy.* Jackson: UP of Mississippi, 1993.

SC Walker Percy. *The Second Coming.* New York: Farrar, Straus, and Giroux, 1980.

SSL Walker Percy. *Signposts in a Strange Land.* Ed. Patrick Samway. New York: Farrar, Straus, and Giroux, 1991.

TS Walker Percy. *The Thanatos Syndrome.* New York: Farrar, Straus, and Giroux, 1987.

WALKER
PERCY'S
VOICES

ONE

A Quality of Consciousness: Walker Percy's Dialogic Art

About a third of the way through Walker Percy's second novel, *The Last Gentleman*, Will Barrett recovers from one of his "spells," fugue states in which he is afflicted with temporary amnesia, not far from a Civil War battlefield in Virginia. Will, as we are told early in the novel, is the last son of "an honorable and violent [southern] family" (9). Yet he lives in an uneasy tension with his heritage, at various times trying to follow in the footsteps of his ancestors and to distance himself from the past. For Will, wandering through an unsettled American landscape in the early 1960s, it is increasingly difficult to assert his patrician heritage in the face of a rapidly changing social structure and the rise of the civil rights movement. And so, unable to come to terms with his past, to comfortably accept or reject his legacy, Will simply forgets it—at least until the tectonic pressures in his unconscious mind build to such a level that he is driven once again to one of the sacred grounds of his inheritance, like this Virginia battlefield where he asserts his identity in oddly stilted language: "My name is Williston Bibb Barrett, he said aloud, consulting his wallet to make sure, and I am returning to the South to seek my fortune and restore the good name of my family, perhaps even recover Hampton plantation [the family estate] from the canebrakes and live out my days as a just man and a little father to the faithful Negroes working in the fields. Moreover, I am in love with a certain someone. Or I shall marry me a wife and live me a life in the lovely green environs of Atlanta or Memphis or even Birmingham, which, despite its bad name, is known to have lovely people" (144–45).

Despite his seeming embrace of his family's patrician values in this passage, Will is as conflicted as ever. What we hear instead of a single-voiced articulation of deeply felt values and beliefs is a kind of pastiche, an awkward conjunction of antebellum gentility and postmodern uncertainty. In the beginning of this passage, Will tries to submerge himself in the ethos and traditions of the old, agrarian South. When he declares his intentions to "recover Hampton plantation" and "restore" his family's "good name," he seems to embrace the collective voice of his "honorable and violent family." But when he speaks of being "a little father to the faithful Negroes working in the fields," his language is too broad to be read without irony, the claim itself exaggerated to the point of caricature. Though I do not think Will is consciously mocking himself here, he cannot repress his knowledge that this sort of paternalism is no longer possible in a South that is slowly being transformed by the civil rights movement (92). Indeed, whenever a tension arises between the values that are ingrained in Will's consciousness and the actual circumstances of life in the United States in the early '60s, the language that he uses to express himself becomes distorted, parodic. Thus, in the middle of the passage, when Will alludes to his love (or perhaps lust) for Kitty Vaught, his flighty inamorata in *The Last Gentleman,* he coyly refers to her as "a certain someone." Because Will is torn between an increasing permissiveness in his culture and his father's almost Manichean code of sexual conduct— "Don't treat a lady like a whore or a whore like a lady"—he adopts a cloying expression of endearment borrowed from "old novels" (97, 51). Even when he surveys the contemporary South in the final sentence of this passage, the tension between his family's values—its belief in what Percy elsewhere describes as the patrician ideal of "toleration and fair-mindedness" (*SSL* 83)—and the violent reality of segregation is too much to bear. So Will brushes aside the "bad name" of Bull Connor's Birmingham and cheerily celebrates its "lovely people" instead, blithely overlooking the fire hoses and police dogs unleashed on peaceful demonstrations.

The tensions in this passage and the stylistic nuances that reveal them are characteristic of both the distinctive landscape of Walker Percy's fiction and of the artistic methods by which he works that landscape. To speak of Percy's artistry first, what we hear in this passage is what the great Russian philosopher and literary theorist Mikhail Bakhtin would call a microdialogue, a kind of internal monologue in which the character's thoughts are saturated with the words and opinions of others (*Dostoevsky* 74). Just as Bakhtin hears in the narrative voices of so many of Dostoevsky's characters "a conflict of

voices," so too is the consciousness of Will Barrett—and of each of Percy's
other protagonists as well—an echo chamber of contending voices, a
cacophony of different values and beliefs (*Dostoevsky* 74). In the passage
above, Will's tentative assimilation of a patrician ideology clearly shows the
influence of his "honorable and violent family," of the voices that he heard
over the course of a privileged youth among a fading aristocracy. But at
the same time, the ironic excesses of his discourse betray another set of
influences. The way that he undermines his own patrician rhetoric suggests
the influence of the many voices heard in contemporary public dialogue that
were critical of the South's rigid segregation and enduring paternalism,
voices to which Will would surely be exposed during his stay in the North.
Indeed, it is possible to say of Will's discourse the same thing that Bakhtin
says of one of Raskolnikov's internal monologues: "Dialogue has penetrated
inside every word, provoking in it a battle and the interruption of one voice
by another" (*Dostoevsky* 75).

At its core—as I will argue over the course of this book—the form and
method of Walker Percy's fiction exemplify Bakhtin's concept of the dialogic novel.[1] The most distinctive artistic quality of Percy's fiction is the interaction of different voices and of what Bakhtin would call "socio-
ideological languages" ("Discourse" 272), roiling and churning through
Percy's supple, nuanced prose. For Percy was not only adept at theorizing
about language—the system itself, langue—in his nonfiction; he was just as
interested in parole, in the quirky, humorous, often poetic ways that the
people he came in contact with used language. And gifted with as deft and
acute an ear as any novelist this side of James Joyce, he was able to marvelously re-create what he heard, from the language of the Mississippi Delta,
where he grew up, to the conversation in the halls of Columbia University's
College of Physicians and Surgeons, where he mastered the arcane vocabulary of science.

Indeed, Percy's extraordinary sensitivity to the way that specific people in
specific places and times use language leads us back to the distinctive landscape of his fiction, for Bakhtin's poetics of the dialogic novel is also ines-
capably a social poetics. As he states at the beginning of his magisterial essay
"Discourse in the Novel," "the study of verbal art can and must overcome
the divorce between an abstract 'formal' approach and an equally abstract
'ideological' approach. Form and content in discourse are one, once we understand that verbal discourse is a social phenomenon—social throughout
its entire range and in each and every of its factors, from the sound image to

the furthest reaches of abstract meaning" (259). Throughout his work,
Bakhtin insists on the social matrix that shapes both language and—perhaps
its most complex expression—literary style. His ideas are profoundly incompatible with a New Critical approach that seeks a state of organic unity
somewhere above and beyond the specific constraints of history and biography and with the closed linguistic loop of poststructuralist thought in which
the unstable signifier leads only back on itself. Bakhtin could never agree
with Derrida's famous dictum, "There is nothing outside the text," because
for Bakhtin, as we will see, the world—in all its inherent contradiction and
heterogeneity—is inevitably present in every phrase that passes through a
speaker's lips, in every sentence a writer composes. The fact of human voices
using language over thousands of years has permeated the language itself.
Simply put, the word cannot be pried loose from its social context. For
Bakhtin, the tensile, multivoiced language that novelists like Percy use in
their fiction is inevitably forged in the crucible of social interaction. As
Bakhtin writes later in "Discourse in the Novel," "The living utterance, having taken meaning and shape at a particular historical moment in a socially
specific environment, cannot fail to brush up against thousands of living dialogic threads, woven by socio-ideological consciousness around the given
object of an utterance; it cannot fail to become an active participant in social
dialogue" (276).

Given Bakhtin's insistence on the social context of language, it is no surprise, then, that the microdialogue we hear in Will's discourse is so deeply
rooted in "a particular historical moment." Will's confusion in the passage
above is representative of all of Percy's protagonists, with one foot planted in
the rich soil and traditions of the Old South and the other poised uncer-
tainly on the shifting ground of a postmodern world dominated by com-
merce, technology, and an increasingly ambiguous moral relativism. Percy
was himself a child of the old southern culture, born into an aristocratic
family that could trace its roots in the American South back to the pre-
revolutionary period. After Percy's death in 1990, the distinguished critic
Lewis P. Simpson wrote that "the last generation of southern writers to write
with a knowledge of the high culture of the patrician South in their bones
has all but disappeared" (927). And yet Percy also recognized that the severe
and honorable traditions he had inherited were increasingly outdated in a
New South that was, in his own words, "happy, victorious, Christian, rich,
patriotic and Republican" (LG 177). He was, if anything, an uneasy patrician. And as his biographers and critics have shown, it was largely out of his

own struggle to at once transcend and come to terms with his legacy as the son of an aristocratic family that Percy arrived at the most momentous decisions of his life: to turn his back on a career in medicine—one of the select professions appropriate for a man of his class—and pursue his vocation as a writer, and, at age thirty-one, in an act that broke radically with the patrician's mild religiosity, to convert to Catholicism.

At some level, that struggle in his own life enabled Percy to document the "particular historical moment" when a gleaming, prosperous New South rose up on the foundation of the Old. Though he often denied Faulkner's influence, it is hard not to see Percy as writing the next chapter in the story that Faulkner began. For Percy's characters do not wrap their fingers through a metal fence like Benjy Compson and look on with a confused sadness at the golf course that was once their patrimony; they boldly march across the fairway with clubs and caddies in tow, as comfortable and easy as the lords of this new world. Indeed, though Percy once in a rare acknowledgment of Faulkner's influence described Binx Bolling, the protagonist of *The Moviegoer,* as a version of "Quentin Compson who didn't commit suicide," that remark is partially misleading (*Con.* 300). Binx is actually of the next generation of alienated young southerners, after Quentin's—and Binx's own suicidal father's–generation. Binx is, unlike Quentin, an inhabitant of the modern South that Quentin anticipated yet could not endure. This story that Percy takes up from Faulkner is embodied in the dialogue of voices and perspectives that we hear in his fiction, where it sounds alongside many other dissonant voices—scientists, believers, moralists, devotees of Hollywood's beautiful illusions—contending for influence in the echoing consciousnesses of his protagonists. In this book, I will describe how that dialogue works, for I believe it is the key to Percy's artistry and achievement as a novelist.

In many ways, it was inevitable that Percy would write dialogic fiction. His particular conception of the novel's function, his conviction about the nature of consciousness, and his enduring devotion to Dostoevsky—the novelist who for Bakhtin best exemplifies the potential of the dialogic imagination–all virtually insured that Percy could write no other kind of fiction. To take the last of these forces first, we have only to note that Dostoevsky's *Notes from the Underground,* a narrative that Bakhtin regards as profoundly dialogic ("The work does not contain a single word gravitating exclusively toward itself and its referential object," Bakhtin writes, "there is not a single monologic word" [*Dostoevsky* 229]), began Percy's long transformation from an uninspired medical student to a novelist. It was one of the first important books that he read during his convalescence from tuberculosis—and one of the books he reread most often (Tolson, *Pilgrim* 183). Indeed, throughout his career, Percy never failed to cite Dostoevsky as one of his most important influences. How could he not, then, have been affected by what Bakhtin calls "the chief characteristic of Dostoevsky's novels," their dialogic form and content (*Dostoevsky* 6)?

More important, though, is Percy's conception of the novel's function in the late twentieth century. In many interviews and essays on his vocation as a novelist, Percy looked back to his medical training and claimed that the novel, in curious times, could function as a diagnostic instrument. As he writes in "Diagnosing the Modern Malaise," "if I believe anything, it is that the primary business of literature and art is cognitive, a kind of finding out and knowing and telling, both in good times and bad, a celebration of the way things are when they are right, and a diagnostic enterprise when they are wrong" (*SSL* 207). And Percy the diagnostician believed that the times in which he wrote were bad indeed. Crudely put, his indictment of the late-modern world (or postmodern perhaps) is as follows. In the late twentieth century, the Judeo-Christian view of humanity as created in the image of God and capable of either sin or salvation has, for the most part, withered away. In its place, the dominant ideology of Western civilization is what might be called a scientific worldview, in which human beings are seen as organisms not qualitatively different from the other organisms that populate the planet. (Though it is not uncommon in the late-modern world to still speak of such things as "the sacredness of the individual," such pieties seem nostalgic at best; they are like vestigial organs, useless remnants of another age.) Moreover, as Percy writes in "Diagnosing the Modern Malaise," "the consciousness of Western man, the layman in particular, has been transformed by a curious misapprehension of the scientific method": he or she regards the scientific method as the ultimate arbiter of truth (*SSL* 210). Yet science, which to a great extent has improved the physical conditions of life for much of humanity, has also left the individual profoundly impoverished, for the scientist, as Percy was fond of pointing out, "cannot utter a single word about an individual thing or creature insofar as it is an individual but only insofar as it resembles other individuals" (*SSL* 211). Consequently, many people in a prosperous consumer society—like the one that Percy's protagonists inhabit—are deprived of some sustaining sense of their own individuality, their own special title to existence, and they find themselves afflicted with a vague, intangible malaise, a sickness unto death. And so for Percy the role of the novelist is to do precisely what the scientist cannot: to explore the nature of individual existence and diagnose its pathology.

In some ways, of course, this concept of using the novel to diagnose the postmodern condition sounds dangerously abstract, yet when Percy is working at the height of his powers, it is not. For his conviction that the special domain of the novelist is individual experience saves him from the sweeping generalizations that, in his own diagnosis of twentieth-century pathology, all too often eclipse the individual. At his best, Percy resists a lofty analysis of this malady in favor of an acute rendering of its symptoms. He adheres to the concrete and the particular because that is the only way to evoke the texture of individual existence.

In practice this approach means that Percy must write a kind of fiction that focuses, first, on the way individuals are fixed in the world, how they perceive and understand experience. As he suggested in "Diagnosing the Modern Malaise," Percy—a diagnostic novelist himself, if ever there was one—begins in the dark burrow of the isolated consciousness that Kafka envisioned and explores what it means to look out at the world from that remove. Relatively early in his career, in fact, in a 1968 interview, he claimed that this emphasis on how the world is perceived by the individual consciousness is the essence of the modern novel:

> Instead of having a large cast of characters, like Tolstoy in *War and Peace,* the tendency now—at least my feeling is—[is] to write from the point of view of one consciousness located in a certain place at a certain time. ... [A] creative work is more apt to be written from the perspective of a single consciousness seeing the world around him. The classical novel took place on a great stage which the reader watched more or less unselfconsciously. In the modern novel, the perspective backs up. What is being presented here is not so much the action on the stage as the experience of the spectator in the privacy of his box. (*Con.* 25)

Though these comments are general in nature, they describe Percy's work as well. He had made that fact clear only moments earlier in the same interview when he explained that the starting point for his fiction was not a theme or an idea but "a situation": "*The Moviegoer,* for example, was conceived by putting a young man in a certain situation, not with the idea of a preconceived story line or certain roster of characters, but with the idea of a young man put down into the world under certain circumstances. In this case the place was Gentilly, a middle class suburb of New Orleans. I'm not primarily concerned with plotting a story. I'm concerned with a certain quality of consciousness put down in a certain place and then seeing what kind of reaction takes place between a character and his environment and the people he meets" (*Con.* 24). If we take Percy at his word here—and I believe we should, even though he made these comments early in his career, before publishing what are apparently more ingenious, plot-driven works like *Love in the Ruins* and *The Thanatos Syndrome*—the imaginative center of his novels is the interaction of the individual's consciousness and the particularities of his or her environment. Percy's fiction, as implied by his comments on the modern novel in general and his own work in particular, dwells heavily on the way that the circumstances of a character's existence resonate in his or her consciousness. But though Percy is of course concerned with "the experience of the spectator in the privacy of his box," he also suggests, in his discussion of the "situation" that inspired *The Moviegoer,* that his character does not just look on at the events on stage in splendid isolation. As Percy makes clear when he speaks of "seeing what kind of reaction takes place between a character and his environment and the people he meets," the character is also affected by what he or she observes. Indeed, although all of Percy's heroes—Binx Bolling, Will Barrett, Tom More, and Lancelot Lamar—try to stand apart from the world by maintaining a proper scientific detachment, they cannot, by theory or force of will, lift themselves out of the crowded world that they share with God's other fallen creatures. Ultimately, the "quality of consciousness" of each of Percy's protagonists is pliant and responsive, both shaping and shaped by the currents of life in which it is immersed.

This interaction has enormous resonance for Percy because of his deeply held convictions about the nature of consciousness and of language and of the vital, inextricable relationship between those two phenomena. To speak of language first, we must note its centrality to Percy's vision of humanity. As he argued throughout his career in his nonfiction, the most important distinction that separates humans from the other creatures that populate the planet is language. Indeed, for Percy, the proper and most accurate term for humanity is not *Homo sapiens* but "*Homo loquens,* man the talker, or *Homo symbolificus,* man the symbol-monger" (*MB* 17). Though some scientists may claim to have taught other species a rudimentary language of signs and gestures, Percy rejects the idea that these apes or pigeons use language as humans do. Rather, he argues that such displays of sign language or tapping out messages on keyboards are really examples of what the philosopher and semiotician Charles Sanders Peirce labeled "the 'dyadic' behavior of stimulus-response sequences" (*LC* 85). In one of his last major public statements, the 1989 Jefferson Lecture sponsored by the National Endowment for the Humanities entitled "The Fateful Rift: The San Andreas Fault in the Modern Mind," Percy told the story of Nim Chimsky, a chimp adopted by a researcher attempting to duplicate the spectacular feats of Washoe, another chimp who had supposedly learned language. But this researcher was disappointed. As Percy tells it, "What he learned was that Nim, though undoubtedly as smart as Washoe, was not really using language. What Nim and Washoe were really doing was responding to small cues by the trainer to do this or that, the appropriate behavior rewarded by a banana or whatever. The trainers were, doubtlessly, not acting in bad faith. What Washoe and Nim Chimsky were exhibiting, however, was not the language behavior of the human two-year-old but the classical reinforced response of the behaviorists" (*SSL* 281–82).

For Percy, the human use of language is markedly different from that of these precocious chimpanzees. Where an ape like Washoe or Nim Chimsky uses gestures and grunts as signs that elicit a particular response to a particular source of pleasure or threat in his environment, humans use words as symbols to name the dazzling multiplicity of things they find in their world.[2] In his essay "Naming and Being," Percy provides a simple example of this distinction: "A father tells his two-year-old child that *this*, pointing to a certain object, is a ball. The child understands him, and whenever his father speaks the word, the child looks for the ball and runs to get it. But this is not naming. The child's understanding is not qualitatively different from the understanding which a dog has of the word 'ball'; it can be construed in terms of response conditioning, sound waves, neural impulses, brain patterns" (*SSL* 130). But then something happens, something that Percy declares is "probably the most portentous happening in the development of the person" (*SSL* 132). The child somehow mysteriously understands that the word *ball* does not necessarily signal that he or she should look for the ball but, rather, "that the sound 'ball' means the round thing" (*SSL* 132). Suddenly, the child has passed over the threshold into a multifarious world filled with things that can be apprehended and known in some deep plenary sense through the names that we together bestow on them. As Percy writes in "Naming and Being," "Naming or symbolization may be defined as the affirmation of the thing as being what it is under the auspices of the symbol" (*SSL* 133).

Perhaps what is most important here—for our purposes at least—is that this process of affirmation is inevitably social. In Percy's words, "an affirmation requires two persons, the namer and the hearer" (*SSL* 133). Indeed, though I referred above to the way that his fiction focuses on "the dark burrow of the isolated consciousness," such terms are, to some degree, misleading. For while Percy's protagonist might very well be isolated in one form or another, his consciousness, in Percy's view, ultimately cannot be, because for Percy consciousness is inherently social. As he repeatedly noted in such essays as "Symbol, Consciousness, and Intersubjectivity" and "Is a Theory of Man Possible?" as well as in the "Semiotic Primer" of *Lost in the Cosmos,* even the etymology of the word *consciousness* is "a knowing-with."[3] We cannot be conscious of something—that is, we cannot attach a name to an object, linking observer, object, and symbol in what Peirce calls "a triadic event"— without implicitly or explicitly addressing that knowledge to someone else: another person who stands before us, an unknown reader (whether real or imagined), even some part of the self engaged in an internal dialogue. (As Percy writes in "Is a Theory of Man Possible?" "I can debate with myself, hassle myself endlessly, and be so thoroughly conscious, knowing-with, that I can't go to sleep. When the dialogue stops, consciousness stops" [*SSL* 125].) The other person is crucial in every act of consciousness because he or she validates through recognition or understanding that fit somehow between the sound *ball,* a little burst in the front of the mouth that settles gently in the back of the throat, and that scuffed round thing lying there in the grass. The other person establishes with me the link between name and thing—an affirmation that is itself an example of what Percy, using the terminology of the philosopher Gabriel Marcel, calls *intersubjectivity,* "that meeting of minds by which two selves take each other's meaning with reference to the same object beheld in common" (*MB* 265).[4] As Percy writes in a crucial early essay, "Symbol, Consciousness, and Intersubjectivity,"

> Denotation, the act of naming, requires the *two,* namer and hearer. My calling this thing a chair is another way of saying that it "is" a chair for you and me. . . . It is inconceivable that a human being raised apart from other humans should ever discover symbolization. For there is no way that I can know this "is" a chair unless you tell me so. But not only are the two a genetic requirement of symbolization—as the presence of two

is a genetic requirement of fertilization—*it is its enduring condition*. Even Robinson Crusoe writing in his journal after twenty years alone on his island is performing a through-and-through social act. Every symbolic formulation, whether it be language, art, or even thought, requires a real or posited *someone else* for whom the symbol is intended as meaningful. (270–71)

What does this belief mean for Percy's fiction? If there are no isolated acts of consciousness, if every thought is in some way addressed to "a real or posited someone else," then the interaction between Percy's protagonist and his environment knows no boundaries. The protagonist's place, his time, the people who surround him, are implicated in every word he speaks, every thought that flashes through his mind. His existence is dialogic, a continuous give-and-take with his environment. And, therefore, if Percy means to explore the nature of individual existence—however well or troubled it may be—he must write a kind of fiction that reflects this truth, that in some fundamental way is itself dialogic.

To understand in more detail the nature of dialogic fiction, we must turn now to the ideas of Mikhail Bakhtin, who described a kind of literature that spoke in many voices while living under a government that tried to compel all of its citizens to speak in a single, uniform voice. Though it is not really accurate, as Bakhtin's biographers Katerina Clark and Michael Holquist note, to see the quiet, circumspect Bakhtin as a dissident intellectual on the order of a Solzhenitsyn (2), Clark and Holquist also suggest that Bakhtin's vision of the novel as a medium in which a single, official language is superseded by the interaction of many different socio-ideological languages serves covertly "as a medium to convey his critique of Stalinist ideology" (268). Indeed, Bakhtin wrote his most comprehensive statement on the dialogic novel, "Discourse in the Novel," in 1934 and 1935, after he had been officially silenced in one of Stalin's purges of the Soviet intelligentsia. In those years, following his arrest in 1929 for participating in various religious discussion groups, Bakhtin was living in exile in Kustani, a small agricultural town in the remote Asian Republic of Kazakhstan, where he survived by taking on the kind of work available to a man with a shadowy political reputation, such as teaching bookkeeping to local pig farmers who were struggling to adapt to Stalin's policy of forced collectivization.

Yet Bakhtin, against all odds, overcame obstacles undreamed of by Western scholars—revolution, war, internal exile—and he produced, often with little hope of publication, a large and varied body of work. In fact, only after decades of neglect, in which his achievements were buried with other victims of Stalin's terror, was Bakhtin rediscovered by Soviet literary scholars at the end of the Khrushchev era, a little more than twelve years before his death in 1975. Beginning with the publication in the Soviet Union of the second edition of *Problems of Dostoevsky's Poetics* in 1963 (the first edition had appeared in 1929, shortly before his arrest, and a favorable review by a communist official probably saved Bakhtin's life), the significance of his work was gradually realized, first in his homeland and then in the West, where Bakhtin's ideas became part of the vogue for literary theory that swept out of France in the late 1960s.

As Clark and Holquist note, however, "Bakhtin did not view himself as primarily a literary theorist. The term that he found closest to what he sought to do was *philosophical anthropology*" (3). Over the course of his life, Bakhtin addressed a wide array of topics, from Freudianism to linguistics to religion, of which literature—and the novel in particular—was only one. Yet throughout Bakhtin's diverse writings there is a powerful intellectual continuity that centers on his view of life itself as an ongoing struggle between those forces that would strive for unity and coherence in human existence and those forces that delight in variety and incongruity.[5] Indeed, Bakhtin's interest in the novel as a literary form reflects this view, for the novel, he contended, was the artistic medium uniquely suited to represent this struggle. As Holquist writes in his introduction to *The Dialogic Imagination,* a collection of four of Bakhtin's key essays on the novel (including "Discourse in the Novel"), all of Bakhtin's work centers on "an almost Manichean sense of opposition and struggle at the heart of existence, a ceaseless battle between centrifugal forces that seek to keep things apart, and centripetal forces that strive to make things cohere. This Zoroastrian clash is present in culture as well as nature, and in the specificity of individual consciousness; it is at work in the even greater particularity of individual utterances. The most complete and complex reflection of these forces is found in human language, and the best transcription of language so understood is the novel" (xviii).

For Bakhtin—who was always interested in the concrete, particular use of language rather than Saussure's abstract system of *langue*—the centrifugal forces he perceived at work in human existence must have first manifest themselves in the diverse, multilingual community of Vilnius, Lithuania, where his family settled in 1904, when he was nine. Vilnius was a city that had known many conquerors, and as a consequence it was a crazy quilt of different traditions and ethnic groups. There, Bakhtin would have heard a kind of linguistic cacophony in which the official language of Lithuania's current rulers, Russian, mingled with its various subject communities' diverse languages: Lithuanian, Polish, and Yiddish. As Clark and Holquist suggest, this smorgasbord of different languages and nationalities seems to have served as a rough model for Bakhtin's concept of heteroglossia, a linguistic phenomenon that is the realization, within the sphere of language, of those centrifugal forces (21–22). For language, as Bakhtin conceives it, is inevitably stratified, dispersed into many separate—though never isolated—languages, so that a single national tongue is itself a polyglot entity comprised of many different types of cultural, ethnic, professional, or generational languages. Yet these separate languages are not merely different linguistic systems; each, in Bakhtin's view, represents a particular perspective on the world, a way of seizing it that is specific to a certain culture or generation. And the interaction of these different socio-ideological languages constitutes heteroglossia, which is itself, as Bakhtin argues in "Discourse in the Novel," the distinguishing feature of novelistic prose:

> The novel can be defined as a diversity of social speech types (sometimes even diversity of languages) and a diversity of individual voices, artistically organized. The internal stratification of any national language into social dialects, characteristic group behavior, professional jargons, generic languages, languages of generations and age groups, tendentious languages, languages of the authorities, of various circles and passing fashions, languages that serve the sociopolitical purposes of the day, even of the hour (each day has its own slogan, its own vocabulary, its own emphases)—this internal stratification present in every language at any given moment of its historical existence is the indispensable prerequisite for the novel as a genre. The novel orchestrates all its themes, the totality of the world of objects and ideas depicted and expressed in it, by means of social diversity of speech types and by the differing individual voices that flourish under such conditions. (262–63)

Ultimately, Bakhtin suggests, the interaction of these different "speech types" or languages allows for what he calls the "dialogization" of the novel's theme (263). Because each of the many languages heard in the novel is linked to a particular culture and a particular way of seeing the world and understanding experience, there is inevitably a dialogue—sometimes tacit, sometimes overt—between these different perspectives.

But the dialogic quality of the novel is not limited to its representation of heteroglossia. In addition to its "diversity of languages," the novel also represents the complex process by which the individual subject, immersed in a world of heteroglot discourse, experiences language. For in Bakhtin's view, the words that we use to express our own beliefs and intentions are themselves contested, shot through with echoes of other voices that we must engage in the very act of using language. As he writes in "Discourse in the Novel,"

> language, for the individual consciousness, lies on the borderline between oneself and the other. The word in language is half someone else's. It becomes "one's own" only when the speaker populates it with his own intention, his own accent, when he appropriates the word, adapting it to his own semantic and expressive intention. Prior to this moment of appropriation, the word does not exist in a neutral and impersonal language (it is not, after all, out of a dictionary that the speaker gets his words!), but rather it exists in other people's mouths, in other people's contexts, serving other people's intentions: it is from there that one must take the word and make it one's own. (293–94)

This struggle to appropriate the words that we use to define ourselves and our own positions on the world is ultimately dialogic, because those words can never be entirely purged of other people's contexts or intentions; an echo or trace will always remain. And an individual's sense of self, which is inevitably expressed in language, is always achieved in relation to those echoes. Does the individual struggle against them and thus use certain words and phrases uncomfortably—as, for example, when we speak ironically and distance ourselves from the literal meaning of our words—or does he or she embrace those echoes, affirming their intentions and assimilating them as his or her own? As Bakhtin suggests, this process constitutes an individual's ideological maturation, his or her formation of a distinctive philosophical position in a clamorous universe of discourse. "The ideological becoming of a human being . . . is the process of selectively assimilating the words of others," he writes in "Discourse in the Novel" (341).

For Bakhtin, the novel is the literary form that can best represent this process. Indeed, throughout "Discourse in the Novel"—and, to a lesser extent, *Problems of Dostoevsky's Poetics*—he argues that the special nature of the novel is its ability to represent the dialogic nature of our life in language. As he contends in "Discourse in the Novel," "The dialogic orientation of a word among other words (of all kinds and degrees of otherness) creates new and significant potential in discourse, creates the potential for a distinctive art of prose, which has found its fullest and deepest expression in the novel" (275). This claim is terribly important because it suggests the unique expressive possibilities of the novel as a form. (It is no accident that Bakhtin speaks of "a *distinctive* art of prose.") For Bakhtin, the novel reveals the stratification of language, the jostle and clamor of many different socio-ideological languages and the perspectives they embody, while demonstrating how one's self and view of the world are formed through dialogue with the countless other perspectives that surround us and echo in our consciousnesses.

I believe that Percy's fiction achieves both of these ends. On a fairly simple level—one easily accessible, perhaps, to a novelist who lived in a region noted for its range of dialects and its deeply ingrained social differences— Percy was keenly aware of the stratification of language. His characters all possess a form of Will Barrett's "radar," "the knack of divining persons and situations," of catching on immediately to the way someone speaks and— through that particular twist of language—the way he or she lives in the world (*LG* 47). In *The Last Gentleman,* Will is so adept at this understanding that within moments of meeting Chandler Vaught, the wealthy patriarch of the Vaught family, and hearing "a lilt in the old man's speech, a caroling in the vowels," Will is able to guess Vaught's northern Alabama upbringing and to reminisce with him as if the two of them were old acquaintances (48). In a short time, in fact, Will ingratiates himself with the rest of the family, though so acute is his radar, so sensitive is he to the most minute verbal cues, that each member of the family takes to him in slightly different way, "each feeling that he was his or her special sort of person." For example, Jamie, the ailing younger son, sees Will as "a fellow technician, like himself an initiate of science," while to Mrs. Vaught he is an heir to the social graces of the Old South, a well-mannered young man from a good family who will maintain the traditions she remembers so fondly. With each of these characters Will speaks a slightly different kind of language. Jamie gives Will a copy of his brother Sutter's article, "The Incidence of Post-Orgasmic Suicide in Male University Graduate Students," with every expectation that the highly tech-nical language of the article will be as comprehensible and meaningful to Will as it is to Jamie himself. But when Will speaks with Mrs. Vaught, his language takes on a different cast; it has a courtly, homespun quality that is reflected in the narrative: "There was a lightness in him: he knew how to fool with her. They could even have a fuss" (62–63).

All of Percy's protagonists have the same ability to catch on to the language of those around them and to hear the intricacies that are encoded in even the simplest exchanges. Early on in *The Thanatos Syndrome,* for example, Dr. Thomas More encounters an old acquaintance, Frank Macon, a black janitor, after Tom's release from prison. (He was sentenced for selling drugs to truckers—a desperate ploy to supplement the income from his failing psychiatric practice.) But when Frank teases More about his release—"I knowed they couldn't hold you! . . . Ain't no police going to hold Doc for long"—More senses a sharper point to Frank's needling than is readily apparent, and his explanation of Frank's intentions exposes the way in which the stratification of language is embodied in the forms of southern life:

> One would have to be a Southerner, white or black, to understand the complexities of this little exchange. Seemingly pleasant, it was not quite. Seemingly a friend in the old style, Frank was not quite. The glint of eye, seemingly a smile of greeting, was not. It was actually malignant. Frank was having a bit of fun with me, I knew, and he knew that I knew, using the old forms of civility to say what he pleased. What he was pleased to say was: So you got caught, didn't you, and you got out sooner than I would have, didn't you? Even his pronunciation of police as pó-lice was overdone and farcical, a parody of black speech, but a parody he calculated I would recognize. Actually he's a deacon and uses a kind of churchy English: Doctor, what we're gerng to do is soliciting contributions for a chicken-dinner benefit the ladies of the church gerng to have Sunday, and suchlike. (11)

As this passage shows, the racial and cultural divisions of the South echo in the subtlest nuances of its natives' speech, and Percy's characters are adept at hearing and interpreting the traces of heteroglossia that flourish in their region's fertile linguistic soil.

But the sensitivity of Percy's characters to the stratification of language leads—indirectly at least—to a more important dialogic quality in his work. Perhaps because Percy's protagonists are so adept at picking up and imitating the way others speak, each character's consciousness is an echo chamber filled with the voices of parents, counselors, friends, lovers, even distant icons of American history and popular culture. Haunted by the storied past of their illustrious families and the tragic history of their native South, acutely conscious of the dreams and foibles of the people who surround them, the minds of Percy's heroes are awash with voices, rife with the clamor of different perspectives. Even the words they use to express themselves come to them wrapped in echoes. (Percy, like Bakhtin, emphasizes the social matrix in which our grasp of language originates. When Percy asserts in "Symbol, Consciousness, and Intersubjectivity" that "there is no way I can know this 'is' a chair unless you tell me so," and when Bakhtin contends in "Discourse in the Novel" that "it is not . . . out of a dictionary that the speaker gets his words," both stress that language is received from other people. Yet as Bakhtin reminds us, one cannot get language from others without also inheriting something of those others' contexts and intentions, and these traces sound in the voices of Percy's protagonists.)

This babel of voices that echoes in the minds of Percy's heroes is their essential condition. This cacophony is the specific quality of consciousness that all of them share. Moreover, the clamorous nature of his protagonists' consciousnesses is also—as I suggested at the beginning of this chapter—the key to Percy's narrative art, for the language of his fiction is dominated by Percy's use of what Bakhtin terms "double-voiced discourse": a kind of language that reveals its own contested status, that is itself the ground of a struggle for ideological dominance within the character's mind. As I noted above, our use of language, in Bakhtin's view, is always, inevitably characterized by a struggle in which we attempt to appropriate the words we will use to express ourselves, either stripping them of other people's contexts or assimilating those contexts as our own. Double-voiced discourse, however, is language in which this struggle is unresolved, in which one hears "a concentrated dialogue of two voices, two world views, two languages" (Bakhtin, "Discourse" 324–25).

In its most intense and inward moments, Percy's prose is always double-voiced. Through his control of diction and phrasing, his mastery of nuance, he enables us to hear this dialogue in the language of his fiction, as in the passage from *The Last Gentleman* that I discussed earlier or in this passage from *Lancelot:* "She [Suellen, one of Lancelot's black servants] had raised me, thousands of Suellens had raised thousands like me, kept us warm in the kitchen, saved us from our fond bemused batty parents, my father screwed up by poesy, dreaming of Robert E. Lee and Lancelot Andrewes and episcopal chapels in the wildwood, and my poor stranded mother going out for joyrides with Uncle Harry" (55). In this sentence, Percy's use of double-voiced discourse enables us to hear again what Bakhtin calls "a micro-

dialogue." Here, the either/or of chivalry or sexuality that bedevils Lancelot
Lamar is embodied in the echoes of his parents' voices that sound in his diction. When Lancelot speaks of his father being "screwed up by poesy," we
hear, in his use of the archaic term "poesy," the voice of his father's quaint,
faded ideals of gentlemanly warriors and religious devotion. Moreover, the
way Lancelot links that archaism with the dismissive and faintly obscene
phrase "screwed up" suggests the collision of Victorian and modern ethos
that is at the heart of his moral confusion. And when, in the same breath, he
also uses his mother's euphemism, "joyrides," to allude to her affair with her
distant cousin, the man politely known as Uncle Harry, her voice too rever-
berates in the narrative with its implications of guilty secrets and repressed
sexuality. In this sentence, then, we hear embodied in two distinct voices—
both of which are subsumed in Lancelot's own voice—the twin poles of the
question that gnaws at him throughout the novel: "Is all niceness or is all
buggery? How can a man be forty-five years old and still not know whether
all is niceness or buggery?" (136–37).

All of Percy's narratives ultimately force his protagonists to sort through
the voices that echo in their minds, identifying with some and rejecting
others. To use Bakhtin's terminology, each of Percy's novels depicts his
protagonist's "ideological becoming," that complex process of self-definition
in which an individual must "selectively [assimilate] the words of others."
Yet in carrying out this project, Percy also dramatically illustrates his diagnosis of our postmodern malaise. For in depicting his characters' struggle to
disentangle their own beliefs from a thick web of others' words and opinions, he also represents the struggle of the individual to formulate a distinctive sense of self in a scientific culture that cannot account for individuals.
After all, what is that process that Bakhtin describes of finding one's own
voice among the echoes that sound in one's consciousness but the struggle
of the individual to define what is unique about himself or herself?

In the end, though, whatever tentative sense of self Percy's characters
achieve can only be sustained in their interaction with others. For as both
Percy and Bakhtin suggest, human beings can never truly see themselves,
never fully grasp their own identities. "In a word, the self can perceive, formulate, symbolize everything under the sun except itself," Percy writes in
"Is a Theory of Man Possible?" "A self stands in the dead center of its universe looking out. The paradox of consciousness is that the stranger we meet
on the street and glance at for a second or two we see more clearly than we
shall ever see ourselves" (SSL 126–27). How, then, can one sustain even a

tenuous sense of self (assuming, that is, that one's self is more than a dissonant chorus of voices articulating radically different beliefs)? Only through
the mediation of another human being, another sovereign subject. Though
Percy is evasive on this point, he speaks suggestively of the role of the other
in an "I-Thou" relationship. In "Symbol as Hermeneutic in Existentialism,"
he describes the other as "the companion and co-celebrant of my discovery
of being" who plays "a unique and indispensable role in the sustaining and
validating of my consciousness" (*MB* 285). On the most fundamental level,
Percy means that the other validates our perceptions by recognizing a world
in common that can be apprehended through the medium of language and
tacitly consenting to the appropriateness of the words we use to symbolize—or name—that world. (And this social interaction is, Percy argues, the
very ground of consciousness. "The *I think* is only made possible by a prior
mutuality: *we name,*" he writes [*MB* 275]. This idea, of course, is the root of
Percy's belief that consciousness itself is a social phenomenon, "a knowing-
with.") But he also suggests that the other plays a crucial role in our formulation of self. For where the other validates our perceptions of a world beheld in common and subsumed under the auspices of the symbol, he or she
may also deny the validity of a false self, an inauthentic formulation of identity. As Percy writes, "Whatever devious constitution of self I have been able
to arrive at, whatever my 'self-esteem,' my impersonation, it melts away before the steady gaze of another" (*MB* 285). Indeed, Percy suggests that what
the other's look ultimately reveals "is literally my *unspeakableness* (unformulability)" (*MB* 285).

The consequences of this phenomenon are harsh, however, with the self
trapped between the Scylla of inauthenticity and the Charybdis of unformulability (a tormented state that Percy explores at length in his wicked
parody of self-help books, *Lost in the Cosmos*). Yet human beings, as his novels
ultimately suggest, can retain sovereignty over their lives and achieve at least
a provisional sense of self that is not wholly false. For what Percy does not
say here—though it is hinted at perhaps by implication—is what Bakhtin
argues at length in his early philosophical essays: that the other who exposes
one's inauthenticity can also delimit and confirm a rough sense of one's own
ultimately unformulable self (for Bakhtin believes that a human being can
never be fully, finally defined; one is always unfinished, capable of change).
Indeed, for Bakhtin, another human being is not a Sartrean antagonist whose
look challenges one's fragile authenticity but a coconceiver of one's self, a
source of one's own identity. Whatever definable self we have is based on the

images of ourselves that we receive from others, he argues. As Clark and Holquist write in their intellectual biography of Bakhtin, "my I-for-myself is always invisible. In order to perceive that self, it must find expression in categories that can fix it, and these I can only get from the other. So that when I complete the other, or when the other completes me, she and I are actually exchanging the gift of a perceptible self. This is what Bakhtin means when he argues that we get our selves from others; I get a self I can see, that I can understand and use, by clothing my otherwise invisible (incomprehensible, unutilizable) self in the completing categories I appropriate from the other's image of me" (79).

Perhaps this is why Percy's novels always end with his characters entering into an intimate relationship or standing on the brink of a profound, potentially life-changing dialogue. Their quest for self at last finds its object in a field of interaction with others, where one's inauthentic self is exposed or one's real self is validated "in the discovering look of another" (*MB* 285).[6] The secret microdialogue of the protagonist ultimately must be echoed in an external dialogue with another character whose essential sympathy with the protagonist may or may not represent the intervention of grace. (Percy explicitly raises this question at the end of *The Second Coming,* a profoundly hopeful work that he once called "my first unalienated novel" [*Con.* 183].) Indeed, dialogue is the message and method of Percy's art. It dominates the language and the structure of his novels, and it also serves as the ultimate object of his characters' anguished searches. In a very real sense, the intense interaction with another troubled soul that ends all of his novels is itself the homeland that his protagonists achieve after many adventures, the welcoming shores on which they may fling their tired spirits. "*L'enfer c'est autrui,*" Percy writes in "Symbol as Hermeneutic in Existentialism," quoting Sartre's despairing view of human interaction. "But so is heaven," he adds (*MB* 285).[7] At its center, Percy's fiction celebrates our interaction with others as the source and guarantor of our identities and as the only earthly paradise we shall know.

TWO

Out of the Evening
Land: *The Moviegoer*

A few pages into Walker Percy's first novel, *The Moviegoer,* the protagonist, Binx Bolling, describes his life in Gentilly, a middle-class suburb of New Orleans:

> Life in Gentilly is very peaceful. I manage a small branch office of my uncle's brokerage firm. My home is the basement apartment of a raised bungalow belonging to Mrs. Schexnaydre, the widow of a fireman. I am a model tenant and a model citizen and take pleasure in doing all that is expected of me. My wallet is full of identity cards, library cards, credit cards. Last year I purchased a flat olive-drab strongbox, very smooth and heavily built with double walls for fire protection, in which I placed my birth certificate, college diploma, honorable discharge, G.I. insurance, a few stock certificates, and my inheritance: a deed to ten acres of a defunct duck club down in St. Bernard's Parish, the only relic of my father's many enthusiasms. It is a pleasure to carry out the duties of a citizen and to receive in return a receipt or a neat styrene card with one's name on it, certifying, so to speak, one's right to exist. What satisfaction I take in appearing the first day to get my auto tag and brake sticker! I subscribe to *Consumer Reports* and as a consequence I own a first-class television set, an all but silent air conditioner and a very long lasting deodorant. My armpits never stink. I pay attention to all spot announcements on the radio about mental health, the seven signs of cancer and safe driving—though, as I say, I usually prefer to ride the bus. (6–7)

Binx is, as he makes out here, very nearly the quintessential suburbanite: living modestly, working steadily, careful to budget his expenses and watch over his health. He is, in his own reckoning, the model of a well-adjusted young man in America in the late 1950s. And yet something is awry here. The very tone in which Binx describes his life, calculated to seem moderate and reasonable, is somehow excessive. When, for example, he tells us "It is a pleasure to carry out the duties of a citizen and to receive in return a receipt or a neat styrene card with one's name on it, certifying, so to speak, one's right to exist," his claim is inflated to the point of absurdity. In much the same way, when he says he owns a "very long lasting deodorant" and then claims that his "armpits never stink," he adopts a blunt, mildly vulgar way of speaking that deliberately undercuts the kind of modesty a product like deodorant is supposed to abet.

What is going on here? This passage—often quoted in the criticism of Percy's fiction, typical of Binx's mind-set at the beginning of the novel—clearly exemplifies the play of voices, the deliberate discordance that is itself the essential quality of Walker Percy's artistic method. For in Bakhtin's terms, this passage is an example of "double-voiced discourse." If we are attentive, we can hear—as Bakhtin does in the exclamations of so many of Dostoevsky's characters—"a conflict of voices" in Binx's utterance (*Dostoevsky* 74). On the one hand, Binx has adopted here the voice of middle-class America. He apparently subscribes to its values and ideology, and he is comfortable using its language to describe himself: "I am a model tenant and a model citizen." On the other hand, another kind of language, one that is more florid and ironic, is also manifest. Even as he proudly describes himself as "a model tenant and a model citizen," he cannot help but chip away at those labels by suggesting, in the same breath, the conformity that they enforce: "and [I] take pleasure in doing all that is expected of me." Indeed, Binx seems to suggest in this passage that "the duties of a citizen" entirely consist of being a thrifty consumer and carrying proper documentation. For him, citizenship is not a solemn participation in democracy; it is human life reduced to cipher, a digit on a credit card.

The easy interpretation of this conflict of voices is that one is more real than the other, that Binx wears the mask of "a model citizen," but his real self speaks in a disaffected voice. Yet it is much too simple to see Binx as a kind of underground man alienated from the society around him and contemptuous of its values. As Richard Pindell notes in "Basking in the Eye of the Storm: The Esthetics of Loss in Walker Percy's *The Moviegoer*," Binx's use of irony is considerably more complex: "Aroused, intelligent, combative, Binx's irony is in a very real way his saving grace. Against the preachers of lifeways, whether the high-minded spokesmen of outworn creeds or the grossly ardent devotees of fashionably and sentimentally conceived self-concept systems, Binx mounts a counterattack. He embarrasses the embarrassers bytaking their words to heart" (109).

In fact, Binx has a genuine appreciation for the comforts and small beauties of life in Gentilly, and that appreciation belies the idea that he has chosen to live there so he can stew in his own sense of alienation. Here, for example, is an admiring description of a new elementary school that sits next to Mrs. Schexnaydre's bungalow: "Everything is so spick and span: the aluminum sashes fitted into the brick wall and gilded in the sunset, the pretty terrazzo floors and the desks molded like wings. Suspended by wires above the door is a schematic sort of bird, the Holy Ghost I suppose. It gives me a pleasant sense of the goodness of creation to think of the brick and the glass and the aluminum being extracted from common dirt—though no doubt it is less a religious sentiment than a financial one, since I own a few shares of Alcoa. How smooth and well-fitted and thrifty the aluminum feels!" (10).

Once again, we can hear an astonishing combination of voices in this passage. Binx is omnivorous in his use of language, taking in and echoing almost everything he hears in his culture, so that a soap commercial ("Everything is so spick-and-span") blends into a sermon ("It gives me a pleasant sense of the goodness of creation"). But what stands out here is the lyrical quality of Binx's attention, his admiration of the symmetry and solidity of the school. As Percy remarked in an interview in 1968, Binx "liked the quality of the sky out there in Gentilly. He liked the new parochial school across the street, made of brick and aluminum and glass. He had an appreciation for these mass manufactured objects. It's very easy to sneer at mass society or the American suburb, but there are many beauties there" (*Con.* 28).

The conflict of voices that sounds in Binx's narrative is ultimately evidence of his tenuous position in a complicated ideological universe. For all his cleverness and his pretense of stability, Binx is buffeted by philosophical and cultural forces that he cannot comfortably reject or assimilate. So, characteristically, he takes a middle course. He adopts a disengaged, ironic posture that admits no allegiances to any ideology but his own bemused skepticism (and, at times, to that vague enterprise he calls "the search," a topic I

will address later). This stance is why Binx is so careful to undercut his description of himself as "a model tenant and a model citizen." He is signaling
to us that he transcends this role. To use the terminology that Bakhtin de-
ploys in *Problems of Dostoevsky's Poetics*, Binx's claim to be "a model tenant
and a model citizen" is an example of "a word with a loophole": "A loophole is the retention for oneself of the possibility for altering the ultimate,
final meaning of one's own words. If a word retains such a loophole, this must
inevitably be reflected in its structure. This potential other meaning, that is,
the loophole, left open, accompanies the word like a shadow. Judged by its
meaning alone, the word with a loophole should be an ultimate word and
does present itself as such, but in fact it is only the penultimate word and
places after itself only a conditional, not a final, period" (233). For Binx, then,
the ironic tones that color his description of his "peaceful" life in Gentilly
function as the loophole through which he escapes self-definition. By making his words inconclusive, their intent ambiguous, he tacitly insists that his
real identity is not contained in his profession or his lifestyle. As Bakhtin tells
us, "The loophole makes all the heroes' self definitions unstable" (234). And
as a consequence, Binx is able to forestall any ultimate decisions about his
identity or his direction in life; he need not embrace any particular creed or
ideology. Rather, like Will Barrett in *The Last Gentleman,* Binx can dwell
perpetually in what Percy calls "the sphere of the possible" (*LG* 10). In
theory at least, Binx's life can assume any configuration that he can imagine.

Of course, such a posture can be enormously liberating. Who would not
like to feel that he or she is capable of anything, that every possibility is still
open? But for Binx, who is nearing thirty when the novel begins, it seems
artificial, a kind of stasis. There is a brittle quality to his life in Gentilly that is
represented in the barrenness of his apartment—which is "as impersonal as a
motel room" (78)—in his inability to sleep soundly, and in the inevitably fu-
tile and awkward course of his various liaisons with his secretaries. (Binx is
an acute, if uncomprehending, observer of the disintegration of these relationships. The pattern is always the same, he explains. Just when his anticipation is at its height, something sours. "The air in the office would grow thick
with silent reproaches," he says. "It would become impossible to exchange a
single word or glance that was not freighted with a thousand hidden meanings" [9].) As we note all these things, we must wonder what has brought
him to such a pass. What has made him cocoon himself in this way, weaving
a protective chrysalis of irony and evasion around his life?

We get our first hint of the answer to this question early in the novel

when Binx returns to the home of his great-aunt, Emily Cutrer, who raised
him after the death of his father. On arriving, Binx is greeted at the door by
Mercer, his aunt's African American butler, whom Emily steadfastly sees as
"a faithful retainer, a living connection with a bygone age" (23). But what is
most notable about this brief yet beautifully realized scene (as no less an authority than Cleanth Brooks has observed, Percy "is our most acute com-
mentator on the social life of the South" [34]) is the exquisite discomfort of
both Binx and Mercer with the roles and behavior that tradition demands of
them. Neither man is quite sure what footing to assume around the other.
As Binx explains, Mercer "is thought to be devoted to us and we to him. But
the truth is that Mercer and I are not at all devoted to each other. My main
emotion around Mercer is unease that in threading his way between servility and presumption, his foot might slip. I wait on Mercer, not he on me"
(22). Indeed, despite Emily's vision of Mercer, neither he nor Binx is comfortable in their roles as servant and master at the time in which the novel is
set, this twilight period in the late '50s between the end of legal segregation
and the rise of the civil rights movement. Binx waits on Mercer, anxious not
to offend him or upset his vision of himself, and Mercer, as Binx knows, "has
aspirations" beyond waiting on Emily Cutrer and her family; he lines his
own pockets "by getting kickbacks from the servants and the tradespeople,"
and he likes to think of himself "as a remarkable sort of fellow, a man who
keeps himself well-informed in science and politics" (23–24). But Mercer
can comfortably assimilate neither the deferential voice of a servant—he
walks a tightrope "between servility and presumption"—nor the worldly
voice of the man of affairs. He speaks tentatively of economic competition
("but they still hasn't the factories and the—ah—producing set-up we has")
and he can't even figure out where to physically position himself in his conversation on world affairs with Binx (23). After Mercer lights a fire in the
hearth, Binx observes that the other man "stands facing neither me nor the
fire but in a kind of limbo" (23).

Of course, this limbo is where Binx dwells as well. In this brief scene, not
only do we see the typically difficult, complex relations between Percy's
white, upper-class protagonists and the African Americans with whom they
interact—which is itself an important thread, as we will see, in Percy's depiction of the changing social landscape of the South—but we also observe the
particular dilemma of Percy's almost preternaturally observant, chameleon-
like heroes. As John Blair notes in "To Attend to One's Own Soul: Walker
Percy and the Southern Cultural Tradition," "For Percy, 'Southernness' is, it

seems, as much a matter of dealing with a bewildering surfeit of changing possibilities for identity as it is a sense of the expectations of a traditional community" (78)—expectations that in *The Moviegoer* are embodied in the voice and character of Emily Cutrer. Indeed, just as Blair argues that "Percy would not deny the applicability of a great deal of what Aunt Emily represents in the novel," so too is Binx affected, almost against his will, by his aunt's expectations of him (79). On seeing her for the first time in the novel and engaging in their usual jousting—she, accurately enough, assails him as the "last and sorriest scion of noble stock"—Binx experiences a kind of epiphany: "In a split second, I have forgotten everything, the years in Gentilly, even my search. . . . This is where I belong after all" (26).

In this unguarded, seemingly uncharacteristic moment, we see how powerfully Binx is tied to his family's past. The Bolling family—like the illustrious Percy family—is an aristocratic southern line filled with civic-minded men, lawyers and politicians and doctors, and its storied past is personified by a photograph on Emily's mantel of several generations of the Bolling family men (including, as we will see later, Binx's father, who is, mysteriously, in Binx's words, "not one of them" [25]). Binx, who is fascinated by the photograph, cannot help but describe the elder generation of Bollings in terms that are inseparable from the lore that has grown up around them: "Judge Anse with his drooping mustache and thin cold cheeks, the hard-eyed one who is still remembered for having publicly described a Louisiana governor as a peckerwood son of a bitch; [and] Dr. Wills, the lion headed one, the rumpled country genius who developed a gut anastomosis still in use" (25). We can hear the voice of the family tradition here, a kind of oral history that Binx recites without question or a trace of his usual irony. But the family tradition of noblesse oblige from which he has walked away weighs heavily on Binx. Indeed, his life in Gentilly is, at bottom, a reaction to this tradition. Binx acknowledges this fact in the first chapter of the novel, when he talks about his profession: "I am a stock and bond broker. It is true that my family was somewhat disappointed in my choice of profession. Once I thought of going into law or medicine or even pure science. I even dreamed of doing something great. But there is much to be said for giving up such grand ambitions and living the most ordinary life imaginable, a life without the old longings" (9). As Binx makes clear here, his life in Gentilly is a renunciation of the "grand ambitions" inculcated in him by his family. What he does not say, though, is why he chose to renounce those ambitions for "the most ordinary life imaginable" or why he is still susceptible on occasion to their allure.

To understand Binx's ambivalence to his family's position and history, we must consider his relationship to his aunt, the most dominant influence in his life. Her importance is manifest from the first paragraph on, when Binx tells us of her summoning him for "one of her serious talks" (3). Though there is a bemused, jaunty tone to Binx's account of his aunt's summons, its position in the novel suggests that her request is more important than Binx would like us to believe. Here is the first paragraph of the novel in full: "This morning I got a note from my aunt asking me to come for lunch. I know what this means. Since I go there every Sunday for dinner and today is Wednesday, it can only mean one thing: she wants to have one of her serious talks. It will be extremely grave, either a piece of bad news about her stepdaughter Kate or else a serious talk about me, about the future and what I ought to do. It is enough to scare the wits out of anyone, yet I confess I do not find the prospect altogether unpleasant" (3). So much is established in this quiet beginning. We see, first of all, Binx's analytical nature, the way he probes and anticipates everything at hand, as he calculates the timing of his aunt's invitation. We are also introduced to the novel's main concerns, the twin threads of its spare plot—Kate Cutrer's growing despair and Binx's own apparent lack of purpose—even as the dramatic climax of the novel is foreshadowed: another "serious talk" with his aunt. But what is most important here is the way this passage suggests both Emily Cutrer's influence on Binx and his attempts to deny that influence.

Of course, the glib tone of the passage is itself a kind of denial of its importance. The offhanded way Binx explains the timing of his aunt's invitation seems to minimize its significance, and the hint at the end of the passage that he even looks forward to their likely confrontation suggests that nothing she can say will be very disturbing. And yet almost none of Binx's assertions can be taken at face value. Here, Percy's use of double-voiced discourse underscores the ideological conflict that runs through the novel, for the way that Binx incorporates certain phrases of his aunt's into his own diction reveals a far greater influence than his facetious tone would otherwise indicate. When, for example, Binx considers the possibility that this "serious talk" will concern him, will be "about the future and what I ought to do," we hear her voice echoing within his own. There is an ominous gravity to the phrase "the future and what I ought to do," a sense of obligation that is

so profound and so severe it seems to toll from deep within the words. However, the leaden quality of that phrase—it is all one unit, as heavy and cum-
bersome as a tombstone—cannot be reconciled with the nonchalance of
Binx's voice. It is clearly an example of his aunt's voice sounding within his
own, and try as he might to neutralize her words by placing them in his own
ironic context, he cannot. The fact that we are aware of his effort indicates
its failure.

As if to confirm her influence on him, Binx shifts suddenly in the second
paragraph to the memory of when his aunt first seemed to speak of what he
"ought to do": the day his older brother, Scott, died of pneumonia. Binx was
eight at the time, and he remembers how Emily broke the news of his
brother's death as they walked behind the hospital where Scott had been
cared for. Binx's memory of the moment is as calm and detached as his anticipation of their "serious talk" in the first paragraph. There is no expression
of grief, neither on the dirty street behind the hospital nor in the long cor-
ridor of memory through which his brother's death is seen. He only seems
disturbed when his aunt begins to speak, and even then it is hard to know
why. Is the source of his emotion the loss of his brother or some hint of the
obligation that his aunt is about to place on him? Binx's account of this exchange provides few answers, on the surface at least: "'Jack,' she said, squeez-
ing me tight and smiling at the Negro shacks, 'you and I have always been
good buddies, haven't we?' 'Yes ma'am.' My heart gave a big pump and the
back of my neck prickled like a dog's. 'I've got bad news for you, son.' She
squeezed me tighter than ever. 'Scotty is dead. Now it's all up to you. It's
going to be difficult for you but I know you're going to act like a soldier.'
This was true. I could easily act like a soldier. Was that all I had to do?" (4).

Binx is here entrusted with the same responsibilities that helped drive
Quentin Compson in *The Sound and the Fury* off the bridge over the Charles
River, the pockets of his Sunday suit weighted with lead. When Binx's aunt
tells him, "Scotty is dead. Now it's all up to you," Binx becomes—like
Quentin—the repository of his family's traditions and the embodiment of
its future. As the oldest son in an old southern family, he is charged with its
continuity, but what does that responsibility entail? All Emily tells him is that
he must "act like a soldier." But what does that mean? In the most basic
sense, her words reflect what Percy has called "the broadsword virtues of the
clan" (*SSL* 84), the martial values so revered in upper-class southern families. (As Lewis A. Lawson notes in his discussion of Bolling family values in
"*The Moviegoer* and the Stoic Heritage," "The crowning demonstration of a

vital family virtue has been the death of a warrior in each generation" [*Following* 74].) For Emily, "to act like a soldier" is certainly to accept one's duty without hesitation or doubt—and perhaps, also, to restrain one's emotions: a soldier does not stop to cry over his brother's death. Moreover, as we will see over the course of the novel, she believes that Binx must continue the family tradition of noblesse oblige, that he must, as she will tell him later, "make a contribution" (53).

But where Emily places all her emphasis on the words "like a soldier," Binx's response—"I could easily act like a soldier"—has a different emphasis. For Binx, whose account of these events is overlaid with his adult perspective, the key word in this phrase is *act*. After all, his world now is dominated by the fantasies he watches on the movie screen, and he is good at maintaining a soldier's stoic pose—whether actually in combat, bleeding on a battlefield in Korea, or joking about his wound years later for the benefit of one of his would-be conquests. Above all, though, Binx's claim of being able to "easily act like a soldier" seems to refer to his relationship with his aunt. As we will see through most of the novel, he is remarkably adept at appearing to sympathize with her values, even though his way of life in Gentilly is at odds with them. Early in the novel, Kate Cutrer, Emily's rebellious stepdaughter and Binx's sole confidante, marvels at his ability to maintain his aunt's trust: "And how do you appear so reasonable to Mother?" (43), Kate asks in a voice that seems to mingle admiration and contempt.

But what is most telling about Binx's response to his aunt's admonition "to act like a soldier" is the question at the end of the passage. Here, in the microdialogue of Binx's consciousness, the voice of the adult who recounts the moment almost merges with the perspective of the child who experiences it. If earlier we could hear the ironic tones of the adult Binx in his assurance "I could easily act like a soldier," the question that follows this assertion—"Was that all I had to do?—has a different tenor. Binx's confusion as an adult is as real as the confusion he felt standing behind the hospital twenty-one years earlier. He still does not know if all he has to do is "act like a soldier." But where as a child he might have wondered if that meant holding back his sorrow over his brother's death, the question has larger implications now. It raises the issue of whether Emily tacitly sanctions the kind of imposture at which Binx excels. When he says "I could easily act like a soldier" and then wonders "Was that all I had to do?" he seems to ask if her real concern is with a kind of gesture, a certain aristocratic demeanor, rather than a deeper sense of engagement with the world. Is all that she really requests of him a type of behavior appropriate to his station as the scion of an old southern family? Does it even matter what motivates that behavior: a feeling of empathy for other human beings or simple adherence to family tradition?

The mingled tones we hear in the last three sentences of this passage, that combination of deference and skepticism, characterize Binx's relationship with his aunt. His affection for her and his desire to win her approval are genuine: he is all too pleased "to act like a soldier." More important, though, as his reaction on entering her house suggests—"This is where I belong after all"—he does find value in her beliefs, for they offer, if nothing else, a clear sense of direction, a way out of the stasis that marks his life in Gentilly. But there is something insufficient about his aunt's perspective that he cannot overlook, and even at those moments when he seems to be on the brink of embracing her values, of assimilating her voice and perspective, his skepticism returns.

When, for example, Binx tries to envision the kind of life she desires for him as they talk after lunch on the day on which the novel begins, his imagination quickly falters. "It seems so plain when I see it through her eyes," he thinks. "My duty in life is simple. I go to medical school. I live a long useful life serving my fellowman. What's wrong with this? All I have to do is remember it" (54). Here, Binx tries to appropriate his aunt's voice and values, so much so that he speaks without irony of "my duty in life," using the kind of exhortatory phrase that comes naturally to Emily. But the terse sentences he uses to sum up this potential life suggest no joy or satisfaction. They are like three doses of bitter medicine that must be swallowed quickly and without protest. Yet Binx is not compliant. When he voices his question, "What's wrong with this?"—which recalls that other nagging question, "Was that all I had to do?"—he rejects his aunt's advice. Once again, we see how he resists Emily's view of duty and tradition.

What is the cause of this resistance? It derives from his aunt's character and the values she received from earlier generations of the Bolling family. As Binx tells us early in the novel, Emily Cutrer is a strong-willed, domineering woman, "soldierly both in look and outlook" (27). (Of course, it is no accident that Binx uses the term *soldierly* to describe her in his narrative. She exemplifies her own counsel, he suggests.) The only daughter in the distinguished Bolling family, her view of the world was entirely shaped by the values and social position she inherited. She is at once a fierce patrician who fervently believes in the tradition of noblesse oblige and an implacable pessimist, watching grimly as the social boundaries inside which she has comfortably spent her life begin to shift and give way. This latter quality colors her most impassioned speeches, such as this bittersweet revery on the disintegration of the Old South: "The world I knew has come crashing down around my ears. The things we hold dear are reviled and spat upon. . . . It's an interesting age you will live in—though I can't say I'm sorry to miss it. But it should be quite a sight, the going under of the evening land. That's us all right. And I can tell you my young friend, it is evening. It is very late" (54).

Here we see some of the limitations of Emily's vision. Though she speaks with power and eloquence, her voice, like Binx's, is in many ways a pastiche of other voices (though those voices are not as heterogeneous and contradictory as the ones that sound in Binx's microdialogue). Her diction is antiquated—"The things we hold dear are reviled and spat upon"—and she does not so much talk to Binx as declaim her ideas for him in the grand, oratorical style of an earlier generation. Then, too, there is a theatrical quality that suffuses the final, doomed cadences of this speech, an infatuation with the poetry of defeat. Yet her pessimism is also bound to a sentimentalized view of the past. It is only possible to see "the evening land" that she mourns if one's perspective of history is narrow: if one sees a courtly way of life but not the social and economic system that was engineered to support it.

All these things contribute to that skepticism with which Binx so often responds to his aunt. He is certainly aware of her tendency to romanticize people and events. As Binx tells us, "She transfigures everyone. . . . All the stray bits and pieces of the past, all that is feckless and gray about people, she pulls together into an unmistakable visage of the heroic or the craven, the noble or the ignoble" (49). More important, though, he perceives, even if he does not consciously articulate it, that there is a profound contradiction at the heart of his aunt's philosophy. Though she repeatedly urges him to spend his life "serving my fellowman," the rigid hierarchical distinctions on which her "evening land" was built cut against the bond of a common humanity that he is supposed to honor. Indeed, as Emily makes all too clear in a long diatribe near the end of the novel, she rejects any hint of egalitarianism:

> "I'll make you a little confession. I am not ashamed to use the word
> class. I will also plead guilty to another charge. The charge is that people
> belonging to my class think they're better than other people. You're
> damn right we're better. We're better because we do not shirk our
> obligations either to ourselves or to others. We do not whine. We do
> not organize a minority group and blackmail the government. We

do not prize mediocrity for mediocrity's sake. Oh I am aware that we hear a great many flattering things nowadays about your great common man—you know, it has always been revealing to me that he is perfectly content so to be called, because that is exactly what he is: the common man and when I say common I mean common as hell." (222–23)

In his sweeping history of the Percy family, *The House of Percy: Honor, Melancholy, and Imagination in a Southern Family,* the distinguished historian Bertram Wyatt-Brown notes, "Class consciousness, based in part upon family pride, was very much a part of the [Percy] family's cultural heritage, one more common than a powerful myth of classlessness in American society would acknowledge" (10). That same sense of class consciousness is certainly manifestly present in the speech quoted above—as it is in virtually all of Emily Cutrer's actions and attitudes. Emily's elitism in this speech shades into outright contempt for those she regards as her inferiors. Yet even here, she continues to speak to Binx of "our obligations either to ourselves or to others," and her ideology virtually deconstructs before our eyes. If one has only scorn for others, then what is the nature of that "obligation?" In fact, the brunt of the obligation that Emily so often invokes is to the traditions of the Bollings's privileged class. Even the most casual aspects of her speech indicate this attitude: the way she places "ourselves" before "others" in her word order. Indeed, as Wyatt-Brown explains in an earlier book, *Southern Honor: Ethics and Behavior in the Old South,* the concept of honor that underlies the "obligation" of which Emily speaks is based less on a strict code of behavior than it is on a perception—first put forth by the individual and then ratified by others—that he or she is, in fact, honorable. As Wyatt-Brown writes, "honor is reputation. Honor resides in the individual as his understanding of who he is and where he belongs in the ordered ranks of society" (*Honor* 14). And so we see that Binx's faint intuition at the beginning of the novel is correct: all he really has to do to please his aunt is to act in a manner that evinces a sense of obligation to others. His motives do not matter; it is enough to offer a series of charitable gestures and then to expect others to recognize and applaud the propriety of those gestures.

As Percy notes in his crucial early essay "Stoicism in the South" (*SSL* 83–88), this attitude, which was itself characteristic of upper-class southerners through much of the twentieth century, was the inevitable consequence of the stoic code that was a crucial part of the ideology and behavior of the southern aristocracy.[1] For the upper-class stoic code was fiercely moral yet grounded its morality in the sense of honor that Wyatt-Brown defines rather than in charity or Christian love. As Percy writes, "The nobility of Sartoris—and there were a great many Sartorises—was the nobility of the natural perfection of the Stoics, the stern inner summons to man's full estate, to duty, to honor, to generosity toward his fellow men and above all to his inferiors—not because they were made in the image of God and were therefore loveable in themselves, but because to do them an injustice would be to defile the inner fortress which was oneself" (*SSL* 85). Of course, we can hear in this passage a nascent version of Emily's voice, as Percy echoes the stoic's injunction "to duty, to honor, to generosity toward his fellowmen." But what is more to the point is the way that Percy clearly identifies the true rationale behind the stoic tradition of noblesse oblige—and, by extension, the rationale behind Emily's advice to Binx: generosity to others is evidence of one's own nobility, a kind of public performance intended to confirm one's honor, not a manifestation of the Judeo-Christian belief in the fellowship of all human beings. As Percy says later in the essay, "it was not the individual, after all, who was intrinsically precious in the Stoic view—rather it was one's own attitude toward him" (*SSL* 85).

Percy goes on to show how the stoic point of view ultimately becomes self-defeating, for it can neither adapt to a changing world—in particular, a more egalitarian culture—nor provide hope for the future. Because the agrarian society in which this stoic code flourished depended on a rigid hierarchy, the leveling effect brought on by the steady encroachment of modern technology and values made that ideology increasingly inadequate. As Percy writes, "like the Stoa of the Empire, the Stoa of the South was based on a particular hierarchical structure and could not survive the change" (*SSL* 85). Upper-class southerners like Emily Cutrer increasingly found that their "inferiors" no longer recognized their leadership or required their generosity. The most glaring example of this change was the civil rights movement, when the African Americans who had depended on the southern gentry for patronage and protection defied their former allies and took to the streets to seek a long-delayed justice. Stoics like Emily saw this civil disobedience as a kind of insolence—an attempt to "blackmail the government"—and many people refused to support the most important moral crusade in modern American history. Instead, they turned inward, retreated to "the inner fortress which was oneself," and cultivated a sense of despair. As Percy says of the upper-class southerner's stoicism, "its most characteristic mood was a poetic pessimism which took a grim satisfaction in the dissolution of its val-

ues—because social decay confirmed one in his original choice of the wintry kingdom of self" (*SSL* 85).

Though these social changes figure more prominently in Percy's second
novel, *The Last Gentleman,* they are the historical context in which the events
of *The Moviegoer* take place. Consequently, Binx's rejection of his aunt's values and his flight to Gentilly must be seen in relation to that context. At
some level, surely, he knows that the role she prescribes for him and the values she would pass on to him are incongruous with the world in which he
has been set down. There is no place any more for the benign, fatherly aristocrat who makes a great show of his generosity and coolly looks down on
its beneficiaries. Moreover, he cannot accept her values because they are
entwined with a melodramatic sense of futility. Even as Emily enjoins Binx
to accept his "obligations," her voice is laced with the same "poetic pessimism" that Percy refers to in "Stoicism in the South." "In this world goodness is destined to be defeated," she insists. "But a man must go down
fighting. To do anything less is to be less than a man" (54). Ultimately,
though, Binx is far too knowing and ironic to embrace this romantic despair. The wan, gray world of suburbs and shopping centers that he inhabits
simply cannot accommodate Emily's vision of a gloomy twilight struggle
between good and evil. Nor is he one to go down fighting for a cause that
was lost long ago, the restoration of Emily's beloved "evening land." And so
he responds to her injunctions with a polite but ironic diffidence: "She is
right. I will say yes. I will say yes even though I do not really know what she
is talking about" (54).

In Binx's rejections of his aunt's exhortations, though, we also note a refusal by Percy of the sort of moralistic voice that will become increasingly
dominant in his later fiction. For Emily Cutrer, as a daughter of the Old
South, imbued with its stern sense of ethics, is what Percy would later call
himself in many interviews and essays: a moralist. Indeed, Emily is the first
of many such moralists who will populate Percy's later work. She anticipates
the bleak disdain of Ed Barrett in *The Last Gentleman* and *The Second Coming*
for the ethical decay of his fellow patricians, the scathing anger of Lancelot
Lamar at the moral rot of contemporary America in Percy's fourth novel,
and even Will Barrett's fierce conviction in *The Second Coming* that he is a
lone pillar of sanity in an insane world. More important, Emily's sweeping
denunciations of the tainted world that will supplant her beloved "evening
land" also anticipate the increasingly critical perspective of Percy's later novels, which become ever more broadly satirical in their depictions of a mor-

ally flawed American culture as Percy's own dismay rises at what he sees as the tragic course of the twentieth century. As Harold Bloom has written, bemoaning what he sees as Percy's own "lost freedom" from "the drive to moralize," "Aunt Emily, the book's moralizer, is a presage of many a Percyian denunciation to come" (Introduction 3). Yet what is most striking about *The Moviegoer* in contrast to Percy's later work is that throughout this novel— even after Binx's final transformation—Percy's protagonist explicitly rejects the stance of the moralist. Over and over throughout the book, Binx refuses to pass judgment on those around him. He may envy them, sympathize with them, or recoil in horror at their seeming blindness, but he never judges or condemns them. In fact, as the totality of Binx's responses and actions makes clear, the insistently moralistic quality of Emily's vision is one of the reasons why Binx finally rejects her ideology in his microdialogue of voices and perspectives. We will see this phenomenon most clearly perhaps when he tries at the end of the novel to explain to Emily his relationship with Kate.

Binx's struggle with his aunt's values is ultimately the novel's dialogic core. I will now examine some of the possibilities Binx explores in an effort to find a credible alternative to his aunt's beliefs. Before moving on, however, it is important to note that *The Moviegoer* is not just a chronicle of Binx's ideological becoming: it is also an artifact of Percy's own development, for the dialogue between Binx and his aunt re-creates Percy's ideological struggle with the man to whom the novel is dedicated, his second cousin and guardian, William Alexander Percy. As Lawson and Jim Van Cleave almost simultaneously noted in late 1970 in their respective essays, "Walker Percy's Southern Stoic" and "Versions of Percy," Emily Cutrer's Stoic beliefs are clearly modeled after those of William Alexander Percy, who took in Walker and his brothers after the suicide of their father and the death of their mother two years later and who became, in many ways, Walker's surrogate father, his beloved "Uncle Will." (Of course, this mirrors the way Emily took in Binx after the death of his father. The biographical parallels in *The Moviegoer* are only loosely disguised.) William Alexander Percy was, as Lawson writes, "virtually a Renaissance man: teacher, decorated military officer, lawyer, poet, and plantation owner" (*Following* 41), and his influence on his adopted son, Walker, was tremendous. As Percy explained in a 1974 interview, "I don't know if you ever had a really great teacher; you're lucky if you have one or two in your lifetime. He was one . . . the sort of man who had this electrical quality. He loved beautiful things—art, music, literature. He could make you see it, see it the way he saw it; he could get you excited about it" (*Con.* 91).

William Alexander Percy certainly helped inspire his adopted son's commitment to literature, just as the stoic philosophy he expressed in his autobiography, *Lanterns on the Levee,* must have illustrated the failure of the creed that Walker Percy would renounce by turns (though never completely, never without at least a respectful affection) in his seminal essay "Stoicism in the South" and later—more dramatically—in *The Moviegoer.* Their relationship was profoundly dialogic, as Percy himself acknowledged in "Uncle Will," a remembrance of his adopted father: "It was usually in *relation* to him, whether with him or against him, that I defined myself and my own direction" (*SSL* 56).

That this dialogue should spill over into Percy's fiction is not surprising. As Bakhtin observes in "Discourse in the Novel," many writers embody the forces that have influenced their beliefs—what Bakhtin calls "internally persuasive discourse"—as characters in fiction, particularly when, as in Percy's case, those forces can only be rejected at great emotional cost. (How could it not have been painful for Walker Percy to break with William Alexander Percy's values? It is a measure of Percy's ambivalence that the work that dramatizes that rejection is also dedicated "in gratitude" to his guardian.) Indeed, the following passage from "Discourse in the Novel" seems to describe the precise impulse that must have driven Percy to embody his Uncle Will's stoic ideology in the stern, "soldierly" figure of Binx's Aunt Emily:

> This process—experimenting by turning persuasive discourse into speaking persons—becomes especially important in those cases where a struggle against such images has already begun, where someone is striving to liberate himself from the influence of such an image and its discourse by means of objectification, or is striving to expose the limitations of both image and discourse. [When an author attempts this kind of objectification,] a conversation with an internally persuasive word may continue, but it takes on another character; it is questioned, it is put in a new situation in order to expose its weak sides, to get a feel for its boundaries, to experience it physically as an object. . . . Novelistic images, profoundly double-voiced and double-languaged, . . . seek to objectivize the struggle with all types of internally persuasive alien discourse that had at one time held sway over the author. (348)

Many of Percy's critics, including Lawson and William Rodney Allen in his biographical study of Percy's fiction, *Walker Percy: A Southern Wayfarer,* have commented at length on the way Percy's struggle with his guardian's values is represented in his fiction. My point here is not to add to their efforts, only to consider them in another light, as further evidence of the dialogic quality of Percy's fiction. For if we see the process of transforming life into art in the manner that Bakhtin describes above, then *The Moviegoer* itself becomes part of the dialogue between Percy and his guardian and a crucial step in Percy's own ideological becoming as well. Seen this way, the novel is not just an acute rendering of the microdialogue that echoes in Binx's narrative; it *is* microdialogue, a double-voiced utterance that is offered both in gratitude and in rejection, that absorbs William Alexander Percy's voice and answers it. Dialogue, then, exists at all levels of the novel: in its language and its structure and in the conditions that led to its creation.

As we have seen, the heart of *The Moviegoer* is the dialogue between Binx and his aunt. Almost everything that Binx does, everything he thinks or says, is in some way a reaction to his aunt's stoic philosophy and the obligation that she sees for him. Even his life in Gentilly as "a model tenant and model citizen" is a kind of elaborate hoax that allows him to reject her values and yet maintain an ironic perspective that enables him to escape self-definition. But there is also a third figure who is implicated in the microdialogue of Binx's consciousness, whose voice is felt most powerfully in its unnatural silence, and who occupies an ideological ground that is somewhere between Emily's unswerving stoicism and Binx's ironic posturing. This figure is Binx's father, who, although long dead, is still an important presence in the novel, a shadowy form who exists for Binx in photographs, documents, a few isolated memories, and other people's apocryphal stories. Over the course of the novel, Binx tries to piece these fragments together so that he can understand his father's unhappy life, for Binx is haunted by an inchoate sense that there is some lesson to be divined from his father's experience.

The first indication of his father's importance to Binx's ideological struggle comes when he arrives at his aunt's home for the lunch and the "serious talk" he referred to in the novel's opening paragraph. Almost immediately, Binx's attention is once again drawn to the picture of his father and the other Bolling men on the mantelpiece. "For ten years I have looked at it on the mantelpiece and tried to understand it," he says (24). The picture shows Binx's father standing with his own father and his uncle, the legendary Judge Anse and Dr. Wills, while on a hunting trip in the Black Forest, but the other men are comfortable with themselves, "serene in their own identities," and Binx's father is not. "[M]y father is not one of them," he says, searching the photograph for a clue to this rift and finding it at last in the expression in his father's eyes: "Beyond a doubt they are ironical" (25). Of course, we recognize right away that the same look must appear in Binx's eyes as well, but Binx neither acknowledges the similarity—this is characteristic, as we will see—nor openly considers the source of that irony. It remains instead for us to trace the look in his father's eyes to his family's history and values.

As we consider the picture of Binx's father that emerges in bits and pieces throughout the novel, it becomes clear that the stoic values to which his family adhered failed him. In a sense, Binx's father did everything right. He lived according to those values, choosing a career in medicine and serving the public, acting in a manner that befitted his station. His only transgression was to marry his nurse, a Catholic woman of common descent (and he can hardly be faulted for doing so, since Emily has done much the same thing by marrying Jules Cutrer, a Cajun merchant). In fact, when Binx considers his father's actions, he contradicts his earlier assertion about his father's relationship to the other men in the photograph on his aunt's mantel: "he is, by every right, one of them," Binx says of his father (27). And yet, once again, Binx's tone is revealing. The insistent note that we hear in the phrase "by every right" acknowledges that this is not the whole truth. Although Binx's father conducted himself in a manner that was virtually indistinguishable from that of the other men in the photograph, the values in which they believed could not sustain him. As Binx knows, and as everything he learns about his father over the course of the novel demonstrates, his father lived in despair. He took little apparent satisfaction in his work or in leisure pursuits like hunting and fishing; he ate without pleasure and hardly slept at all. The only time he seemed happy was when World War II began and he volunteered for service in the Royal Canadian Air Force. But even that soldierly act was not without its shadows, for there are hints that he was not just motivated by a sense of duty or a hatred of fascism. Going to war was also a way of escaping the conditions that oppressed him, escaping them once and for all. As Binx says, in a carefully worded sentence, "He was commissioned by the RCAF in 1940 and *got himself killed* before his country entered the war" (25, emphasis added).[2]

Binx's father is ultimately an enigma. The "ironical" look Binx sees in his father's eyes suggests that at some level the older man recognized the inadequacy of his family's values, but the events of his life demonstrate nothing but obedience to those values. Even his death is ambiguous: it can be seen as an act of rejection, a kind of suicide, or as a final, fiery embrace of "the broadsword virtues of the clan" (*SSL* 84). (No death could be more fitting for a man of his station than to fall in battle against such a clear-cut evil.) And as a consequence of this ambiguity, Binx's legacy from his father is uncertain. Does his father hand down to him irony or despair? What does his example teach Binx? To struggle against his family's values, or to submit to them?

Because of these unresolved questions, Binx is careful to distance himself from his father. Despite his curiosity about his father's life and his apparent desire to claim his father as a confederate in his own ideological struggle, Binx refuses to acknowledge any resemblance to his father. Though both his aunt and his mother (who has remarried and started another family) compare him to his father, Binx rarely responds to these comments. More important, in the few times that Binx himself recalls his father, his memories inevitably point up the differences between them. When, for example, Binx remembers how his father tried to cure his insomnia by sleeping in the rose garden outside their home, Binx disparages his father's efforts. Although the memory is occasioned by Binx's insomnia, his own sleeplessness is not a link to his father but a source of their differences.

> [My father] made a mistake. He was trying to sleep. He thought he had to sleep a certain number of hours every night, breathe fresh air, eat a certain number of calories, evacuate his bowels regularly and have a stimulating hobby (it was the nineteen thirties and everybody believed in science and talked about "ductless glands"). I do not try to sleep. And I could not tell you the last time my bowels moved; sometimes they do not move for a week but I have no interest in such matters. As for hobbies, people with stimulating hobbies suffer from the most noxious of despairs since they are tranquilized in their despair. I muse along as quietly as a ghost. Instead of trying to sleep I try to fathom the mystery of this suburb at dawn. Why do these splendid houses look so defeated at this hour of the day? Other houses, say a 'dobe house in New Mexico or an old frame house in Feliciana, look much the same day or night. But these new houses look haunted. Even the churches out here look

haunted. My poor father. I can see him, blundering through the patio
furniture, the Junior Jets and the Lone Ranger pup tents, dragging his
Saskatchewan sleeping bag like the corpse of his dead hope. (86)

The explicit focus of this passage is the distinction that Binx makes between
his father and himself. In a tone that ranges from mockery to sorrow, Binx
contrasts his father's obsessive concern with hygiene with his own indifference to such matters. But this passage also depicts that obscure project that
Binx calls "the search." Indeed, it even suggests—implicitly at least—that
Binx's search is a consequence of his father's despair.

Binx's father, as he is pictured here, emerges as a man who believed—or
at least wanted to believe—the accepted wisdom of his time. Like so many
others, he conceived of life as a series of purposeful activities that would
bring contentment if they were rigorously pursued. Each day for him was
supposed to be another stage in a long journey toward self-fulfillment. But
this system failed him. For as Binx's mother makes clear late in the novel,
Binx's father seemed uncertain of what activities he should take up, what
goals he should pursue. Even the rational, disciplined routine that Binx describes here eventually seemed inadequate, and his father gave up trying to
eat because he lost interest. As Binx's mother says, "It was like he thought
eating was not—*important* enough. You see, with your father, everything, every second had to be—" (153). Though she does not finish her thought, her
meaning is clear enough: Binx's father felt obligated—virtually to the point
of neurosis—to use time wisely. In a sense, he must have lived in time like
Faulkner's Quentin Compson (another anxious aristocrat of the same generation as Binx's father). Intensely conscious of his heritage, Binx's father saw
himself as part of a tradition that he was bound to uphold, however much he
might have questioned the value of that tradition. And his actions, his attempts to live a purposeful and productive life, were important precisely because they were the living extensions of that tradition.

Binx, however, does not live in time like his father. As we have seen, he is
at best ambivalent to the claims of the past. And so, like Quentin Compson,
he seeks to escape time, though he does not kill himself. Instead of commit-
ting suicide, Binx in effect places himself outside of time by inhabiting what
Percy calls "the posture of objectivity" (and here we see again the accuracy
of Percy's claim that Binx is a version of "Quentin Compson who didn't
commit suicide"). The posture of objectivity, a term Percy coins in "The
Message in the Bottle," is a mode of existence in which one determines "to

stand outside and over against the world as one who sees and thinks and knows and tells" (*MB* 128). It is the characteristic stance of the scientist or the philosopher, of anyone who abstracts from existence and seeks to discover general truths about the world and his or her place in it. In this mode of being, though, a radical separation occurs between oneself and the world. For the person who occupies the posture of objectivity, the world becomes a kind of laboratory filled with objects to be observed and studied, and the observer is necessarily detached from those objects. As Percy says, "one condition of the objective method of the sciences is the exclusion of oneself from the world of objects one studies" (*MB* 129). But the pure, abstracted observers' realm, that zone of objectivity they must somehow create, also removes them from the dimension of time. For though the world may change, though the objects one studies may change, observers must not. They must remain a fixed point in a world of flux to accurately observe the process of change that sweeps over everything else. And, the ultimate goal of observers' work is a kind of information that can be discerned anywhere and at any time and is of the same abstract importance to all who receive it. (After all, the essence of scientific truth is that it is repeatable.)

We see Binx inhabit the posture of objectivity in the passage quoted above, as he wanders the streets of Gentilly and tries "to fathom the mystery of the suburb at dawn." Binx examines the neighborhood with a measured, dispassionate curiosity and never openly acknowledges that he lives here too, that this mystery concerns him as well. "Why do these splendid houses look so defeated at this hour of the day?" he asks coolly, as if to frame the question for further study. Indeed, Binx is so detached here that he is all but oblivious to the specific fact of his physical existence. He ignores the rhythms of his body, the need to sleep and to defecate at regular intervals (and here is further evidence that Binx does not live in time like his father, for those rhythms are, of course, time-bound: they are the body's inner clock). Binx is all too correct when he says, "I muse along as quietly as a ghost." He is so divorced from his physical existence and the actual conditions of his life—the fact that he is not some wandering anthropologist but that he also lives in this neighborhood—that he is very nearly all spirit, all mind. (There is a hint, however, that Binx's ghostly existence ties him to the particular sadness of the suburb, for he calls the houses and churches "haunted," suggesting perhaps that they are tenanted by ghosts like him. Is it possible, Binx seems to ask, that the other residents of Gentilly are as detached from the world as he is?)

Binx's exploration of the neighborhood is a part of what he calls "the search," a vague activity that occupies many of his evenings and lingers in the back of his mind for much of the novel. Though Binx never clearly defines his search, the narrative is peppered with little maxims, such as this one, that hint at its methods and its purpose:

> The search is what anyone would undertake if he were not sunk in the everydayness of his own life. This morning, for example, I felt as if I had come to myself on a strange island. And what does such a castaway do? Why, he pokes around the neighborhood and he doesn't miss a trick.
>
> To become aware of the possibility of the search is to be onto something. Not to be onto something is to be in despair. (13)

Of course, the activity that Binx describes here is exactly what he does when he walks through Gentilly at dawn, musing on the obscure sorrow of the houses; and the search, as he defines it here, is a minute phenomenological exploration of the world around him—though to what end he does not say. But the tone of the passage also mirrors Binx's detachment as he tries "to fathom the mystery of the suburb at dawn." When Binx says, "The search is what anyone would undertake if he were not sunk in the everydayness of his own life," his phrasing is characteristic of a man who occupies the posture of objectivity. Binx effaces his own individuality here: he does not speak for himself but for "anyone," pronouncing a kind of universal truth. Binx only refers to himself in this passage as an example of the general principle that he wants to define, and he shifts quickly from the first person back to the generic *he*—a transition that exemplifies Percy's view of the occupant of the posture of objectivity, who has "abstracted from his own predicament in order to achieve objectivity" (*MB* 130).

Binx lives in the posture of objectivity most fully when he is engaged in the search, and the detached, "scientific" voice that he uses to describe his quest embodies that point of view. When Binx makes sweeping, impersonal pronouncements like those in the last two sentences of this passage—"To become aware of the possibility of the search is to be onto something. Not to be onto something is to be in despair"—he not only mimics a scientist's diction and tone but also assimilates the scientist's point of view: his or her detachment and drive to generalize, to seek the broadest and most inclusive level of truth. This link between Binx's narrative voice and his perspective is an example of what Bakhtin means in "Discourse in the Novel" when he speaks of "language conceived as ideologically saturated, language as a world view" (271). In simple terms, Binx cannot use the language of science without also assuming—in part, at least—a scientific worldview.

Ultimately, this scientific voice that Binx uses to describe his search functions as a counterbalance to his aunt's voice in the microdialogue that inheres within his consciousness. As we have already seen, Binx is strongly influenced by his aunt's stoic perspective; her voice echoes in his mind and sounds in his narrative, often alongside this scientific voice. But where those traces of Emily's voice call him to the world and remind him of his obligations as an individual whose life is linked to a tradition of noblesse oblige, the scientist's voice speaks from somewhere outside the day-to-day world and deliberately obscures all references to himself as an individual. (After all, what good is information that is only true for himself? He seeks general laws, universal truth.) This balance between voices and the tension that it creates is central to *The Moviegoer.* Though the novel's external conflict focuses on Binx's conduct—the way he resists his aunt's ideology by moving to Gentilly—the real tension in the novel arises from the dissonance created by these voices and the perspectives that they embody.

But Binx's scientific voice is not merely addressed to his aunt; it accomplishes more than balancing her stoicism. That voice is also a response to his father's despair. As Binx tells us again and again, the search—even the possibility of a search—is the only real alternative to a life of despair. And so it is only natural that the voice that chronicles his search is in some way addressed to his father, whose memory embodies the face of despair for Binx. We can sense this quality of Binx's scientific voice, this direction, in that passage where his observations of Gentilly at dawn are intertwined with his memories of his father's insomnia. Even though Binx does not directly speak to his father in this passage, that omission is only a semantic disguise. He certainly speaks *at* his father if not *to* him. For the cool, detached voice that Binx uses here evokes a perspective that is pointedly, willfully different from his father's, and this difference is obviously intended to redeem Binx from his father's despair.

Binx's scientific voice has many purposes, as we have seen, but this use is perhaps the most curious, the way it functions as a rejoinder to his father. In essence, when Binx uses this scientific voice, he participates in a dialogue that lacks all the usual requisites of dialogue, a phenomenon that Bakhtin calls "hidden dialogicity": "Imagine a dialogue of two persons in which the statements of the second speaker are omitted, but in such a way that the general sense is not at all violated. The second speaker is present invisibly, his words are not there, but deep traces left by those words have a determining influence on all the present and visible words of the first speaker" (*Dostoevsky* 197). This passage describes the interaction between Binx and his father. There is no trace of the other's voice. Binx never remembers anything his father said, so there are not even echoes in his own voice, any words or images that are clearly borrowed from his father, despite the fact that Binx was fourteen when his father died and that he can easily recall things his mother said to his father, such as the way she gently mocked his plans to sleep in the garden: "Honey, I'm all for it. I think we all ought to get back to nature and I'd be right with you, Honey, if it wasn't for the chiggers. I'm chigger bait" (72). This glaring discrepancy between Binx's careful re-creation of his mother's voice—right down to her tart, folksy tone—and the complete absence of his father's suggests that Binx deliberately eliminates his father's voice from his memory and from the narrative that records his experience. All the same, however, Binx's father is a very real presence in Binx's consciousness—as his consuming need to learn about his father's life attests—and Binx's scientific voice makes us aware of that presence by subtly responding to it. In effect, this voice enables us to hear his father's silence even as his father's anguished life is absorbed into Binx's scientism. As Binx says early on, "Any doings of my father [are] in the nature of a clue to my search" (71), yet the peculiar nature of Binx's fascination strips away the filial connection to his father's sufferings, leaving only a series of impersonal observations to be noted in a willfully detached, almost clinical voice.

But although the search is clearly Binx's alternative to his aunt's beliefs and his father's despair, it is not only a reaction to those forces. It is also a way of reaching out to and experiencing the wider world in which he finds himself. How the search functions in this context and how it is also deeply and irremediably flawed by the scientific posture that Binx adopts are the issues we must now consider.

Binx's reawakening to the possibility of a search initiates the transformation of his character that will occur over the week in his life that the novel details. Though other things tug at Binx—the fact that he will turn thirty at the end of the week, his aunt's desire for him to choose what she sees as a more suitable career—the possibility of a search galvanizes him, initially "complicates" his "peaceful existence" in Gentilly (10).

That possibility is revived by the memory of being wounded in Korea. On the morning on which the novel begins, Binx awakes "with the taste of it in my mouth, the queasy-quince taste of 1951 and the Orient" (10). The idea of a search first occurred to Binx in Korea, after he was shot and lay bleeding on the ground. At that moment, as he regained consciousness, he saw the world around him with extraordinary vividness. The overwhelming sense of routine—what Heidegger called "the everydayness"—that would otherwise cloud his vision was momentarily dispelled.[3] "Six inches from my nose a dung beetle was scratching around under the leaves. As I watched, there awoke in me an immense curiosity. I was onto something. I vowed that if I ever got out of this fix, I would pursue the search. Naturally, as soon as I recovered and got home, I forgot all about it" (11). The idea implied here, that the world can be regained through an ordeal, is expressed throughout Percy's writings. (In his third novel, *Love in the Ruins,* Percy's psychiatrist hero, Dr. Thomas More, will literally prescribe various ordeals for his alienated patients.) Later in *The Moviegoer,* Kate Cutrer will also attest to this idea when she describes the aftermath of the car accident that killed her fiancé: "I remember at the time of the wreck—people were so kind and helpful and *solid.* Everyone pretended that our lives until that moment had been every bit as real as the moment itself and that the future must be real too, when the truth was that our reality had been purchased only by Lyell's death. In another hour or so we had all faded out again and gone our dim ways" (81). But as both Binx and Kate admit, the effects of such moments are short-lived. Many years intervene before Binx recalls that feeling of being "onto something," before the idea of a search again becomes a reality for him.

It is significant, though, that Binx's memory of Korea is not by itself the catalyst for his search. That memory seems to stir up a sense of possibility in Binx, but the possibility remains undefined until he spots a small pile of his belongings on his bureau. "They looked both unfamiliar and at the same time full of clues," Binx explains. "I stood in the center of the room and gazed at the little pile, sighting through a hole made by thumb and forefinger. What was unfamiliar about them was that I could see them. They might have belonged to someone else. A man can look at this little pile on his bureau for thirty years and never see it. It is as invisible as his own hand. Once I saw it, however, the search became possible" (11).

Binx is struggling here to recall the clarity with which he saw the world when he was wounded in Korea, but he can only achieve that clarity now by distancing himself from his possessions. (In Korea, of course, reality was frighteningly immediate. The dung beetle that he saw so clearly was only six inches from his nose, and he watched it as he lay in his own blood.) Here, as so often in Percy's fiction, the protagonist's literal point of view reveals his state of mind. When Binx looks at the pile on his bureau through the aperture created by his fingers, he mimics the perspective of a researcher looking through a scientific instrument (and he anticipates the way a young Will Barrett will try to "recover" the particular reality of the world around him by looking at it through an expensive German telescope in *The Last Gentleman* [30]). Once again, Binx occupies the posture of objectivity, and his own experience is abstracted, generalized. "A man can look at this little pile on his bureau for thirty years and never see it," he says, transforming himself from a particular individual into "a man," an anonymous representative of his species.

There is, of course, tremendous irony in what occurs here. Though the search is Binx's way of regaining the world, of re-creating the immediacy with which he saw things when he was wounded in Korea, he distances himself now from what he tries to see. It is as if, when he is away from the battlefield, this detachment is the only way of establishing that there is in fact a world "out there" to be regained. Under ordinary circumstances, Binx implies, reality must be mediated for us, distilled and focused through specific instruments or techniques, because things can only be seen clearly if they are seen under conditions of the most rigorous objectivity.

In fact, this gesture shows us—as if we needed any confirmation—just how deeply Binx has been affected by the scientific temper of his age. When he is puzzled by the presence of those odds and ends on his bureau, he reflexively adopts the perspective of a scientist. He does not stop to think or question his actions: he forms that aperture with his fingers and begins to generalize about what he sees through it. But as we are drawn deeper into Binx's narrative—this event takes place in the first few pages—we see that his attitude toward science and scientism is both complex and contradictory. Despite actions like this, despite the scientific voice that he uses to discuss his search, Binx repeatedly denies that he has any aptitude for science. When, for example, he tells us that his aunt insists he has "a flair for research," he responds, "If I had a flair for research I would be doing research" (51). Binx dismisses his aunt's comment out of hand, as if it is another attempt to "transfigure" those around her, and he goes on to relate an anecdote, obviously intended to disprove his aunt's assertion, about a summer in which he attempted to study "the role of acid-base balance in the formation of renal calculi" (51). Despite his ability to adopt the language of science and frame the problem in a suitably technical manner, he quickly became distracted by the way "the August sunlight came streaming in the great dusty fanlights and lay in yellow bars across the room" (51). For Binx, during that summer, "the singularities of time and place" (52) were more compelling than any knowledge produced by experimentation. And yet we learn later that his interest in science was not merely the enthusiasm of a single season. When Binx and Kate walk by one of the science buildings at his alma mater, Tulane, while coming home from a movie late at night, he tells her, "I spent every afternoon for four years in one of those laboratories up there" (81). Surely, then, there is a basis for his aunt's conviction.

How can we resolve these contradictions? The answer is suggested by a long passage in which Binx distinguishes between what he calls the "vertical search" and the "horizontal search":

> Until recent years, I read only "fundamental" books, that is, key books on key subjects, such as *War and Peace,* the novel of novels; *A Study of History,* the solution of the problem of time; Schroedinger's *What is Life?,* Einstein's *The Universe as I See It,* and such. During those years I stood outside the universe and sought to understand it. I lived in my room as an Anyone living Anywhere and read fundamental books and only for diversion took walks around the neighborhood and saw an occasional movie. Certainly it did not matter to me where I was when I read such a book as *The Expanding Universe.* The greatest success of this enterprise, which I call my vertical search, came one night when I sat in a hotel room in Birmingham and read a book called *The Chemistry of Life.* When I finished it, it seemed to me that the main goals of my search were reached or were in principle reachable, whereupon I went out and saw a movie called *It Happened One Night* which was itself very good. A memorable night. The only difficulty was that though the universe had been disposed of, I myself was left over. There I lay in my hotel room with my search over yet still obliged to draw one breath and then the next. But now I have undertaken a different kind of search, a horizontal search. As a consequence, what takes place in my room is less important. What is important is what I shall find when I leave my room and wander in the neighborhood. Before, I wandered as a diversion. Now I wander seriously and sit and read as a diversion. (69–70)

This passage certainly affirms that Binx—at one time, at least—uncritically embraced the perspective and the methodology of science. His "vertical search" was nothing less than a far-reaching scientific inquiry into such broad questions as the composition of the universe and the logic of history. But the aim of this passage is ostensibly renunciation. Binx expresses here the criticism of science that is at the heart of Percy's diagnosis of the twentieth century's odd pathology. Just as Percy argues in such essays as "The Delta Factor" (*MB* 3–45) and "Diagnosing the Modern Malaise" (*SSL* 204–21), Binx realizes that science can identify the components of life itself yet say nothing about him as an individual. And so, Binx is "left over" after he finishes *The Chemistry of Life,* the universe "disposed of" and himself a mystery.

But although Binx purports to turn away from scientific inquiry in this passage, the habits of his mind are too ingrained to be broken. He gives up the traditional subject matter of science, a world that can be grasped empirically and quantified, but he does not stop thinking like a scientist. For as we have seen, Binx adopts a scientific voice and perspective when he conducts what he calls here the "horizontal search." Indeed, the language that he uses to discuss his search does not just evoke a certain kind of objectivity that is suited to scientific research; it is literally borrowed from the scientist's vocabulary, which Binx must have absorbed in college and in the course of his "vertical search." As careful attention to Binx's language shows, the terms he uses to describe what he does while he is engaged in his search are determinedly scientific. At one point, for example, he calls his activities "my little researches" (63)—which, of course, contradicts his assertion that "If I had a flair for research, I would be doing research." At another point in the novel, when Binx returns to a movie theater where he has not been for fourteen years, he speaks of carrying out "a successful experiment in repetition" (79). Even the language that he uses in the passage quoted above suggests a mind disciplined by science. The terms he invents to distinguish between the two kinds of search show us his need to categorize different kinds of experience, and his determination to "wander seriously" is also perhaps scientific. After all, the word *wander* suggests a kind of aimless, casual rambling about, yet Binx has a clear aim when he roams the streets of Gentilly and at least a vague plan to achieve that aim. For him, it seems, to "wander seriously" is to wander methodically.

Thus, Binx's search is an attempt to apply the methods of science to a realm of experience that is beyond the conventional domain of science. In effect, he brings the mind-set of the "vertical search" to the work of the "horizontal search," even though they are fundamentally incongruous. Why does Binx cling so stubbornly to this scientific point of view? Because, for one reason, he finds the detached perspective of a scientist to be comforting. As we have seen, there is an element of self-interest in Binx's determination to inhabit the posture of objectivity, for it removes him from the dimension of time and the confusion of his heritage. But Binx is also simply a product of the modern age. He succumbs to what, in "Diagnosing the Modern Malaise," Percy tentatively calls the "idolatry" of science that characterizes the twentieth century (*SSL* 210). Like so many other inhabitants of a technological society, Binx cannot help but believe that science is the only reliable channel to truth. He epitomizes the condition of the layman that Percy describes in "The Delta Factor": Binx believes, as his language and his actions demonstrate, "that only science can utter the true word about anything" (*MB* 22). And so, when he tries to grasp the strange, idiosyncratic reality of that pile of things on his bureau, he forms an aperture with his fingers and tries to look at it like a scientist.

Ultimately, however, this brief gesture, which makes the search "possible," also encapsulates its profound flaw (11). For we see here a contradiction between the aim of his search—which is nothing less than to regain the world, to experience it as vividly as he did in Korea—and the method of his search: his insistence on remaining a detached observer. As long as this contradiction exists (and there is no indication that Binx is even aware of it, much less that he will resolve it), his search is doomed to failure. He will always place out of his reach that which he wants to gain. And this contradiction is the source of a tension in the novel that is as fundamental as the tug-of-war between Emily's stoicism and Binx's resistance to her values. Just as there is a tension between Binx's and his aunt's ideological perspectives, there is also a constant tension within his narrative voice that reflects this contradiction between his desire to regain the world and his unwillingness to surrender his detachment. We can hear a conflict in the prose of the novel between a kind of language that aspires to poetry, that strives to embody the concreteness and idiosyncrasy of things, and another kind of language that is limited to analysis, that dissolves concreteness in theories and generalities.

When, for example, Binx conducts his "successful experiment in repetition," which takes him back to a movie theater near Tulane after fourteen years, this conflict is apparent in his summary of the results of his "experiment": "There was this: a mockery about the old seats, their plywood split, their bottoms slashed, but enduring nevertheless as if they had waited to see what I had done with my fourteen years. There was this also: a secret sense of wonder about the enduring, about all the nights, the rainy summer nights at twelve and one and two o'clock when the seats endured alone in the empty theater. The enduring is something which must be accounted for. One cannot simply shrug it off" (80). Here we see Binx on his search at his most characteristic. He perceives the world around him with the eye of a poet, but he interprets what he sees with the mind of a scientist. Binx is at his most lyrical when he describes the "secret sense of wonder about the enduring" of the theater, but his voice changes completely in the final two sentences of this passage. After beautifully and concretely evoking the passage of time—though time as a phenomenon that is solely to be observed, not as something that is felt, that affects the observer—he says, in his most detached and clinical voice, "The enduring is something which must be accounted for." And, immediately, the idea of "enduring" seems to dissipate the reality of this particular theater. The broken seats, the musty darkness: all are forgotten or lost in themselves as Binx begins to theorize.

This tension between being in the world or apart from it cannot be sustained indefinitely, however. Like the ideological tension that characterizes Binx's relationship with his aunt, it must be resolved if he will ever transcend the stasis in which we find him at the beginning of the novel. For we come to see that Binx's life, as it is initially revealed to us, is predicated on a refusal to choose between one stance, one way of being in the world, and another—just as, within the microdialogue that we hear in his narrative, he refuses to choose between the voices that echo in his consciousness. Binx will not become the patrician that his aunt would like him to be; he will not embrace the despairing, sentimental values of a disintegrating class system. But neither will he articulate his disenchantment with those values or cease trying to "appear so reasonable" to his aunt. Similarly, though Binx's dream of Korea has jarred him to life again, has recalled him to the beauty of the world around him, he will not see himself as a part of that world; he will only look on abstractedly, half desirous and half skeptical. Indeed, at the beginning of the novel, Binx dwells between possibilities, in a no-man's-land where he only defines himself by what he is not.[4] But this position is untenable. The action of the novel ultimately forces that realization on Binx, transforming his consciousness and the weave of voices in which his consciousness is manifest. Now let us see how that occurs.

Perhaps nowhere are the stresses in Binx's life more apparent than in the movie theaters where he spends so much of his time and in the personal relationships that are affected by his moviegoing. He is, of course, an ardent moviegoer. As Lawson notes in "Moviegoing in *The Moviegoer*," movies and references to the movies suffuse the novel. "During the eight days of the novel proper," Lawson writes, Binx "refers to twelve specific and several unidentified movies and to thirty-seven actors and eight actresses. During the same time, he goes to the movies no less than four times, including a drive-in on Saturday night" (26). But for all his love of the movies, Binx's experience of them, like so much else in his life, is curiously split between involvement and detachment.

His posture as a moviegoer certainly embodies the detachment that informs his character. In the theater, Binx is contemplative, passive, separated in space and time from the events he watches so closely—a stance that approximates the way he sees the world from the posture of objectivity. Indeed, it is no exaggeration to say that Binx's abstracted way of looking at the world is shaped as much by his moviegoing as his scientific training. For to maintain his detachment from the world around him, everything he sees must be transformed into a sort of tableau contrived for his amusement. The world must be held back, partitioned off, like the life that is contained within the borders of the movie screen. As Lawson notes in "Moviegoing in *The Moviegoer*," because of the detachment necessitated by the scientific method, Binx "will apprehend his world as he views a movie. . . . In the novel, then, moviegoing characterizes the alienated man's fascinated gaze at a distant reality, stresses the sense of apartness that he feels" (30).

But although Binx's posture in the theater embodies his carefully maintained detachment, moviegoing is also his most passionate occupation. As Binx says, in his usual arch tone, "The fact is that I am quite happy in a movie, even a bad movie. Other people, so I have read, treasure memorable moments in their lives: the time one climbed the Parthenon at sunrise, the summer night one met a lonely girl in Central Park and achieved with her a sweet and natural relationship, as they say in books. I too once met a girl in Central Park, but it is not much to remember. What I remember is the time John Wayne killed three men with a carbine as he was falling to the dusty street in *Stagecoach,* and the time the kitten found Orson Welles in the doorway in *The Third Man*" (7). We can hear Binx's characteristic irony in his description of the "memorable moments" he should have experienced in his life. As the phrases "so I have read" and "as they say in books" indicate, he is clearly mimicking and mocking the popular literature of his time. (When, for example, he appropriates the phrase "a sweet and natural relationship," it

manages to sound both saccharine and prurient at the same time.) But none
of that irony is expended on the films that linger in his imagination. The
specificity of the images that Binx remembers shows us his involvement in
the films he sees. Though he can sometimes be critical of the movies' sentimentality—the ebullience of a Jane Powell musical repels him: "the despair
of it is enough to leave you gone in the stomach," he says (74)—Binx is nevertheless powerfully affected by the romanticism of the movies. Reel life has
a sense of mystery and potency to it that surpasses anything in real life.

The source of this power for Binx is the sense of a heightened reality that
is created by the artifice of the movies. Early in the novel, for example, he
spots William Holden, who is making a film in New Orleans, walking down
the street. In a brief but marvelously detailed scene, Binx watches Holden's
effect on the other passers-by, who somehow feel impoverished or threatened by Holden's presence. As Binx says, watching one young man react to
the movie star, "He can only contrast Holden's resplendent reality with his
own shadowy and precarious existence" (16). This statement is deliberately
paradoxical, though. How can a man who makes his living pretending to be
other people be more real than anyone else? The answer to this paradox is
linked to the concept of everydayness, that sense of grinding routine that
makes one's life and everything touched by it seem unreal. Though everydayness oppresses the day-to-day world in which Binx and the other passers-
by on the street exist, it has no place in the cinematic world that Holden
seems to inhabit.[5] For the movies create a world in which every action, no
matter how mundane, is romanticized, made larger than life. And, purged of
everydayness, the movies can seem more real than the world in which they
are seen. That world is just a dim, faded counterpart whose essential poverty
is illuminated by the light that emanates from the screen.[6]

Indeed, Binx is so convinced of the peculiar "reality" of the movies that
the extravagant romanticism of Hollywood becomes another voice echoing
in his consciousness. Throughout *The Moviegoer*, Binx tries to assimilate—
not altogether successfully—the voices, the gestures, even the behavior of
the characters on the screen. For example, early in the novel, he keeps "a
Gregory Peckish sort of distance" from his newest secretary, Sharon Kincaid
(68). Later, however, when they work late one night and he wants to hint
that he is not quite all business, he contrives "to stand at the window, loosen
my collar and rub the back of my neck like Dana Andrews" (105). In the
most blatant sense, Binx uses these gestures from the movies as tools of seduction, but he is taken in by his own illusions. Ultimately, as we will see, his

undoing is a consequence of his attempt to live up to the imitations of life that he sees on the screen.

Though Binx lavishes these borrowed gestures on virtually every young woman he encounters, only Kate Cutrer, his most frequent companion at the movies, is exempt from them. Although Kate is surely desirable—Binx, who has a mild obsession with women's buttocks, calls hers "marvellously ample and mysterious" (42)—he does not attempt to seduce her. Unlike Sharon Kincaid, who is merely an object of desire for him, an unwitting participant in his attempts to relive what he sees on the screen, Kate is much more of an equal. She is his sole confidante, the only person who knows of his search, and she accompanies him on many of his "researches," such as his "experiment in repetition."

What is the source of this bond between them, which transcends both his usual reserve and his persistent desire? At the most basic level, Kate shares Binx's alienation, his sense of separation from the society at large and the strict, simple values proffered by his aunt. But where Binx conceals that alienation beneath his "reasonable" facade, Kate makes no such effort. She fights bitterly with Emily and drifts from one course in life to another, alternating between manic enthusiasms and a bottomless, suicidal despair. (In fact, when Emily summons Binx for "a serious talk" at the beginning of the novel, it is because she has found a bottle of barbiturates that Kate had tried to conceal. Much of the plot of the novel—such as it is—revolves around Emily's fears for Kate and her efforts to enlist Binx in Kate's care.) At another level, though, Kate, like Binx, often tentatively assimilates the voices of those around her. Just as Binx echoes Emily's stoicism or the scientific texts he has absorbed in his "vertical search" or the gestural language of the movie stars who shape his desires, Kate adopts the clinical language of her analyst or the jargon of one of the occupations she has halfheartedly taken up. Early in the novel, for example, Binx describes the way she appropriates the diction and tone of a social worker: "Her voice has suddenly taken on its 'objective' tone. Since she started her social work, Kate has spells of talking frankly in which she recites case histories in a droning scientific voice" (44). Indeed, Kate's consciousness seems as much an echo chamber of voices as Binx's is, and her character and ideology are as protean as his. Over the course of the novel, we will see Kate take on a variety of different stances and voices as she too struggles to "selectively [assimilate] the words of others" (Bakhtin, "Discourse" 341).

But perhaps the most important link between Binx and Kate is that Kate, like Binx, has experienced an event that ruptured the normal course of life. A few years earlier, she was in a car accident that spared her but killed her fiancé on the eve of their wedding. That accident affected her in the same way that Binx's experience in Korea affected him: by revealing the tenuousness of life, it exposed the way everydayness cheapens existence and obscures our awareness of the world around us. But where Binx was able to forget that knowledge for a while at least, until his dream of Korea brought it back to him, Kate has never been able to ignore or accommodate it. That knowledge is the reason why she struggles as she does and flirts with the idea of suicide—"suicide is the only thing that keeps me alive," she says at one point (194)—for she desperately needs to hold on to the clear, vivid sense of the world that she experienced so briefly and to find a way of living authentically that is commensurate with it. As Kate says to Binx, pointing to all they have in common, the accident "gave me my life. That's my secret, just as the war is your secret" (58).

When Kate says this, though, Binx does not acknowledge its truth. He responds, "I did not like the war" (58), a comment that may be true in general sense—no one likes war—but is false in its refusal to admit what Binx has told us in the first chapter of the novel, that being wounded was "one of the best" times in his life because it enabled him to conceive his search (10). This exchange illustrates an important aspect of Binx's relationship with Kate. Throughout the novel, she confronts him with a series of truths that he will not acknowledge. Early on, for example, she tells him that, despite his ability to "appear so reasonable" to Emily, he is really like Kate, "but worse. Much worse." Binx, however, refuses to even consider the thought: "She is in tolerable good spirits," he tells us. "It is not necessary to pay much attention to her" (43).

Kate's role in the novel is to reveal the limits of Binx's self-knowledge. Though she is commonly made out to be dependent on him, a high-strung woman who will fly apart without his steady, reassuring touch, she is, in fact, the galvanizing force in the novel.[7] As Sheila Bosworth argues in "Women in the Fiction of Walker Percy," "For all her apparent fragility, Kate is 'onto something,' and Binx, sensing this, must take her hand before he can make that great leap from the aesthetic sphere of the consumer [where he indulges in his moviegoing and his various "researches"] 'clear across the ethical' [where Emily would have him dwell in service to his fellow man] . . . into the spiritual sphere of the giver" (78). Indeed, for a writer who is often accused—with some justification—of doing poorly by his female characters, Kate is one of two glorious exceptions in Percy's body of work (the other being Allison Huger in *The Second Coming*). At almost every turn she initiates the action that requires Binx to confront the tensions in his life that he will not resolve. And, equally important, she exposes the various guises that constitute his inauthentic attempts to formulate a sense of self. She bitterly scorns the "reasonable" facade he presents to Emily, and she questions the image he creates of himself through his search, that of a man who has discovered the secret of rising above despair and everydayness. When, for example, they talk about the search after his "experiment in repetition," her doubts become clear. Though Binx is reluctant to engage her at first—"I would as soon not speak to her of such things, since she is bound to understand it as a cultivated eccentricity," he thinks (82)—Kate presses on and soon enough draws him out on the characteristics of "the vertical search":

> "If you walk in the front door of the laboratory, you undertake the vertical search. You have a specimen, a cubic centimeter of water or a frog or a pinch of salt or a star."
> "One learns general things?"
> "And there is excitement to the search."
> "Why?" she asks.
> "Because as you get deeper into the search, you unify. You understand more and more specimens by fewer and fewer formulae. There is the excitement. Of course, you are always after the big one, the new key, the secret leverage point, and that is the best of it."
> "And it doesn't matter where you are or who you are."
> "No."
> "And the danger is becoming no one nowhere."
> "Never mind."
> Kate parses it out with the keen male bent of her mind and yet with her womanish despair. Therefore I take care to be no more serious than she. (82–83)

Binx condescends here to Kate's "womanish despair," but she perhaps sees more than he realizes. As her reactions a few sentences later suggest, Kate seems to hear the note of abstraction in his voice and to perceive that he is already in danger of "becoming no one nowhere," despite his insistence that he has renounced "the vertical search." (It is no accident that Binx volun-

teers the information "And there is excitement to the search." We can hear a
quickening of interest in his voice as he describes the quest for "the secret
leverage point.") Indeed, after they exhaust this subject, she turns on him,
verbally and then physically challenging his detachment:

> "You're a cold one, dear."
>
> "As cold as you?"
>
> "Colder. Cold as the grave." She walks about tearing shreds of flesh
> from her thumb. I say nothing. It would take very little to set her off on
> an attack on me, one of her "frank" appraisals. "It is possible, you know,
> that you are overlooking something, the most obvious thing of all. And
> you would not know it if you fell over it."
>
> "What?"
>
> She will not tell me. Instead in the streetcar, she becomes gay and
> affectionate toward me. She locks her arms around my waist and gives
> me a kiss on the mouth and watches me with brown eyes gone to
> discs. (83)

Binx, typically, refuses to hear Kate's accusation that he is as "cold as the
grave." Her outburst is merely another symptom of her volatile emotional
state, he implies. But when she suggests that his search is misguided, that he
is "overlooking something, the most obvious thing of all," she seems to
genuinely engage his attention; there is no dismissive reference to her psychological condition or her "womanish despair" now. Instead, at this moment, Kate's voice seems to embody what Bakhtin calls "the penetrative
word" in *Problems of Dostoevsky's Poetics:* "a word capable of actively and con-
fidently interfering in the interior dialogue of the other person, helping that
person find his own voice" (242). For Kate's taunts finally do affect Binx. He
acknowledges by his simple admission of curiosity that it is at least possible
that she is right, that there is a flaw in his search that she perceives and he
does not.

Binx and Kate's dialogue is ultimately the most important external dialogue in the novel. Although his aunt's voice is a crucial part of the internal
dialogue that resonates in his consciousness, their actual exchanges are far
more limited. Because he will not reveal his true feelings, Binx refuses to
engage her in honest, open dialogue. Instead, he assumes a kind of polite but
evasive diffidence that makes a true give-and-take impossible. By contrast,
however, Binx's dialogue with Kate is far more direct and truthful, if only
because she sees through his poses and will not hesitate to challenge him. In

a sense, their dialogue is similar to the "special type of dialogue" that Bakhtin finds in Dostoevsky's *Crime and Punishment* between Porfiry, the detective, and Raskolnikov:

> Porfiry speaks in hints, addressing himself to Raskolnikov's hidden voice. Raskolnikov tries to perform his role with calculation and precision. Porfiry's goal is to force Raskolnikov's inner voice to break out in the open, to create interruptions in his deliberate and skillfully performed replies. For this reason the words and intonations of Raskolnikov's role are continually invaded by the real words and intonations of his true voice. Porfiry too occasionally allows his true face, the face of a man already certain, to peek out from behind his assumed role of unsuspecting investigator; suddenly, amid each conversant's fictive replies, two real rejoinders, two real discourses, two real human views meet and intersect each other. As a result the dialogue from one plane—the role-playing plane—passes from time to time to another plane—the real, but only for a moment. (*Dostoevsky* 261)

Of course, this analogy is limited, and there are important differences. Though Kate sometimes assumes an artificial voice or set of mannerisms, she does not play a role in her dialogues with Binx, as Porfiry pretends to be an "unsuspecting investigator" in his confrontations with Raskolnikov. But the point here is the edgy, erratic quality of the dialogue that Bakhtin describes, the way it can shift suddenly from the artificial to the real. We certainly see this quality in Binx and Kate's exchange after his "experiment in repetition." Though initially Binx's abstracted posture as a moviegoer and a searcher is nearly inviolate, though his real self seems out of reach, Kate eventually breaks through his reserve and touches the core of uncertainty that is concealed beneath his calm, detached manner.

The effect of this breakthrough, though, is quite different from that of Porfiry on Raskolnikov. Where Porfiry is in the most literal sense Raskolnikov's antagonist, one who must discover what the other hides so that he can be punished for his crime, Kate is Binx's closest companion, and her efforts at forcing him to speak honestly are conjoined with a kind of offering. For if we consider all of Kate's actions in this exchange—both what she says and what she does, the way she becomes "gay and affectionate" on the streetcar—we see that she embodies the possibility of intimacy for Binx: real intimacy that is both psychological and physical rather than merely sexual.

This possibility becomes clear the night after his "experiment in repetition," when Kate comes to see him on the crest of one of her enthusiasms. Even as she explains to Binx the revelation that has come to her—"a person does not have to *be* this or *be* that or be anything, not even oneself. One is free" (114)—the wave of exaltation that has carried her along begins to recede. She becomes nervous, uncertain; in Binx's terms, she starts "overtaking herself" (115). But as she begins to slip over the edge, into a deep depression, Binx does a curious thing. He takes "her cold hands" and tells her about a plan he has begun to formulate to build a service station on the vacant lot across the street (115). As he explains this idea, however, he quietly suggests that she could come live with him:

> "We could stay on here at Mrs. Schexnaydre's. It is very comfortable. I may even run the station myself. You could come sit with me at night, if you liked. Did you know you can net over fifteen thousand a year on a good station?"
>   "You sweet old Binx! Are you asking me to marry you?"
>   "Sure." I watch her uneasily.
>   "Not a bad life, you say. It would be the best of all possible lives." She speaks in a rapture—something like my aunt. My heart sinks. It is too late. She has already overtaken herself.
>   "Don't—worry about it." (116)

Binx's suggestion is hardly a declaration of love—the fifteen thousand dollars his station might earn seems at least as alluring to him as his life with Kate—and yet his suggestion that Kate could share his life as the owner of a prosperous new Shell station is a half step out of the stasis in which he has lived so long. Binx thus moves, ever so cautiously, toward a decision that would transform his life, though typically he expresses that possibility in the vaguest terms—"We could stay on here at Mrs. Schexnaydre's"—as if to leave himself a way out, an escape route back to his old life. Here again, as so many other times in the novel, it is up to Kate to make explicit what Binx will only hint at, to express what he deliberately leaves unsaid: "Are you asking me to marry you?" And yet the possibility that they will marry exists only for a moment. Kate cannot sustain it. When she speaks of it as "the best of all possible lives," her language becomes double-voiced and the idea of marriage loses its authenticity. For Kate, at this moment, marriage is imbued with all the honorific qualities that Emily and others have no doubt ascribed to it. She seems to quote from Emily here, to emulate her voice and manner, as Binx himself implies when he says that Kate "speaks in a rapture—something like my aunt." But by doing so Kate makes it impossible for marriage to be *her* choice. "The best of all possible lives" is too steeped in Emily's values for Kate to claim it as her own. It would only be a way of deferring to Emily's wishes, to Emily's vision of Kate, and so it slips from her grasp. What is Binx's reaction, though, to this fleeting chance for a new life? "My heart sinks," he tells us as Kate's attention seems to wander from his proposal. But the reason for his despair is unclear. We cannot be sure if he grieves over her unwillingness to marry him or his own inability to stop her from "overtaking herself."

His actions the following day certainly outwardly suggest that his proposal was largely an attempt to forestall her depression. On Saturday morning, after a few hours of desultory work in the office, he convinces his secretary, Sharon, to go with him to the Gulf Coast for the remainder of the weekend. Except for an attempt to call Kate before he leaves, Binx seems completely unaffected by their exchange the night before. His tentative vision of a new life is apparently left far behind as his MG storms toward the coast and he and Sharon gradually shed their office demeanor. But though he does not even mention his proposal, it is possible to see his pursuit of Sharon as a reaction to the events of the previous night. At the conclusion of the novel, after a bitter falling-out with his aunt, he tries to stanch his despair by giving in to desire. "Whenever I take leave of my aunt after one of her serious talks, I have to find a girl" (228), he says, pointing to a pattern in his behavior that is evidenced earlier as well. As soon as Binx edges close to the real issues that perplex his life—such as the static quality of his existence in Gentilly or, perhaps, the true depth of his feelings for Kate—he looks for a diversion, a poultice of flesh to cover the wound that has been exposed. And so, just as he tells himself after he leaves his aunt at the end of the novel that "Nothing remains but desire," all he can do after his attempt to reach out to Kate fails is leave New Orleans and try to consummate his desire for Sharon (228).

In keeping with these clouded motives, Binx's relations with Sharon on this trip show him at his most inauthentic. Though he speaks of acting "on impulse" when he embraces her while they are lying on the beach, very little of his behavior here can truly be called impulsive (135). Rather, Binx creates a version of himself over the course of the day that is a synthesis of poses, of borrowed words and gestures. Even when they are involved in a slight traffic accident that jars his war wound, the pain that tears through his shoulder becomes "a lovely checker in a lovely game," as it affords him the chance to take on a role out of a movie: the tight-lipped, battle-scarred vet-

eran (126). Gradually, however, even Binx becomes seduced by his own behavior, and the promise of success in his pursuit of Sharon inspires a kind of
spurious lyricism in him: "Joy and sadness come by turns, I know now.
Beauty and bravery make you sad, Sharon's beauty and my aunt's bravery
and victory breaks your heart. But life goes on and on we go, spinning along
the coast in a violet light, past Howard Johnson's and the motels and the
children's carnival. We pull into a bay and have a drink under the stars. It's
not a bad thing to settle for the Little Way, not the big search for the big
happiness but the sad little happiness of drinks and kisses, a good little car
and warm deep thigh" (135–36).

Binx's language here is as artificial as his gestures earlier in the day, an uneasy synthesis of the voices that sound in his consciousness. In the beginning
of this passage, he echoes his aunt's weary, vaguely self-satisfied fatalism. Just
as Emily assures him, "In this world goodness is destined to be defeated" (54),
he tells himself that joy and sadness are hopelessly intertwined and that disappointment is the inevitable consequence of "victory" (which is itself a
dubious term for the seduction of his secretary; Binx makes out his relations
with Sharon to be a test of wills, a sexual competition that undercuts his lyrical mood). Moreover, like his aunt, Binx "transfigures" those around him; he
lapses into the same kind of sentimentality that he had earlier pointed out so
clearly in her, a hoary romanticism that turns "all that is feckless and gray
about people . . . into an unmistakable visage of the heroic or the craven, the
noble or the ignoble" (49). Here, Binx works the same alchemy as his aunt,
as he elevates Sharon (whom he had earlier described as "not really beautiful" [65]) into an emblem of beauty and transforms his aunt—the privileged,
insular daughter of a wealthy family—into an exemplar of bravery. But in
the third sentence of the passage, another voice is heard. "But life goes on
and on we go," he proclaims, in a style that recalls the happy-go-lucky antics
of the characters in the Jane Powell musical he had disliked so intensely a
few days earlier. Here, though, the jaunty optimism of the movie's "wake up
and sing number" is tempered by the melancholy Binx has inherited from
Emily (73). The bright technicolor aura of the movie is replaced by a more
subdued "violet light" as Binx—temporarily at least—rejects Hollywood's
overblown romanticism, "the big search for the big happiness" (135–36). Yet
even as he turns his back on those fantasies, we hear still another voice, that
of a man who occupies the posture of objectivity. "It is not a bad thing to
settle for the Little Way," Binx says, transforming this particular experience—
"the sad little happiness of drinks and kisses, a good little car and a warm

deep thigh"—into a general principle that others can emulate. (Live for the moment, he seems to say. It is best to renounce the grand ambitions of people like his aunt.) Once again, he abstracts from his own experience and, like a good scientist, affixes a label to his discovery. Binx calls this rapprochement with a life of diminished expectations the "Little Way," and even the capital letters that he uses to denote the formality of this title suggest his distance from his experience. They give his actions an official status as an existential phenomenon that others can identify and repeat at will.

His plans to seduce Sharon are thwarted, though, when he takes her to what he assumes will be his mother's deserted fishing camp and instead finds his mother and his five half brothers and sisters, the Smith family, very much in residence. The weekend suddenly takes a more serious turn. As Binx says when they arrive, the lights of the fishing camp are "ablaze like the Titanic" (136), and the intimations of disaster are appropriate. His plans for Sharon are ruined, and his flight from the despair that followed his proposal to Kate has only led him inadvertently back on himself. In the Kierkegaardian terms that are often applied to Percy's fiction (and that the author himself uses quite comfortably), what had begun as a "rotation," a brief journey that is calculated to divert one from ordinary life and thus combat everydayness, has become an existential "repetition," a confrontation with one's past.[8]

Binx's relationship with his mother, like so much of his life, comprises ordinary courtesies and an oblique deferral of the deeper feelings that give those gestures meaning. Though he struggles at times to evoke the correct sort of affection, to speak in the voice of a proper son—"Sometimes I feel a son's love for her, or something like this, and try to give her a special greeting," he says (137–38)—his mother does not encourage any such display. Haunted by her own griefs, the deaths of a husband and two sons (Binx's brother, Scott, and Duval, the eldest of Binx's half brothers and sisters), she resolutely "veers away from intimacy" and becomes instead a conduit to his past—in particular, to his father (149).[9] On Sunday morning, after he and Sharon have spent the night (in separate quarters, of course), his mother tells him how the start of World War II in Europe ended a severe depression in which his father would not eat or get out of bed. And as she talks, the knowledge that Binx has only hesitantly expressed before becomes unavoidable. Going to war, he realizes, fulfilled his father's secret yearning: "He had found a way to do both, to please them and please himself. To leave. To do what he wanted to do and save old England doing it. And perhaps even to carry off the grandest coup of all: to die" (157). Here, as Allen writes in *Walker Percy: A*

Southern Wayfarer, Binx discovers the object he has been warily stalking for much of the novel, "the body of a suicide" (34).

This discovery is made, though, in the midst of one of the novel's most lyric scenes. As Binx and his mother talk, their voices "ringing around the empty room of the morning" (149), her stories about his father are counter-pointed by the beauty of the environment in which they are placed and the quiet and isolation of the morning. While they speak, they stand on the edge of the dock looking out on the marsh, and their conversation is interspersed with images of astonishing precision and clarity. Even as his mother recalls his father's eye for natural beauty—"Look at such and such a tree over there," she says, mimicking him, "look at how the sunshine catches in the water in such and such a way" (150)—Binx demonstrates that he shares his father's sensibility: "It is possible to squint into the rising sun and at the same time see my mother spangled in rainbows. A crab spider has built his web across a finger of the bayou and the strands seem to spin in the sunlight" (149–50).

Indeed, Binx demonstrates over the course of this scene how much he is like his father. Not only does he share his father's sensitivity to the beauty of his environment, but he casually acknowledges that he too has felt the same kind of lassitude that paralyzed his father before the war. For Binx, though, that lassitude came in the wake of an experience on the battlefield. After being separated from his company in Korea, Binx experienced a strange kind of listlessness that he struggles to define for his mother: "What I am trying to tell you is that nothing seemed worth doing except something I couldn't even remember. If somebody had come up to me and said: if you will forget your preoccupation for forty minutes and get to work, I can assure you that you will find the cure for cancer and compose the greatest of all symphonies—I wouldn't have been interested. Do you know why? Because it wasn't good enough for me" (158). The odd calm that Binx describes here seems to be a kind of battle fatigue, the reaction of a mind that has been overloaded with impressions and demands to which it must instantly respond. (This state is apparently very different from the mood that gripped Binx when he was wounded. At this moment, nothing seems to have mattered to him; when he was wounded, everything did.) But what is striking about Binx's story is its implicit purpose: to explain not only his feelings when he was separated from his companions in Korea but his father's too, as he lay in bed for days on end before the outbreak of World War II. Binx has heretofore studiously avoided commenting on any resemblance between himself and his father.

Now, however, he deliberately makes such a comparison. Why has this change occurred—particularly just when Binx has discovered the extent of his father's despair? It is difficult to say. Perhaps his quiet, halting acknowledgment of this resemblance is only the inevitable consequence of an effort to understand his father's suffering. Perhaps Binx's recognition of his father's desire to leave is too familiar to be overlooked, too much like the feelings that have shaped his own life in Gentilly. Whatever the reason, though, this much is clear: Binx moves closer to allowing his father's voice to sound in his consciousness and, further, to assimilating it—with all the consequences that may entail.

In a sense, this exchange between Binx and his mother early Sunday morning is the eye of the storm that sweeps over him in the course of the novel and transforms his life. But the calm that prevails in this remarkable scene cannot last. Sooner or later, the despair that Binx holds at bay must catch up with him. Ironically, though, the instrument through which it strikes is the character with whom he is most openly affectionate: his half brother, Lonnie.

Lonnie is a fourteen-year-old who is afflicted with a wasting, degenerative disease that has confined him to a wheelchair and will inevitably take his life. In *Walker Percy: Books of Revelation,* Gary Ciuba argues that all of Percy's major characters live a kind of apocalyptic existence in which the traditions and habits that make up their old worlds are swept away so that they may experience a kind of "unveiling," a renewed and cleansed vision that reveals new possibilities for communion with others and, ultimately, with God (3). Perhaps no other character in Percy's fiction so epitomizes this idea as Lonnie Smith. As Ciuba writes, "Binx's half brother lives in the advent of the eschaton. . . . Although Binx often longs to be an Anyone living Anywhere, Lonnie dwells at the most specific moment possible—the days before death—and in one place all his own, the breakdown of his own body. He suffers from a malady but not from the malaise. Although his illness might easily have driven him into the arrogance and acrimony of his own suffering, he has turned personal disaster into way of living ultimately, not unto himself but under God" (76). Indeed, prior to Lonnie's appearance in the novel, the possibility of faith has been at best remote. Citing opinion polls that show that "98% of Americans believe in God," Binx early on dismisses the issue. "Who wants to be dead last among one hundred and eighty million Americans?" he asks (14). Yet Lonnie's devout Catholicism has an entirely different effect on Binx. As Binx says when he considers Lonnie's belief that his sufferings are a kind of penance for others' sins, "I would not mind trading places with him. His life is a serene business" (137).

Like Binx, Lonnie is an avid moviegoer, and when Binx and Sharon take him and his brothers and sisters to the Moonlite Drive-In on Saturday night to see *Fort Dobbs,* a Western with Clint Walker, Lonnie's special bond with Binx is clearly demonstrated. While they lie on the hood of Binx's car, Binx and Lonnie watch each other watch the movie and furtively signal their recognition of the special moments in the film that both of them love: "he looks around at me with the liveliest sense of the secret between us; the secret is that Sharon is not and never will be onto the little touches we see in the movie and, in the seeing, know that the other sees—as when Clint Walker tells the saddle tramp in the softiest easiest old Virginian voice: "Mister, I don't believe I would do that if I was you"—Lonnie is beside himself, doesn't know whether to watch Clint Walker or me" (143–44). At this moment, Binx and Lonnie embody Gabriel Marcel's concept of intersubjectivity, which Percy has adapted in his essays and his fiction. In his description of the sense of intimacy that is engendered by intersubjectivity, Martin Luschei in *The Sovereign Wayfarer* virtually takes as his model Binx and Lonnie's silent exchange at the drive-in: "The mainspring of intersubjectivity is the shared secret. Two people who have an intimate relationship often feel a kind of unity that excludes a third person, centered on a secret shared by those two, whether merely a few allusions or jokes or some painful, incommunicable experience" (54).

Lonnie ultimately brings out a warmer, less guarded side of Binx. In contrast to Binx's difficult relationship with his mother and his contrived affection for Sharon, his feelings for Lonnie are not complicated by false expectations or a hidden agenda. When talking to Lonnie, Binx neither assumes a pose nor tries to take on some obligatory role. He speaks directly and affectionately, without even the defensiveness that clouds his relationship with Kate. And Lonnie, for his part, is equally direct. He is perhaps the only character in the novel whose voice is not distorted by echoes of other people's words or subtle references to other contexts, other relationships. Though Lonnie, as Binx notes, "uses the peculiar idiom of the catechism in ordinary speech," such terms as "an habitual disposition" or "a jocose lie" do not seem borrowed or false when Lonnie speaks them, because he has achieved his ideological becoming and assimilated the language of the church as his own (163). As Ciuba argues, "because Lonnie's life is centered on the Logos, his words are renewed not just in sound but in their very essence" (78). Purified by a faith that is forged in the crucible of his suffering, Lonnie's words are univocal, and, consequently, they are restored to meaning. As Binx says, "Lonnie's monotonous speech gives him an advantage, the same advantage foreigners have: his words are not worn out. It is like a code tapped through a wall. Sometimes he asks me straight out: do you love me? and it is possible to tap back: yes, I love you" (131).

But for Binx, who is used to surveying the world from the safe distance afforded by the posture of objectivity, this kind of intimacy is unsettling. Even the analogy he uses in the passage above suggests his caution: when he expresses love, he taps out his message in code. So it is not surprising, then, that his caution gets the better of him when he and Sharon prepare to leave on Sunday afternoon. After saying their goodbyes, Binx is called back by Lonnie. "'Wait,'" Lonnie says, using the same word that Will Barrett cries out in *The Last Gentleman* when he tries to prevent his father's suicide. In *Walker Percy: A Southern Wayfarer,* Allen says that "this all-important word in Percy's fiction" is "uttered time and time again by characters reaching out in the deepest need for human contact" (70). Here, though, Lonnie seems to only want to continue the religious talk in which he and Binx engaged earlier. When Binx once more starts to leave, however, Lonnie calls out again:

> "Wait."
> "What?"
> "Do you love me?"
> "Yes."
> "How much?"
> "Quite a bit."
> "I love you too." But already he has the transistor in the crook of his wrist and is working it furiously. (165)

In the space between Lonnie's assertion—"I love you too"—and Binx's observation—"But already he has the transistor in the crook of his wrist"—a pall descends on Binx's heart. The preposition *but* is steeped in doubt. For Binx, Lonnie's shift in attention is a shadow that falls over his declaration of love, obscuring it. Never mind that Lonnie's fleeting attention is probably just a sign of the child who lingers in the wreck of his body; Binx chooses to regard Lonnie's actions as a comment on the strength or the significance of his feelings.

Why is Binx so quick to make this assumption? Because everything he has experienced so far argues against the viability or even the importance of love. His proposal to Kate—perhaps his most explicit declaration of affection until this exchange with Lonnie—could not stop her from "overtaking herself." His relationship with his mother is distant, and their guarded conversation on Sunday morning only proved that the love of family—if it could even be said to have existed—was insufficient solace for his father's despair. Even Binx's relationship with Sharon has not led to the romantic or sexual intimacy for which he had hoped. But, most important, perhaps, his and Lonnie's feelings for each other—no matter how strong or how pure—cannot disguise Lonnie's frailty. How insubstantial love must seem when it is weighed against the ravages of Lonnie's illness. How quickly, also, is love absorbed into the routine, the mundane details of life. In less than a second, Binx and Lonnie's special relationship is eclipsed by Lonnie's attention to his radio and the necessity of Binx's departure.

No wonder, then, that in the next sentence his car is "infested with malaise" (166). At this point in the novel, Binx's strategies for outrunning his despair have given out. On the way back to New Orleans, he and Sharon occupy one car in a long train of vacationers making their way miserably back to the city, "all with the same vacant headachy look" (166). Even Binx's "little red MG," which he had earlier said was "immune to the malaise," cannot protect them from its ill effects (122).

Binx's depressed and diminished state leaves him ill prepared for what he finds when he returns to New Orleans. On arriving at Emily's home, he is greeted by Sam Yerger, a journalist and novelist and old family friend. In contrast to Binx, whose sense of self is now more muddled and obscure than ever, the "rumpled and red-eyed" and "bearish-big" Sam is, in Binx's words, "as always, of a piece" (167–68). Indeed, we quickly learn that Binx has long been susceptible to Sam's Hemingwayesque persona.[10] He describes Sam as having a "larger-than-life plenitude" and later says that the stories Sam tells about his various adventures in Mexico and Venezuela "used to arouse in me an appreciation so keen and pleasurable that it bordered on the irritable" (168, 180). But if Sam's voice had once registered in Binx's consciousness as a model of "a Stoic sort of gracefulness," Binx's use of the past tense in his description of the pleasure he took in Sam's stories indicates that Sam's Hemingwayesque stoicism has no more impact on him now than Emily's characteristic exhortations to "live by his lights [and] go down fighting" (169, 54). For Binx has clearly learned to distrust the doomy romanticism implicit in such typically gnomic utterances of Sam's as "Always cherish your woman, Binx" (169). Even now, Binx fails to respond in kind to the urgency in Sam's manner when Sam tells him about Kate's apparent overdose of sleeping pills the night before and his and Emily's plan to spirit her away to New York for treatment by a famous European analyst. While Sam paces furiously as he speaks, Binx sits "hunched over and bemused by the malaise" (170), and when he is sent off to find Kate he immediately tells her almost everything that Sam has just told him about her actions. "I tell her the truth because I have not the wit to tell her anything else," Binx explains (176), referring obliquely to his own exhausted state at this moment. But surely Binx also confides in Kate because the despair in her voice resonates more deeply with him than Sam's tacit appeal to Binx's sense of duty and the self-conscious drama of Sam's account of the previous night—it is narrated as skillfully as any of the stories that used to appeal to Binx, with extravagant references to Kate's charm and her doctor's "nerve" and his own "importunate sense of something wrong" (173, 172).

Indeed, the distance between Binx's and Kate's alienated perspectives and the values of Emily and Sam is epitomized by Binx and Kate's literal perspective as they talk to one another. After Sam sends him to find Kate, Binx comes upon her in "a dark little mezzanine" off of the stairway "wherefrom the view of the house, the hall and the dining room, seems at once privileged and strange" (175). From this "privileged" vantage, Binx and Kate watch the rest of the family at dinner below like moviegoers screening a film. As Binx himself acknowledges, Kate observes Sam "like a theatre-goer in the balcony" (177). But we see not only Binx and Kate's detachment from the others in this scene. As all of their voices overlap, the conversations in the dining room and on the mezzanine playing off of and counterpointing one another in a virtuoso display of Percy's novelistic skill and his keen ear, the microdialogue in Binx's consciousness is externalized. We hear Kate's narrative of her struggle with despair, a struggle that is much like Binx's. (When she says that she took "six or eight" sleeping pills only to "break out, or off, off dead center" [181], like a wounded man, we cannot help but think of Binx's struggle to regain the vision he experienced when he was lying in his own blood in Korea.) And we hear Sam "spieling in pretty good style" for Emily and the others, as the southern traditions and manners that still pull at Binx play out in the dining room (180).

Binx, of course, fails miserably in the duties that Sam had entrusted to him. Even when Sam gives him specific instructions, all he remembers is "that they were delivered in the tone of one of my aunt's grand therapeutic schemes" (183). Instead of helping to get Kate to New York, as Sam and Emily had hoped, Binx agrees—without telling anyone else, a fateful omission that will come back to haunt him—to allow Kate to accompany him on a business trip to Chicago.

Soon enough, they are heading north on what will prove to be a nightmarish journey. From the moment they step on the train, an air of foreboding prevails. Their sleeping compartments, Binx notes, "turn out to be little coffins for a single person" (184). Even the countryside through which they pass is transformed into a region of the dead. From the windows of the train, a cemetery in Metairie becomes a city unto itself: "In the gathering dusk the cemeteries look at first like cities, with their rows of vaults, some two- and three-storied and forming flats and tenements, and the tiny streets and corners and curbs and even plots of lawn, all of such a proportion that in the very instant of being mistaken and from the eye's own necessity, they set themselves off into the distance like a city seen from far away" (185). Of course, this elaborate conceit requires an effort of mind to bring it off. A cemetery—even in Metairie, where bodies are entombed above the marshy ground—does not necessarily resemble a city, despite being seen at night from the window of a speeding train. The mind works on a brief, blurred impression and transforms it according to the dictates of imagination and emotion. Binx, in other words, chooses to confuse cemeteries and cities, to see roomettes as coffins, and to describe the train's passage over a stretch of elevated tracks above the cemetery as riding "at a witch's level above the gravelly roofs" (185). Why do these dark images occur to him now? We must remember that it has only been a few short hours since Binx, in his conversation with his mother on Sunday morning, offered his first acknowledgment of his likeness to his father. And in doing so, Binx took his first tentative steps toward assimilating his father's voice in the microdialogue of his own consciousness. The morbid images that haunt Binx are the graphic manifestations of that voice. Though any specific verbal traces of his father's voice are deliberately censored from Binx's narrative, the darkness that veiled his father's sight and no doubt helped to drive him to his doom manifests itself now in what Binx sees from the train. In effect, these nightmarish images alert us to a shifting balance in his microdialogue. The further Binx travels from New Orleans, from the South itself, where the history and traditions that pull at him are rooted, the more his aunt's exhortations recede in his consciousness. We hear no echoes of Emily's voice in Binx's account of his trip to Chicago, and, consequently, Binx acts in a way that is increasingly at odds with any vestige of her stoic code.

But these somber images also suggest that events are quickly reaching a crisis. As the night proceeds, Kate intermittently steals off to the bathroom to take more of her pills, and her moods change quickly. When Binx finds her in her roomette at one point, she speaks wistfully of his proposal, nearly in tears. Then, suddenly, she rails at him:

> "Can't you see that it is much too late for such ingenious little schemes?"
>
> "As marrying?"
>
> "The only way you could carry it off is as another one of your ingenious little researches. Admit it."
>
> "Then why not do it?"
>
> "You remind me of a prisoner in the death house who takes a wry pleasure in doing things like registering to vote. Come to think of it, all your gaiety and good spirits have the same death house quality. No thanks. I've had enough of your death house pranks." (193)

Kate's speech is a crucial moment in the novel. Though she has always served to warn us of the limits of Binx's self-knowledge, she makes clear now the consequences of his behavior by taking the death imagery that permeates his narrative and fashioning it into an indictment of his life in Gentilly and his "search." (That Kate somehow manages to draw from the same well of imagery as Binx is an indication, also, of how psychologically close they are.) This is why she asks him to "admit" that he could only marry her if it was one of his "ingenious little researches." Kate tries to force Binx to acknowledge the extent of his abstraction, how it corrupts even his most intimate relations. But her final analogy is still more damning. When she compares him to "a prisoner in the death house who takes a wry pleasure in registering to vote," we cannot help but recall Binx's claim at the beginning of the novel to be "a model tenant and a model citizen" (6). Yet that passage, in which he spoke so fondly of carrying out "the duties of a citizen," rings very differently now, when it is overshadowed by Binx's and Kate's despair (6). What had once seemed a clever and amusing facade, a way of playfully forestalling more important choices, now seems pathetically inadequate—in Kate's words, a "death house prank."

But the truth of Kate's attack is blunted perhaps by the manner in which she expresses it, for her language in this scene is often borrowed, inauthentic. When, for example, she explains why she will not marry him, her speech becomes a broad parody of middle class slang: "I'm not up to it. Having a little hubby—you would be hubby, dearest Binx, and that is ridiculous—did

I hurt your feelings? Seeing hubby off in the morning, having lunch with the girls, getting tight at Eddie's and Nell's house and having a little humbug with somebody else's hubby, wearing my little diaphragm and raising my two lovely boys and worrying for the next twenty years about whether they will make Princeton" (194). The way Kate expresses her vision of married life washes it in the worst kind of hypocrisy. And her manner of speaking also enables Binx to ignore her attack, because he is never so aloof from her as when he coolly analyzes the echoes that sound in her speech. As Binx says when she leaves him again to go to the bathroom, "None of this is new, of course. I do not, to tell the truth, pay too much attention to what she says. It is her voice that tells me how she is. Now she speaks in her 'bold' tone and since she appears to be more composed . . . than her words might indicate, I am not seriously concerned about her" (195).

Kate only breaks through to Binx, at last, when she seduces him. Yet even that act is oddly stilted, for Kate first broaches the possibility of it in a voice that is dominated by double-voiced discourse. When Kate accompanies Binx back to his roomette still later in the night and lies with him arm in arm on his bed, she tells him about declaring her intention to her psychiatrist a few days earlier of "having a little fling" (198). As she explains to Binx, "I'm talking about some plain old monkey business . . . like a comic book one of your aunt's maids showed me last week in which Tillie the Toiler and Mac—not the real Tillie, you understand, but a Frenchy version of Tillie— go to an office party and Tillie has a little set-to with Mac in the stockroom and gets caught by Whipple" (198–99). Kate's manner of speaking here is frank and businesslike—"I'm talking about some plain old monkey business"—but her language is surprisingly coy, not at all like the cool, clinical "sex books" that were popular in the late 1950s. (Binx, at one point, imagines a passage from a typical such work, *Technique in Marriage* by Dr. and Mrs. Bob Dean: "Now with tender regard for your partner remove your hand from the nipple and gently manipulate—" [190].) When Kate speaks of enjoying some "monkey business" or "a little set-to," her expressions are stilted, artificial. She seems at once to parody her own frankness and slightly retreat from it behind a veil of euphemisms. Indeed, there is even a plaintive quality to her bold demeanor that we hear in her final, desperate question to Binx: "So—when all is said and done, that is the real thing isn't it?" (199). For Kate, who has searched for some kind of authentic experience, sexuality presents itself as her last, best hope.

But "the real thing" fails. Though Binx complies with her wishes, striving dutifully like a good soldier, he is not the adroit lover he would like to be. Burdened with the responsibility of being either as stubbornly virtuous as the movie stars he admires, like Clark Gable in *It Happened One Night,* or as reliably virile as the protagonist of a John O'Hara novel, Binx is neither, and this, in a sense, is a sort of death. In his essay "The Man on the Train," Percy speaks of a typical moviegoer who, like Binx, attempts to emulate the "gestural perfection" of the characters on the screen (*MB* 94). But "gestural perfection," Percy warns, is "an aesthetic standard which is appropriated by the moviegoer at a terrific cost in anxiety" (*MB* 94). When that standard cannot be maintained, the moviegoer is caught up in "a spiral of despair whose only term is suicide or total self-loss" (*MB* 95). And so, when Binx fails to make love to Kate with the ease and dispatch of one of his heroes, he suffers a loss of self that is a kind of death.

This failure signals the beginning of Binx's emergence from his old life. Though other things must happen to complete that process, he now sheds the irony and the self-protectiveness that once insulated him from the world. We hear this change when he tries to explain what went wrong in his tryst with Kate. Binx's language is still full of echoes—he even addresses his account to Rory Calhoun, a movie star who was infamous for his roguish sexuality—but Binx's tone in this passage is startlingly different.[11]

> Flesh poor flesh failed us. The burden was too great and flesh poor flesh, neither hallowed by sacrament nor despised by spirit (for despising is not the worst fate to overtake the flesh), but until this moment seen through and canceled, rendered null by the cold and fishy eye of the malaise—flesh poor flesh now at this moment summoned all at once to be all and everything, end all and be all, the last and only hope—quails and fails. The truth is I was frightened half to death by her bold (not really bold, not whorish bold but theorish bold) carrying on. I reckon I am used to my blushing little Lindas from Gentilly. Kate too was scared. We shook like leaves. Kate was scared because it seemed now that even Tillie the Toiler must fail her. I never worked so hard in my life, Rory. I had no choice: the alternative was unspeakable. Christians talk about the horror of sin, but they have overlooked something. They keep talking as if everyone were a great sinner, when the truth is nowadays one is hardly up to it. There is very little sin in the depths of the malaise. The highest moment of a malaisian's life can be that moment when he manages to sin like a proper human. (200)

Of course, what strikes us first in this passage is the presence of a new voice within his microdialogue, for Binx—the skeptic, the searcher—now speaks in a religious voice. There is a penitential sound to his refrain "flesh poor flesh," and the long second sentence, with its liturgical rhythms, reads like a prayer. Why does he speak in this voice at this moment? In his essay "Notes for a Novel about the End of the World," Percy defines the word *religious* "as signifying a radical *bond* . . . which connects man with reality—or the failure of such a bond—and so confers meaning to his life—or the absence of meaning" (*MB* 102–3). In this context, Binx's religious voice here signals the failure of such a bond. Kate—and perhaps he also—had looked for this act to be "the real thing," to connect them to reality in some vital yet intangible way. But as Binx says, "the burden was too great"; sexuality alone could not "be all and everything" for Kate and him. Indeed, there is even a kind of nostalgia for the clear moral strictures that religion once provided, because those boundaries would at least have lent some meaning to their act. De-prived of the name *sin,* purged of any declarations of affection—"Just don't speak to me of love, bucko," Kate told him earlier (198)—and so steeped in anxiety that even physical pleasure is impossible, Binx and Kate's awkward coupling leaves them exposed to "the cold and fishy eye of the malaise."

But this apparent disaster is redeemed—in part, perhaps—by its effect on Binx, because there is also a new directness and honesty in his narrative. When he says, "The truth is I was frightened half to death by her bold . . . carrying on," his undisguised sexual anxiety is radically different from the evasions he used to conceal his feelings earlier in the novel. Even when he was overcome by despair after leaving his mother's fishing camp, the reasons for his mood were rendered elliptically. Binx refused to trace his despair to his visit or the emotions it provoked; he explained his unease in general terms rather than as the result of a specific set of circumstances acting on a specific individual: "Sunday afternoon is always the worst time for malaise," he insisted (166). By contrast, Binx is far more direct here. Moreover, this passage is characterized by a relative absence of his usual abstraction. Binx only slips into his familiar detached voice in the final sentence—"The high-est moment of a malaisian's life can be that moment when he manages to sin like a proper human"—and even then the theory he advances clearly arises from his own experience. Binx makes no attempt here to obscure the per-sonal nature of this observation.

Binx and Kate's stay in Chicago is notable for his increasing dependence on her. "Kate takes charge of me with many a cluck and much fuss, as if she had caught sight in me of a howling void and meant to conceal it from the world," Binx says (202), and his analogy is far more truthful than he would like it to be. But the climax of the novel occurs after Binx and Kate have been called back to New Orleans by Emily, who has tracked them to Chicago and is furious with Binx for this apparent breach of trust. "Do you have any notion of how I felt when, not twelve hours after Kate has attempted suicide, she vanishes without a trace?" (222), Emily asks in the midst of a long, bitter denunciation of his conduct. Both Binx and Emily ultimately recognize in this scene—their last "serious talk"—that they do not share a common language. As Emily says, "All these years I have been assuming that between us words mean roughly the same thing, that among certain people, gentlefolk I don't mind calling them, there exists a set of meanings held in common, that a certain manner and a certain grace come as naturally as breathing" (222). Indeed, throughout this exchange, Binx struggles to adopt a voice and a manner of speaking that will frame his conduct in terms Emily can understand: "I try as best I can to appear as she would have me, if not right, then wrong in a recognizable, a right form of wrongness. But I can think of nothing to say" (222).

Binx's inability to explain his behavior to Emily is a decisive moment in the novel. Until now, his rejection of her values has been tentative, compromised by his desire to appear reasonable to her as well. Yet at this moment he finds that he cannot express himself in her aristocratic language. Though he can mimic her way of speaking well enough for small talk and the expected courtesies, the lofty abstractions that fill her speech and the ethical conviction that animates her do not convey his sense of the world. Emily—again the moralist in the stoic tradition of the Old South—speaks of *right* and *wrong* or *noble* and *ignoble,* but Binx does not live in the simple, hierarchical world those terms evoke, a world where moral distinctions are as rigid and clear-cut as class lines. When, for example, she asks him, "Do you condone your behavior with Kate?" (225), he is clearly puzzled. Though he knows his actions were questionable, the word *condone* frames the issue entirely as one of conduct, whether he adhered to an ethical code of behavior. Yet Binx— who has consistently rejected the stance of the moralist—was not concerned with morality when he slept with Kate; he was virtually driven into her arms by a mutual sense of existential terror.

In Bakhtin's terms, Binx stands now on the verge of his "ideological becoming." He recognizes that he cannot assimilate his aunt's beliefs. But if he turns away from her stoic ideology, what is left for him? Binx struggles with

this question as he sits in the schoolyard across from his apartment shortly
after his aunt dismisses him.

> Today is my thirtieth birthday and I sit on the ocean wave in the
> schoolyard and wait for Kate and think of nothing. Now in the thirty-
> first year of my dark pilgrimage on this earth and knowing less than I
> ever knew before, having learned only to recognize merde when I see
> it, having inherited no more from my father than a good nose for
> merde, for every species of shit that flies—my only talent—smelling
> merde from every quarter, living in fact in the very century of merde,
> the great shithouse of scientific humanism where needs are satisfied,
> everyone becomes an anyone, a warm and creative person, and prospers
> like a dung beetle, and one hundred percent of people are humanists
> and ninety-eight percent believe in God, and men are dead, dead, dead;
> and the malaise has settled like a fall-out and what people really fear is
> not that the bomb will fall but that the bomb will not fall—on this my
> thirtieth birthday, I know nothing and there is nothing to do but fall
> prey to desire. (228)

Because of its emphasis on the significance of this day, there is an odd formality to this passage, as if it were an official confession. In a sense, Binx
seems to want to expunge the guilt that he could not explain to his aunt,
and so he engages in a kind of intellectual mortification, scourging himself
again and again with his admission that he knows "nothing." But his guilt is
not due to a simple moral lapse, like the things of which Emily accuses him;
rather, it is a consequence of his self-deception. Throughout the novel, he
has refused to see the paucity of his methods for holding off despair: the futility of his "Little Way" and the narrow, limited reach of his search. (It is a
fine idea in principle perhaps, but the actuality does not lead to much.) Now,
however, with his admission that he knows "less than I ever knew before,"
he acknowledges the truth of what Kate has told him all along, that his despair is as bad as hers and that his stratagems for evading it are nothing more
than "death house pranks."

In this remarkable passage, Binx implicitly denies that he has ever been
"onto something," as he once claimed that his search proved him to be, and
his language is purged not only of all traces of his aunt's stoicism but of the
scientism associated with his search as well (13). Yet the passage is still
double-voiced. His language is filled with traces of many different voices,

from the benign, vacuous humanism that Binx parodies to the first clear echo of his father's voice, completing the tentative assimilation of this voice that began in his conversation with his mother. His ability to "recognize merde" is inherited from his father, Binx insists, and he both embraces and flaunts that gift in the fierce contempt that roils through the long second sentence. But what is most striking—particularly in light of the absence of his usual abstraction—is the presence, again, of what can only be termed a religious voice. Binx's admissions of his failings ring of the confessional. His conclusion, "on this my thirtieth birthday, I know nothing," seems like a formal gesture of contrition—or it would, if not for the tag that follows: "and there is nothing to do but fall prey to desire." (It is as if he is embarrassed by his penitent tone and deliberately chooses an ironic form of chastisement to compensate for it.) Most of all, however, his initial reference to his life as a "dark pilgrimage" suggests that he now sees his existence in a religious context, though one in which faith is still profoundly uncertain.

Binx is clearly moving away from the posture of objectivity in this passage. The lack of abstraction and the bitter, personal tone suggest that he no longer stands "outside and over against the world" (*MB* 128) in the characteristic mode of the scientist. But despite the religious echoes in this microdialogue, he is by no means a believer either. If his life is a pilgrimage, it is shrouded in doubt, and he is as yet a pilgrim only in the sense that he longs for direction and faith. Binx is at his lowest ebb here, and he initially tries to console himself by falling back on another of his old tricks, masking despair with desire. But Binx's pathetic gambit of trying to seduce (over the telephone, at that) either Sharon or her roommate is quickly made unnecessary. For hope soon arrives in the person of Kate, who had promised to meet him earlier as he left his aunt's home. While Binx and Kate sit in her car outside a church where people are arriving to celebrate Ash Wednesday, they speak again of marriage. Although all of their previous conversations on the subject ended unresolved, Kate is astonished that Binx did not explain himself to Emily by announcing their plans to marry, because Kate now takes it for granted that they will and has told Emily so. This announcement functions as both a reprieve for Binx—Emily has asked to see him again—and a prod. For this decision, confirmed at last, enables him to make a larger decision. He knows now, or seems to know, how he shall live his life: "There is only one thing I can do: listen to people, see how they stick themselves into the world, hand them along a ways in their dark journey and be handed along, and for good and selfish reasons" (233).

Despite his apparent earlier rejection of his aunt's values, Binx seems now to accept her ideal of service. Though his resolution to "listen to people, see how they stick themselves into the world" sounds like a continuation of his search, and though he again briefly entertains the idea of opening a gas station, he quickly tells Kate that he will bow to Emily's wishes and go to medical school. Is this decision another attempt to seem reasonable, to please his aunt? At first glance, it certainly seems to be. Yet the language in which he expresses his decision has no trace of the aristocratic "obligations" of which Emily speaks (223). Rather, Binx's vision of service, "to hand [others] along a ways in their dark journey and be handed along," is one of fellowship and interdependence. Though he assimilates something from his aunt here, the ideal of service itself, her voice does not echo in his own, for he does not speak of reaching down to others from his own exalted station but of helping them along on a common path. And this vision is expressed in the religious voice we heard in Binx's monologue on the ocean wave: the "dark journey" he speaks of here is the same as his own "dark pilgrimage."

Much has been said in the criticism of Percy's work about Binx's transformation at the end of *The Moviegoer*. In *The Sovereign Wayfarer*, for example, Luschei speaks of Binx making Kierkegaard's "leap of faith" (106). I want to emphasize, however, how Binx's transformation is embodied in Percy's language, in the play of voices that characterizes his narrative. Moreover, Binx's transformation, which is accomplished through a dialogic process, is itself inalterably joined to an affirmation of the abiding value of dialogue. It is no accident that the moment of Binx's transformation is also the moment when his union with Kate is finally affirmed. In the simplest sense, each of these events reinforces the other. Kate's love is literally Binx's salvation in the depths of his despair, and the faith that underpins his determination to help others in "their dark journey" enables him to accept Kate in all her frailty. Indeed, as J. P. Telotte argues in his essay, "A Symbolic Structure for Walker Percy's Fiction," the act of communication between two individuals is consistently portrayed in Percy's work as a restorative of the most profound human values: "Provided that man can open himself up to the intersubjective possibilities of communication, if he braves the risk of caring for others, the possibility remains that he may re-establish that most fundamental of human communities, 'the I-Thou' relation espoused by Martin Buber" (175).

Both the possibility and the elusiveness of faith coalesce for Binx in the image of a heavyset, well-dressed black man leaving the church in front of which Kate's car is parked. Because of the man's skin color Binx cannot tell if there are ashes on his forehead, and his whole demeanor—"more respectable than respectable . . . more middle class than one could believe" (233)—seems too worldly and stolid to embody the faith that Binx seeks. Indeed, in one of Percy's later, more satirical works like *The Second Coming,* this man might be an object of satire, a Christian in name only whose outward piety is inextricably linked to his inward conformity. Yet here, the incongruity between this man's workaday manner and his presence outside the church becomes a mystery over which Binx lingers in the final sentences of his narrative of this pivotal week:

> It is impossible to say why he is here. Is it part and parcel of the complex business of coming up in the world? Or is it because he believes that God himself is present here at the corner of Elysian Fields and Bon Enfants? Or is he here for both reasons: through some dim dazzling trick of grace, coming for the one and receiving the other as God's own importunate bonus?
> It is impossible to say. (235)

As this passage demonstrates, Binx's transformation has not silenced the microdialogue in his consciousness. There is a conflict of voices in this passage that recalls the tension between lyricism and analysis that was a consequence of Binx's search. Just as he wanted to regain the world through the medium of the search but distanced himself from it with the scientific, analytical consciousness he brought to his "researches," Binx perceives the possibility of faith here in all its "dim dazzling" glory, but—as of yet—he cannot quite affirm its reality. The skepticism bred in him by his scientific training is still too strong, and so the lavish language in which he evokes "God's own importunate bonus" is balanced by the detached, interrogative form of the sentences in which it appears and by the equivocal statements that bracket his musings: "It is impossible to say."

The extent of Binx's transformation is only made clear in the epilogue, which advances the story a year. Much has changed in that time: he and Kate have married, he has begun medical school, his uncle and Lonnie have died. Yet not only the circumstances of his life are different; Binx too has changed, though it is difficult at first to say how. The language of his narrative is still sly and allusive, and he still observes and analyzes others' behavior. When, for example, in the flashback that ends the novel, Kate decides to see Lonnie before he dies, Binx describes her action in the same condescending tone he used before as "an extravagant womanish sort of whim, what I call privately a doubling, or duplication" (238). But though he still watches others and invents terminology to classify their behavior, he no longer speaks of carrying out any "researches." Indeed, all of the pretensions regarding his search—the sweeping generalizations, the grandiose claims as to its effects—have disappeared and been replaced by a newfound humility and reticence. As Binx tells us, "As for my search, I have not the inclination to say much on the subject. For one thing, I have not the authority, as the great Danish philosopher declared, to speak of such matters in any way other than the edifying. For another thing, it is not open to me even to be edifying, since the time is later than his, much too late to edify or do much of anything except plant a foot in the right place as the opportunity presents itself—if indeed asskicking is properly distinguished from edification" (237). Of course, Binx acknowledges the influence of one of Percy's greatest "spiritual fathers" here. But more important is the implication of Binx's citation from Kierkegaard. For in alluding to Kierkegaard's decree that one cannot speak of religious matters "in any way other than the edifying," Binx admits that the focus of his search has shifted from a world of concrete, observable phenomena to a more elusive spiritual realm. In effect, he has traded the mantle of the scientist for the staff of the pilgrim.

One consequence of this shift is the complete disappearance in his narrative of the willfully impersonal, detached voice he used to discuss his search before. Binx no longer abstracts from his own experience and speaks of himself in vague, generic terms as "a man" or "anyone." His voice in the epilogue is uniformly specific and personal. Even when he talks about the search, he explains its new difficulties in individual terms: "*I* have not the inclination to say much more on the subject. . . . *I* have not the authority . . . to speak of such matters in any way other than the edifying . . . . [I]t is not open to *me* even to be edifying" (my emphasis). This shift is certainly very important. For as Bakhtin tells us again and again throughout his writings, a change in voice such as this indicates a change also in the way one exists in the world. Binx no longer holds himself apart from the world, a detached observer composing grand theories about alienation (as a general condition) and despair (as a common ailment). Rather, he now exists in the world as an individual whose struggles—however representative they may be—are always, inevitably personal.

Binx's new placement in the world is clearly manifest in the last scene in the novel, which takes place on the day before Lonnie's death. Kate has just left his hospital room, horrified at his condition, and Binx has charge of

Lonnie's brothers and sisters. Of course, this scene recalls Binx's memory at the beginning of the novel of his brother's death and of Emily's injunction to him "to act like a soldier" (4). Like Emily, who told him in plain terms, "Scotty is dead" (4), Binx is direct and honest with the children when they ask if Lonnie will die. But Percy's emphasis, in setting up this parallel, is to contrast Binx's and Emily's manner. For Binx does not offer the children a stoic's cold comfort. When one of them asks if Lonnie will no longer be crippled when he is resurrected at the Second Coming, Binx assures them he will be healed. And in doing so, Binx makes clear his new orientation in the world, one determined by faith rather than stoicism or science.

This does not mean, though, that all of Binx's difficulties have been resolved. Kate, in particular, is as uncertain of herself as ever and needs much care and reassurance (it is as if, now that she and Binx are married, Percy cannot imagine her being as independent and forceful as he once depicted her), and Binx, as we have seen, still analyzes and labels her behavior. But their love is founded on a true interdependence. For each's fragile sense of self is dependent on the confirmation offered by the other. Just as Kate exposed Binx's various impostures earlier in the novel, her love and affection now validate the very different self he presents to the world: the medical student, the devoted husband, the quietly believing Christian whose faith underpins these different facets of his identity. Similarly, Kate, whose sense of self was as elusive and unstable as Binx's, finds herself in her interaction with him. She no longer tries to overcome her anxiety through dramatic gestures, like her attempts at suicide or her impulsive decision to have "a little fling." Rather, she struggles with her fears from day to day and looks to Binx for support and reassurance. Indeed, as Lawson writes in "Walker Percy's Indirect Communications," in language that strikingly echoes Bakhtin's vision of human interdependency and dialogue, Binx and Kate "are conscious now that they exist, for they see confirmation of their existence in the eyes of the other. And that last phrase is not conceit; they literally depend upon the recognition of themselves they see in each other's eyes for their feeling of authenticity" (*Following* 22–23).

Perhaps the best measure of Binx's change, this pilgrim's progress, is found in the last sentence of the novel, when his relation to the children, his half brothers and sisters, is transformed. As Binx watches Kate walk off, a cape jasmine flower that he had given her held aloft like a magic token, he says, "my brothers and sisters call out behind me," (242). With a shift of a word, the nascent religious voice that we heard earlier at last takes precedence in his microdialogue. For by omitting a simple adjective, Binx quietly declares that his relation to these children is no longer so tenuous, so provisional. And, by extension, perhaps, he also embraces his other brothers and sisters: the sad, fractious family of humanity. Where once he fixed his sight on the distance between himself and others, now he sees the web of creation that binds them.

THREE

White Man's Burden:
The Last Gentleman

Walker Percy's second novel, *The Last Gentleman*, is a far more expansive book than *The Moviegoer.* It is as if Percy, having mastered the craft of writing a novel, was determined to press up against the limits he had imposed on himself in his previous book. Though the principal theme of *The Last Gentleman* is the same as that of *The Moviegoer*—as Percy explained, "A great deal of *The Moviegoer* and *The Last Gentleman* have to do with the differences between me and my uncle. The whole thing is a dialectic between his attitude, which *was* a Southern patrician paternalism, and the attitude of the two young men in these novels, a more detached, alienated point of view" (*Con.* 91)—Percy's canvas in his second novel is much larger. Everything that lingered in the background of *The Moviegoer* comes into a sharper focus here: the storied past of an aristocratic southern family, the inadequacy of their stoic ideology, the changes wrought in the South by the civil rights movement. And while *The Moviegoer* is a spare, undramatic work, *The Last Gentleman* features a complex plot filled with character and incident. In contrast to Binx Bolling's story, which is tightly focused in space and time, *The Last Gentleman* details a long odyssey that carries its protagonist across much of the United States.

Technically, Percy's second novel is also more elaborate, as he abandons—in part at least—the safe haven of a first-person narration. *The Last Gentleman* is dominated initially by an omniscient narrator who comments in a discursive fashion on the background and the psychological difficulties of the novel's protagonist, Will Barrett. As Percy acknowledged in an interview in 1973, "I wanted [Will] seen as a patient, an ill man suffering all kinds of difficulties. In the first person it would have been incoherent because he has this in and out of amnesia" (*Con.* 83). But the method of the novel gradually changes, as the influence of the narrator recedes and we see events almost exclusively through Will's perspective. In "Narrative Triangulation in *The Last Gentleman*," Simone Vauthier observes that by the end of the book the omniscient narrator has virtually disappeared: "Almost transparent, he leaves us to face the characters' words, their few gestures . . . and to decipher the meaning of the scene" (72). Indeed, the narrator's voice, so powerful in the opening pages of the novel, is gradually replaced by Will's, which is woven into the book's third-person narration through the use of what is conventionally called "free indirect style" or what Bakhtin in "Discourse in the Novel" terms "character zones." Through this technique, Percy incorporates significant words or phrases of Will's into what is ostensibly the language of the narrator (and thus Percy is able to duplicate something of the effect of a first-person narrative). As Bakhtin writes, "Such a character zone is the field of action for a character's voice, encroaching in one way or another upon the author's voice" ("Discourse" 316).

But if there are important differences in the scope and technique of Percy's first two novels, both works ultimately pursue the same end: to dramatize a young man's ideological becoming, his formation of a distinctive point of view amid a clamor of other voices and beliefs. Like Binx Bolling in *The Moviegoer,* Will Barrett in *The Last Gentleman* is a young man whose consciousness is virtually overrun with other people's words and intonations. Will's mind is an echo chamber resounding with voices: "the old sad poetry" of his father's stoic code (318); the voice of the scientist, the man who transcends the brute facts of the world and observes all from a privileged, detached vantage; the prosperous though faintly strident tones of the modern South; and the dim promise of grace that haunts the conclusion of the book, the whisper that eludes Will's understanding yet lingers in his consciousness. Over the course of the novel, Will must bring this cacophony of voices into some kind of balance. He must pick and choose among them, appropriating the language of some and rejecting that of others, to achieve his ideological becoming.

The novel opens almost at the moment when the process of becoming begins in earnest. On the first page, the narrator who guides us through Will's life in the opening chapter assures us that an event is about to occur that will alter his future. Until now, we are told, Will has lived in "a state of

pure possibility, not knowing what sort of man he was or what he must do, and supposing therefore that he must be all men and do everything" (4). But within moments, the narrator explains, something will happen that will force Will to choose between the voices that echo in his consciousness (for to exist in a state of pure possibility is to assume that all of those voices speak with equal validity, that all of the paths they suggest are equally probable): "Thereafter he came to see that he was not destined to do everything but only one or two things" (4).

The event that initiates this change in perspective is "a bit of accidental eavesdropping" in which, while gazing through an expensive telescope that he has recently bought, Will spots a young woman concealing a note in a loosened mortar of a bench in Central Park (3). This chance occurrence sets in motion the novel's loose-jointed plot and leads to Will's involvement with the Vaughts, a wealthy and eccentric southern family. For when he sees Kitty Vaught, an attractive young woman, recover the note, he is instantly infatuated. Soon enough, through a series of coincidences, Will makes the acquaintance of the family and is hired—more or less—by Kitty's father, Chandler Vaught, to be a companion to her younger brother, Jamie, who is stricken with leukemia. Over the course of the novel, Will must balance his attraction to Kitty with his obligation to Jamie, a conflict that is taken advantage of by Rita Vaught, Kitty's sister-in-law and the woman who initially left the note in Central Park. Rita, who seems to desire Kitty herself, is jealous of Will and schemes to separate him from Kitty. Ultimately, however the most important members of the Vaught family are Jamie and Kitty's old siblings, Sutter—Rita's estranged husband—and Valentine. When Will f lows the Vaughts back to the South, these characters contend for influe over him. Sutter, a failed doctor now employed as a pathologist, seer offer a kind of elliptical wisdom, and Val, who outraged her parents by verting to Catholicism and entering the novitiate, charges him with responsibility. Her insistence that Will see to Jamie's baptism lead novel's powerful conclusion.

Though I will discuss this web of relationships in greater detai course of this chapter, it is important to first understand the tensic consciousness, for these competing claims have brought him to that he is, at the beginning of the novel, almost paralyzed. F description of him, lying on the ground in Central Park beside two qualities above all are emphasized about him: an inten and an overriding passivity. Like Binx Bolling, Will is cha

almost chronic wariness, an edgy sensibility that is alert to the most minute tremors of experience yet reluctant to act on what he perceives. As the narrator says of him, "What distinguished him anyhow was this: he had to know everything before he could do anything" (3).

This watchfulness is, in a sense, an inherited trait. Will is the last heir of an old southern family, the last gentleman in a long line of wealthy patricians. But the family history is one of decline, in which the capacity to act is increasingly blocked by a paralyzing sense of self-consciousness. As the narrator explains, in what is perhaps the quintessential description of the families of Percy's protagonists (and the Percy family too),

> Over the years his family had turned ironical and lost its gift for action. It was an honorable and violent family, but gradually the violence had been deflected and turned inward. The great grandfather knew what was what and said so and acted accordingly and did not care what anyone thought. He even wore a pistol in a holster like a Western hero and once met the Grand Wizard of the Ku Klux Klan in a barbershop and invited him then and there to shoot it out in the street. The next generation, the grandfather, seemed to know what was what but he was really not so sure. He was brave but he gave much thought to the business of being brave. He too would have shot it out with the Grand Wizard if only he could have made certain it was the thing to do. The father was a brave man too and he said he didn't care what others thought, but he did care. More than anything else, he wished to act with honor and to be thought well of by other men. So living for him was a strain. He became ironical. For him it was not a small thing to walk down the street on an ordinary September morning. In the end he was killed by his own irony and sadness and by the strain of living out an ordinary day in a perfect dance of honor. (9–10)

In this passage, the narrative voice remains largely aloof from the voices of the characters whose lives it chronicles. Though we hear traces of other voices—such as Will's great-grandfather who "knew what was what" with a moral certainty so absolute that any specifics were superfluous—the narrator's need to isolate and explain Will's family history necessitates that the voices of Will's ancestors be muffled. (There is, for example, an almost patronizing quality to the description of Will's father's tortured attempts to achieve "a perfect dance of honor" that is incompatible with Ed Barrett's own voice.) Yet through the detached, omniscient stance of the narrator we

see here how in Will all the confusion and self-consciousness of his father and grandfather have been distilled into an almost total passivity, an unwavering inclination toward observation rather than action. As the narrator says of Will, "he did not know what to think. So he became a watcher and a listener and a wanderer. He could not get enough of watching" (10).

Will's complex relationship to his family's storied past is the core of the novel—it underlies his passivity and figures prominently in the babel of voices that sounds within his mind—but this relationship must be seen in its historical context. *The Last Gentleman* takes place in the early 1960s and is set against the background of the civil rights struggle that divided the South, a struggle that rages on the periphery of the novel's action. For Percy, the civil rights struggle was—beyond its moral and political importance—the culmination of "a momentous change" in the social landscape of the South (*SSL* 83). In his seminal essay "Stoicism in the South," Percy noted the breakup of the traditional coalition of southern blacks and the wealthy, landed gentry that had protected black rights: "until a few years ago, the champion of Negro rights in the South, and of toleration and fair-mindedness in general, was the upper-class white Southerner. He is their champion no longer. He has, by and large, unshouldered his burden for someone else to pick up" (*SSL* 83). This disavowal, though, was not an isolated event, not merely the southern aristocrat's response to "the insolence of his former charge . . . the Negro's demanding his rights instead of being thankful for the squire's generosity" (*SSL* 86). In fact, the civil rights movement was only the last in a series of indignities that had begun in the first few decades of the century, when upper-class southerners were politically rejected in favor of the kind of populist epitomized by Huey Long. Percy's great-uncle, LeRoy Percy, experienced just such a defeat in a U.S. Senate race in 1911 at the hands of James Vardaman, an overt racist known to his supporters as the "White Chief."[1] These political defeats and the eventual rejection of the traditional system of paternalism by southern blacks resulted in a crisis for upper-class southerners like the Percy family and its fictional counterpart, Will Barrett's "honorable and violent family." Because southern honor, as Bertram Wyatt-Brown explains, depended on "the evaluation of the public" (*Southern Honor* 14), the entire ideological structure on which patricians had constructed their sense of identity and value was jeopardized by these rejections. The chivalric code of conduct and its underpinning of stoic philosophy by which patricians had lived for generations were no longer tenable. As Percy observed in "Stoicism in the South," writing on the eve of the civil rights crusade, "neither the ethos nor the traditional world-view of the upper-class white Southerner is any longer adequate to the situation. No longer able to maintain a steadfast and temperate position, he finds himself caught up in violent and even contradictory crossmovements" (*SSL* 89).

Such is the position of Will Barrett in *The Last Gentleman*. Like his father and grandfather, Will is burdened with an ethos and a code of conduct that are increasingly inadequate to respond to the complexities of the twentieth century. It is no longer so easy to know, as Will's great-grandfather did, "what was what," yet Will struggles alternately to live up to the traditions that haunt him and to escape from them. Thus, following in the family custom, he goes to Princeton for his education, even occupies the same dormitory room that his grandfather did earlier. But unlike his father and grandfather, Will does not measure up. Overpowered by the hoary traditions of the school and the family's unspoken admonition that he cherish this, "the prime and pride of youth" (13), Will drops out in his junior year and flees to New York City to live at the YMCA, finding a kind of freedom in the anonymity of city life. This tension in Will's actions—now embracing his inheritance, now rejecting it—persists for years, but it is most powerfully manifest in what the narrator gently calls Will's "nervous condition." Will, we are told, experiences "spells," something like a minor form of epilepsy that has developed in adulthood into occasional periods of amnesia (10). Of course, that amnesia—which the narrator clearly implies is a form of "emotional illness" (12) and not physiological in origin—is the most literal sign of Will's desire to erase the past, to wipe the slate clean and start his life afresh. (One of the epigraphs of the novel, taken from Kierkegaard, seems to endorse this desire: "If a man cannot forget, he will never amount to much.") Yet even the demons of Will's subconsciousness offer their obeisances to the past. When his memory returns, Will is as liable as not to come to himself while wandering on one of the battlefields of the Civil War.

For Will, the conflicting claims of his inheritance are most painfully embodied in his father's voice. Throughout the novel, Will is continually "put in mind" of his father's voice by a series of Proust-like triggers (95). A scrap of paper with a passage from Montaigne on it, the closeness of a summer night, the path along the levee into his hometown: all serve to evoke the past, to force Ed Barrett's voice on his son's mind. Indeed, though Will is described at the beginning of the novel as "not [knowing] what to think" and therefore being "a watcher and a listener and a wanderer" (10), whatever context he has for understanding the turbulent world in which he finds himself has been shaped in a large measure by what he remembers his father telling him.

For Ed Barrett, like other sons of the Old South, standards of individual morality were determined by one's place in the social hierarchy. We see this in the first of the memories of his father that abruptly surface in Will's consciousness, almost involuntarily, over the course of the novel. When, early in the book, on a hot summer night like the ones years earlier that Will spent on his front porch listening to his father declaiming about morality, Will wants to see Kitty, he suddenly remembers his father's stern condemnation of the sexual behavior of the white men and women in their hometown. Walking up and down the sidewalk in front of their home, Ed Barrett railed against the behavior of the white couples parked in their cars at night overlooking the levee. Such actions, of course, could be expected and tolerated from blacks; for Ed undoubtedly, as for William Alexander Percy, another southern patrician who bemoaned the passing of the Old South, black "vices [had] the charm of amiable weakness" (William Alexander Percy 21). But the same such behavior in whites was both intolerable and destructive of the intricately calibrated social order in which Ed believed. For whites to adopt the sexual freedom of blacks would, in Ed's eyes, lead to chaos. "One will pick up the worst of the other and lose the best of himself," Will remembers Ed saying. "Watch. One will learn to fornicate in public and the other will end by pissing in the street" (97).

To some degree, Will still believes this—or at least wants to—at the beginning of the novel. This is why he proposes to Kitty only a few pages later in the same sort of stern formal voice that his father used. "Let's go home, either to your home or mine, and be married," Will declares (100), and the link he makes between their marrying and returning "home" only emphasizes how much this decision represents an embrace of his father's beliefs. Indeed, by acting the gentleman and echoing his father's voice, Will does return in his manner and his forms of expression to the idealized South that his father envisioned for him. Even the way he speaks of marriage in the passive voice—"Let's . . . be married"—suggests that this decision is, at bottom, an act of acceptance of his rightful role and responsibility.

Ultimately, though, Will must be wary of his father's influence, for Ed Barrett's bleak vision of the Götterdämmerung of Southern values was so overwhelming that he finally took his own life with a Greener twelve-gauge shotgun. This fact is not revealed, however, until late in the novel. Will has literally repressed his awareness of it, though the memory lingers near the surface of his consciousness. When, for example, he sees Sutter Vaught idly brandishing a pistol, "aiming it here and there, laying the muzzle against his cheek," Will becomes "extremely agitated" without knowing why (206).

Over the course of the novel, Will must come to grips with his father's suicide; he must acknowledge the reality of his father's action without embracing the sentiment and values that motivated it. This dual imperative is why,
as the novel progresses, Will must painstakingly reconstruct the events leading to his father's death in his own unreliable memory. But it is also the
source of "the dread in his heart" that attends his intermittent memories of
his father striding up and down the sidewalk in front of their house, declaiming about the moral decline of the South or the vast indifference of the
universe (316). Though there is something grand and seductive about Ed
Barrett's speech, his despair is inalterably joined in Will's mind to its violent
consequence. And so, as much as Will parrots his father's voice and seems to
affirm the values he upheld, Will also often maintains a subtle distance from
those values by overlaying his expressions of them with his own exaggerated, faintly ironic accents.

The same halfhearted assimilation of another's voice occurs in Will's relationship with his psychiatrist, Dr. Gamow, who is himself "a father of sorts"
to Will (39). At the beginning of the novel, Will has been in analysis for five
years, with little to show for it beyond the depletion of his inheritance. There
is no evidence that Dr. Gamow has ever inquired into Will's past in any sys-
tematic way or that he even knows of what is surely the most profound psychological event in Will's life, his father's suicide. As the narrator tells us, "A
laborer digging in a ditch would know more about his partner in a week
than the doctor had learned about his patient in a year" (32). Why should
Will admire a man who has failed him so miserably (and whom he has been
able to bluff and elude for years)? In his own way, Dr. Gamow presents a
model of behavior that is as seductive to Will as his father's stern code of
conduct. In his ability to transcend his patients' sorrows, his seemingly in-
violable detachment, Dr. Gamow epitomizes "the posture of objectivity"
that is characteristic of a scientist. And for Will, Dr. Gamow's aloof, dispassionate manner suggests a way of stepping back from the whirl and confusion of history. If, as Percy asserts in "The Message in the Bottle," "one condition of the practice of the objective method of the sciences is the exclusion
of oneself from the world of objects one studies" (MB 129), then by emulat-
ing Dr. Gamow's scientism, Will can achieve what Binx Bolling achieves
through his "little researches" (MG 63): he can separate himself from his
family's troubled past and from the obligations that that past seems to impose on him.

This desire is the source of Will's declaration to Dr. Gamow at the end of the first chapter: "He told Dr. Gamow he had reached a decision. It seemed plain to him that he had exhausted the resources of analysis—not that he had not benefited enormously—and in the future he thought he might change places with the analyst, making a little joke of it, heh-heh. After spending almost five years as an object of technique, however valuable, he thought maybe he'd go over to the other side, become one of them, the scientists. He might even have an idea or two about the "'failure of communication' and the 'loss of identity' in the modern world." (34). Though Will's speech is filtered through the narration here, creating what Bakhtin terms a character zone, we can see how he tentatively appropriates Dr. Gamow's vocabulary and ideological perspective. When Will alludes to his own theories about "the 'failure of communication' and the 'loss of identity' in the modern world"—which, according to the narrator, are two of Dr. Gamow's "favorite subjects" (34)—Will's language again becomes double-voiced. Will tries both to appropriate Dr. Gamow's language and to set himself apart from that language. The same undercurrent of self-mockery that runs through the entire passage—so that each assertion is immediately qualified or undercut by Will's attempt to "[make] a little joke of it"—here finds expression in the quotation marks that enclose the lofty terms he takes from Dr. Gamow. Though Will is sincere in his desire to "go over to the other side" and become a scientist, an implicit skepticism—surely based on the failure of his own analysis—attaches to his words and prevents him from wholeheartedly appropriating Dr. Gamow's language.

As Bakhtin suggests in "Discourse in the Novel," not all words in all contexts "submit" to this process of appropriation: "many words stubbornly resist, others remain alien, sound foreign in the mouth of the one who appropriated them and who now speaks them; they cannot be assimilated into his context and fall out of it; it is as if they put themselves into quotation marks against the will of the speaker" (294). So it is with the language that Will borrows from Dr. Gamow. Because of his knowledge of Dr. Gamow's failure in treating him—however much Will might resist acknowledging that failure—Will cannot use such expressions of Dr. Gamow's as "the 'loss of identity' in the modern world" without some measure of irony coloring his words, almost involuntarily.

Despite this fact, however, it would be a mistake to underestimate Will's fascination with what Percy calls "the objective method of the sciences." Will clearly conceives of himself as a practitioner of science, someone in step with the zeitgeist of the twentieth century. After all, he has learned scientific

principles through his long tutorial with Dr. Gamow. (At least this is how
Will seems to construe this process: as an alternative to his abortive career at
Princeton. When he cuts off his analysis, Will thinks of leaving "his alma
mater, sweet mother psychoanalysis" [39].) And he has been trained as "a
humidification engineer" (18). In preparation for a job at Macy's, where he
monitors the store's air-conditioning console from midnight until eight in
the morning, Will took a six-month course in "Temperature and Humidification Control" (18). Through a kind of fusion of this technical training and
the process of analysis, Will is, in his own eyes, schooled in the values and
methodology of science. As he thinks at the end of the first chapter, "I am
indeed an engineer . . . if only a humidification engineer, which is no great
shakes of a profession. But I am also an engineer in the deeper sense: I shall
engineer the future of my life according to the scientific principles and the
self-knowledge I have so arduously gained from five years of analysis" (40).
Indeed, so strong is his conviction that he is a kind of scientist and that
his life can be made as orderly as a diagram or a mathematical formula that
that belief is refracted through the narrative. Will is almost never referred to
by name in the novel—it is as if his name is too bound up with his
family's troubled past to use without invoking that past—but he is referred
to instead by a series of designations, the most common of which is the
"engineer."[2]

Another manifestation of Will's scientific bent is his most conspicuous
possession, the telescope beside which he is lying on the first page of the
novel. Will buys the telescope when he becomes convinced that the world is
so sunk in everydayness that it is no longer "accessible" to ordinary sight;
only "special measures," such as the telescope with its intricate network of
lenses and prisms, can enable him to "recover" the reality of the seemingly
mundane phenomena that surround him (30). Of course, the view through
the telescope is itself a metaphor for the posture of objectivity; even as it
heightens and concentrates Will's sight, the telescope isolates the object of
his vision in its aperture, radically distancing him from what he sees. But the
telescope is more than just an emblem of Will's scientific mind-set. The instrument also leads to his involvement with the Vaught family when he accidentally spots Rita leaving the note for Kitty. Though that incident in itself arouses Will's curiosity, only when he sees Kitty a few moments later is
he drawn inevitably into the Vaughts' chaotic orbit. When he spies Kitty
through his telescope, Will falls in love "at first sight and at a distance of two
thousand feet" (7).

It is no accident that Will instantly falls in love with a woman he sees from a vast distance through the medium of the telescope. Perhaps as a consequence of its ability to recover the reality of the world around him, the telescope somehow transforms what is fixed in its sight. As the narrator tells us, "It was as if the telescope created its own world in the brilliant theatre of its lenses" (4). So it is that Kitty—a slight, unprepossessing character whose beauty is more insisted on than described—becomes, through the artifice of the telescope, a reflection of Will himself. He sees in her "a certain bemused and dry-eyed expression in which he seemed to recognize himself! She was a beautiful girl but she also slouched and was watchful and dry-eyed and musing like a thirteen-year-old boy" (7). But though Will sees a kindred soul, a woman who is as "watchful" and "bemused" as himself, Kitty is only intermittently what she appears to be in the "theatre" of the telescope's lens. When the novel moves to the South, she sheds the nervous mannerisms that were magnified by the telescope, thereby becoming a more conventional southern belle. "I want to have beaus," she insists. "I want to go to dances and get a tremendous rush. That's what my grandmother used to say: I went to such and such a dance and got a tremendous rush" (163). Of course, Kitty's ambitions are expressed here in language that is as double-voiced as Will's declaration that he will restore Hampton Plantation—and in this perhaps, she is indeed a kindred soul, someone as haunted by an idealized image of the past as he is. But she is also not, by any means, the same woman here as the one he thought he saw through the telescope. That figure was a chimera, a fantastic alloy of Will's desires and the telescope's power.

Will's relationship with Kitty is deeply problematic for him. All too aware of the increasingly flexible sexual mores of American culture in the early 1960s, he is alternately hounded by desire and curbed by his father's rigid code of sexual conduct, a struggle that results—once again—in a distorted quality to his language. When, for example, he proclaims his love for her at a lunch counter in Manhattan, the narrative reflects Will's chivalric intentions: "What he wanted to tell her but could not think quite how was that he did not propose country matters. He did not propose to press against her in an elevator. What he wanted was both more and less. He loved her. His heart melted. She was his sweetheart, his certain someone. He wanted to hold her charms in his arms. He wanted to go into a proper house and shower her with kisses in the old style" (68). The language here—which constitutes another character zone—partakes of nineteenth-century propriety and florid romance novels, a combination of moral rectitude and mawkish sentiment that passes beyond the bounds of credulity. But that is the point, of course. At some level, Will knows that this sort of grand declaration of love "in the old style" is impossible to sustain in the twentieth century. So he subverts his own intentions, fosters "a conflict of voices" within the passage, by self-consciously using a series of tinny clichés to describe his feelings. Ultimately, though, no matter how much Will suspects the inadequacy of his ancestors' view of sexual morality, he cannot wholly disavow that view. He is virtually paralyzed by his father's distinction between "gentlemen," who condescend to satisfy their sexual needs with prostitutes so that they will not compromise the purity of the women they love by lusting after them, and "fornicators," who have intercourse indiscriminately. When Will later meets Sutter Vaught, who, he has been told, "went to the bad on liquor and women" (79), Will looks to the mercurial pathologist to sanction his own desires. But Sutter, who rebuffs almost all of Will's questions, will have nothing to do with such a request. "I can't help you," he insists. "Fornicate if you want and enjoy yourself but don't come looking to me for a merit badge certifying you as a Christian or a gentleman or whatever it is you cleave by" (216).

Will's confused desire for Kitty, though, drives the plot in the first half of the novel and finally lures him back to the South. For when Rita arranges for the Vaughts to receive a phony message saying that Will has decided not to take the position as Jamie's companion that Mr. Vaught had offered earlier, they leave New York City without him, and he sets out in pursuit on a journey that will ultimately lead him to confront his father's suicide and his own legacy as the last gentleman.

Instead of returning him to a familiar world, however, a realm in which he knows the correct signals and codes of behavior, Will's journey takes him through a baffling landscape in which nothing is what it seems or should be. Immediately on leaving New York, he is picked up by what appears to be a "light-colored high-stomached Negro" (120). But though Will had earlier been so attuned to the polyphony of voices and dialects around him that he could identify Mr. Vaught's northern Alabama upbringing after only a few words of acquaintance, this light-skinned black man is something else altogether. "The driver did not speak as one might expect him to, with a certain relish and a hearkening to his own periods, as many educated Negroes speak. No, his speech was rapid and slurred, for all the world like a shaky white man's" (121).

In fact, Will's companion is revealed to be Forney Aiken, a white photographer who, while struggling to salvage his career from the ruins of alcoholism, has had his skin artificially darkened to penetrate the "cotton curtain" and write an exposé of Southern racism (124). As Jay Tolson writes in *Pilgrim in the Ruins,* "For this episode, Percy blatantly lifted from John Howard Griffin's autobiographical account of his pigmentational masquerade as a black man in the South, *Black Like Me.* Percy did so for satirical reasons. He wanted to poke fun at the bizarre extremes to which well-meaning white liberals would go to establish their solidarity with blacks, extremes which tended to be as artificial as Forney Aiken's skin tone" (308). In many ways, though, Percy's satire of naive liberalism is the least interesting thing about Forney, who is as obvious a target for Percy's ire as the pun that constitutes his name. More interesting, though, is the way that Forney initiates Will into a world of skewed racial and cultural roles. For if the world of his father was one of carefully prescribed identities, themselves articulated through an elaborate system of gestures and formal courtesies, in the polarized American landscape through which Will travels, these settled roles and expectations no longer exist. Will's world instead is characterized by masquerades and mistaken identities. It is not only that Will is baffled by Forney's deception or the way that Kitty veers back and forth between nostalgic gestures and tentative attempts to prove herself sexually. Even Will himself, despite what he conceives to be an ingenuous and friendly persona, is capable of being misperceived, as when he is embroiled in a bitter confrontation after being mistaken for an integrationist realtor in a northern suburb.

But Will's confusion only worsens after he reunites with the Vaughts and returns to the South, for the land to which he returns is not the one he remembers. It is not the declining, unhappy land of his father's mournful reveries, but a new South, a "happy, victorious, Christian, rich, patriotic and Republican" region, in which the antebellum plantation of Will's nostalgic fancies has been replaced by the Vaughts' suburban home, "a castle fronting on a golf links" (177, 180). In this new South, commercialism has overtaken stoicism; even the idealized past of Ed Barrett and his heroic forefathers has been commodified in the form of costumed salesmen, complete with "Reb-colonel hats and red walking canes," at "the Confederate Chevrolet agency" owned by Kitty's father (251). Perhaps most of all, though, Will discovers that in this new South the old paternalistic relationships of white gentleman and black servants are no longer stable or clear-cut.

We see this phenomenon most clearly in Will's relationship with David Ross, one of the Vaughts' black servants, who possesses a singular inability to grasp "either the Negro way or the white way" (187). Will's usual equanimity, the bemused detachment with which he usually greets everyone and everything, is undone by David's hapless ingenuousness. Will is appalled by David's "innocence," his seeming inability to recognize exploitation or aggression and his utter failure to mimic the sly, accommodating ways of other blacks—who are adept at giving their white employers and charges the impression of always dwelling "in loving and familiar territory" (189, 186). Indeed, Will marvels that David cannot even do a decent job of polishing the silver like a proper servant.

But Will's uncharacteristic irritation with David comes from something deeper than his annoyance at the blots of polish on the Vaught silverware. This ire proceeds from a muffled recognition of himself in the other, an implicit dialogic link between them, for Will is a lot more like David than he will admit. It is not only that David is as bad at being a servant as Will is at being a master. They also share some of the same eccentricities. Just as David doesn't transmit the same comforting signals to whites as do other, older blacks, Will confounds the Vaughts' servants by not behaving like other whites. "He actually looked at them," we are told (186). Then, too, when Will says that David is "like a rich man's son," squandering money on foolish schemes to sell electronic kits or ice cube dispensers, Will seems to forget that he abruptly spent the last of his inheritance on his telescope (188). Will dimly seems to recognize that David, like himself, can neither play the role that tradition once assigned him nor fit comfortably in the new world that is emerging around him. And in recognition of this fact—implicitly at least—Will finally tells David, "Do like me. . . . Watch and wait. Keep your eyes open" (217).

Yet David's innocence also seems to make Will feel most keenly his own inability to do what the patrician had always done, to stand between "his helpless 'freedmen'" and the whites who would abuse them (SSL 85). David's terrible vulnerability only reminds Will of his own inability to embrace and echo his father's beliefs. And so Will alternately rages at David—"Oh Christ, David, this goddamn innocence, it's going to ruin us all"—and then dismisses any lingering sense of responsibility for him—"Why should I, for Christ's sake, sit here all asweat and solicitous of his vulnerability. . . . [I]f he gets hurt: well, I'm not well myself" (189, 190).

The anachronistic quality of the code of behavior of Will's heroic ancestors is further underscored by what he sees in his classmates from the university where he enrolls on his return to the South. These young men, whom we are told are "from [Will's] country, though he did not know them" (255), are characterized in language that is strikingly similar to that used earlier to describe Will's great-grandfather, who "knew what was what and said so and acted accordingly and did not care what anyone thought" (9). In a similar fashion, Will's classmates "knew what they were, how things were and how things should be" (255). Of course, the parallel words and the crisp decisive rhythm in both descriptions suggest that these young men carry on the traditions of Will's storied ancestors. And yet they are flawed models of continuity. For as much as Will would like to emulate them, he is confounded by the hatred they espouse when they talk about a black student integrating the university. For Will, who is "so mystified by black and white alike that he could not allow himself the luxury of hatred," these young men who are "lordly in theirs" (256), seem to represent a devolution of the once tolerant patrician tradition. Typically, though, he cannot acknowledge the conflict between the present reality and the idealized past, and so his language again becomes distorted as he praises his classmates in flowery, extravagant terms borrowed from old books: "They're good chaps and so very much at one with themselves and with the dear world around them bright and sure as paradise" (256).

Will's historical confusion and the failure of his patrician legacy ultimately leave him open to the potential influences of the two most important members of the Vaught family, Valentine, Kitty's older sister, and the mysterious Sutter. Their dual significance is emphasized by the architecture of the novel when they are introduced in back-to-back chapters. But if Will—as we will see—is drawn to Sutter, Will takes an instant dislike to Val, a sort of nun in training, who immediately antagonizes him when, only moments after they have exchanged introductions, she asks him to tell Jamie "about the economy of salvation" if no one else is with him when he is dying (201). Will is scandalized by Val's request since his scientism makes no allowances for religion except as the source of some gauzy ethical precepts. Her request only stirs up in Will a memory of his father's scorn for "Catholic monkey business"— "how do you expect me to tell him what I don't believe?" Will replies (202)—and he momentarily assimilates his father's voice when he refuses Val "with the same species of satisfaction that Ed Barrett once refused a request from a Catholic priest" (203). Indeed, until the conclusion of the novel, Will seems to thoroughly reject Val's voice and values. We never hear any of her religious language echo in his consciousness.

It is otherwise with Sutter, however, about whom Will has already conceived a powerful curiosity based on what he has heard others say about the

eldest of the Vaught children. From the first casual mention of Sutter, when
Jamie gave Will a copy of Sutter's article, "The Incidence of Post-Orgasmic
Suicide in Male University Graduate Students," to a stray remark of Kitty's
that "Sutter could look at you and tell what was wrong with you" (110), Will
seems to have become convinced that Sutter can help Will resolve his own
problems: his confusion about sexuality, his "nervous condition," and—perhaps at some unconscious level that is jarred by the title of Sutter's article—
his long-repressed grief over his father's suicide. We see this conviction quietly take hold in Will's mind early in the novel as he lies with Kitty in
Central Park after a halfhearted attempt at making love: she recounts the
events of a fateful week at Rita and Sutter's home in New Mexico during
the previous summer, when Rita and Sutter's marriage collapsed and the
first signs of Jamie's illness appeared. As Kitty tells Will of a dispute between
Rita and Val over the religious beliefs of a Native American boy employed
by Rita, Will interrupts Kitty repeatedly, sidetracking her from her story, to
ask almost obsessively, "What did Sutter say?" (112). In this scene, long before Will even sees him, Sutter's voice already resounds in his consciousness,
exemplifying what Bakhtin terms "internally persuasive discourse": the
words of others that influence our own beliefs, that in some fundamental
way both accord with our sense of the world and help us define how we see
the world ("Discourse" 342).

Indeed, Bakhtin's distinction—carefully laid out in "Discourse in the
Novel"—between "internally persuasive discourse" and "authoritative discourse" is the key to understanding Sutter's importance to Will. In Bakhtin's
view, "an individual's becoming, an ideological process, is characterized by a
sharp gap between these two categories" (342). We first awaken to ideological life, Bakhtin argues, when we begin to discriminate between these types
of discourse. Authoritative discourse is that which is handed down by one's
elders; it is the beliefs and values we inherit, the fixed points on the moral
compass we are given as children. As Bakhtin writes, "The authoritative
word demands that we acknowledge it, that we make it our own; it binds us,
quite independent of any power it might have to persuade us internally; we
encounter it with its authority already fused to it. The authoritative word is
located in a distanced zone, organically connected with a past that is felt to
be hierarchically higher. It is, so to speak, the word of the fathers. Its authority was already *acknowledged* in the past" (342). Of course, the ideals of Will
Barrett's "honorable and violent family" embody Bakhtin's concept of authoritative discourse. As in Bakhtin's definition, the patrician values that Will

has inherited are "organically connected with a past that is felt to be hierarchically higher"; they are the last vestiges of an Edenic past, a lost world of honorable men and faithful servants and virginal women. Moreover, as those values are passed on to Will in the cold, despairing voice of Ed Barrett, they become quite literally "the word of the fathers."

In marked contrast, though, to authoritative discourse, internally persuasive discourse is "denied all privilege, backed up by no authority at all" (Bakhtin, "Discourse" 342). Where authoritative discourse issues from some mythic, golden age, internally persuasive discourse is always a part of and speaks to the contemporary world. Its power derives not from some halcyon source but from its fundamental truthfulness and its relevance to our lives. Indeed, we affirm the truthfulness of internally persuasive discourse by the way we assimilate it to our own ends, the way it interacts with our own voices: "In the everyday rounds of consciousness, the internally persuasive word is half-ours and half-someone else's. Its creativity and productiveness consist precisely in the fact that such a word awakens new and independent words, that it organizes masses of our words from within, and does not remain in an isolated and static condition [as does authoritative discourse, which, Bakhtin says, "enters our consciousness as a compact and indivisible mass" ("Discourse" 343)]. It is not so much interpreted by us as it is further, that is, freely, developed, applied to new material, new conditions" ("Discourse" 345).

In *The Last Gentleman,* the words of Sutter Vaught are internally persuasive for Will. Despite the fact that Sutter is regarded by others as a failure—once a brilliant diagnostician, he is now assistant coroner at the local hospital—and thus is "denied all privilege, backed up by no authority at all," Will fastens on Sutter as a kind of guru. As Will explains to the other man, "I can tell when somebody knows something I don't know" (209). Why does Will respond to Sutter in this way? All the things he has heard about Sutter from the other characters certainly have prepared the ground for this leap of faith. And, to an extent, Will accords Sutter a degree of authority simply because he is, like Dr. Gamow, "one of them, the scientists" (34). But Will's bond with Sutter is ultimately based on Marcel's concept of intersubjectivity. Both Will and Sutter perceive a kind of emptiness, a spiritual and psychological void, in the consumer society that thrives around them. When Will roams fitfully through New York City in the early pages of the novel, he is sensitive to a malaise that seems to hang over everything, raining down on him in the form of "ravenous particles" that leach the color from paintings and make

the world around him inaccessible without the help of his telescope (25).
And yet he can find no one who will confirm his impressions until he meets
Sutter, who obliquely signals that, yes, there might indeed be something arid
and sorrowful in the lives of those around them. For example, when Will
watches his classmates celebrating on the night before a football game and
then wonders aloud, "Why do they feel so good and I feel so bad?" Sutter's
response is at once bracing and evasive. "The question is whether they feel
as good as you think," he says, "and if they do, then the question is whether
it is necessarily worse to feel bad than good under the circumstances" (257).

In many ways, that response typifies Sutter's own existential perspective,
for he is all too aware of the abyss that waits for those whose lives are drained
of significance by everydayness and conformity. By nature abstracted, a man
given to observation and theorizing, as the abstruse meditations in his casebook will show, Sutter can transcend the quotidian reality of everyday life
when he is engaged in the pursuit of objective knowledge. But that detachment exacts a price too, for Sutter finds it virtually impossible to repair the
Cartesian split between subject and object. In effect, he can study the world
but not live in it, and when he tries to reenter the world from what he calls
"the orbit of transcendence" (331), he is lost. Religion will not avail for him;
at best it is simply passé in a scientific age, and at worst it is the province of
hypocrites who combine their piety with a disguised lewdness. For Sutter,
the only way to live in his own skin is by indulging in its pleasures. In an age
that only recognizes a physical reality that can be certified through the ob-
jective-empirical techniques of science, sexuality, Sutter believes, is "the sacrament of the dispossessed" (269). Yet the redemption it offers is only temporary. Once the physical experience is consummated, the mind is cut loose
from the body again, set free to scale the heights of abstraction and wander
the earth like a disembodied spirit.

Of course, the effect of this philosophy is to profoundly isolate Sutter,
who seems, when we first meet him, almost incapable of dialogue. It is no
accident that Will's first view of Sutter has him lofted ten feet off the ground
on a balcony of the Vaught's garage. Such a perspective signifies Sutter's abstraction and isolation. And, indeed, Sutter's manner around others reinforces
that sense of isolation. He typically separates himself from the rest of his family, even in social situations. Though we are told in the scene where Will's
classmates are celebrating on the night before a football game that "Jamie
and Sutter had been in deep talk . . . for a good half hour," all that Percy
allows us to hear of Sutter's exchanges with others are arch remarks and

ironic rejoinders (254). The only dramatic evidence of any possibility of a genuine dialogic interaction is found in the sections of Sutter's casebook addressed to Val, in which he argues with her beliefs. But we have no way of knowing whether Val has ever actually seen those passages or whether Sutter is merely rehearsing what he would say if he could bring himself to engage her in dialogue. No wonder, then, that Sutter once tried to take his life and that he continues to flirt with suicide over the course of the novel. Only in response to Will's insistent requests for aid and counsel is Sutter gradually, almost involuntarily, drawn out of his own isolation.

Ultimately Sutter's role in the novel is to act as a galvanizing force in the process of Will's ideological becoming. (In this, he is like *The Moviegoer's* Kate Cutrer, who, in a slightly different way, forces Binx to confront his demons.) Sutter encourages Will—sometimes tacitly, sometimes explicitly—to trust his impressions of the culture in which he is immersed. More important, though, Sutter gives Will license to act. When, late in the novel, Sutter decides to take Jamie with him to the dude ranch in New Mexico where he works as house physician—to insure that Jamie will, as Sutter sees it, be allowed to die with dignity—Sutter at last uses the authority that Will has accorded him. In a surprisingly gentle act, Sutter takes Will aside on the night before he leaves and for once responds to his plight without sarcasm or ambiguity. After Will indicates that he is about to suffer from one of his "spells," Sutter seems to hypnotize him and then hints that something will happen the next day, that Will's status will be changed. "For the next few days you may have a difficult time," Sutter warns. "Now I shall not tell you what to do, but I will tell you now that you will be free to act" (261).

This prediction of Sutter's is, in many ways, the turning point in the novel, for Will does indeed become a more active and decisive character hereafter. When he wakes up the following morning and finds that Jamie and Sutter are gone, Will is quick to follow them, even though he knows that his pursuit of them will jeopardize his fragile relationship with Kitty. Indeed, whether or not he will admit it, Will tacitly decides that his relationship with Sutter and his obligation to Jamie are more important than the vaporous emotion that constitutes his "love" for Kitty. Though he readily responds to Kitty's seeming offer to accompany him to New Mexico, they are quickly separated. When Kitty asks him to stop at the campus where they have enrolled for classes so that she can pick up her textbooks to prepare for a test—which she will miss if she goes with Will—they become embroiled in a race riot that is patterned after the violence surrounding James Meredith's arrival at Ole Miss.[3] In the midst of the chaos, Kitty is confined in her sorority house and Will is accidentally knocked unconscious. When he comes to, his amnesia has conveniently taken hold, and Kitty is no more than an unspecified flicker of memory. Just as Will's amnesia manifests his desire to be free of the burden of his family's history, here it functions as a way for Will to unconsciously divest himself of a failed love. It is certainly a convenient device to rid Percy of a problematic character. As he has often claimed in interviews, "I don't know enough about women," and so he allows Kitty to drift out of the novel (*Con.* 212).

When Will sets out in pursuit of Sutter and Jamie, he is aided by two very different kinds of guides that he finds in Sutter's apartment: a map that indicates Sutter's route and the casebook referred to earlier, in which, between summaries of autopsies, Sutter muses on such topics as the loss of sovereignty over one's own experiences in an age of specialists, the failure of Christianity, and the conflict between immanence and transcendence—that is, between being in the world or abstracted from it. In a 1967 interview, Percy described the casebook as "a possible weakness in the book" but said that the only alternative "was long Dostoevskian conversations" (*Con.* 14). Whether the casebook is a flaw in the novel, Percy's reference to Dostoevsky is revealing, for it confirms the dialogic significance of the casebook. Just as those conversations in Dostoevsky speak directly to each character's inner life, echoing in his or her microdialogue, so does Will's exposure to Sutter's ideas—he is compelled to read all of the casebook over the course of his wanderings—affect him profoundly. In the truest sense, the casebook functions as internally persuasive discourse for Will, not because he accepts all of Sutter's ideas without question but because Sutter's words goad him to think anew. Its effect on Will is precisely that which Bakhtin describes for internally persuasive discourse: "it awakens new and independent words, . . . it organizes masses of our words from within" ("Discourse" 345).

Indeed, when Will comes across his own name in the casebook, something is surely triggered in him. As Sutter argues with his sister, Val, the object of many of his harangues in the casebook, over the futility of anything she could tell Will to ease his difficulties from her perspective as a Catholic, Sutter proves a more effective advocate of Val's beliefs than Val herself. Addressing Val, Sutter writes,

> So you say to him: Look, Barrett, your trouble is not due to a disorder of your organism but to the human condition, that you do well to be afraid

and you do well to forget everything which does not pertain to your salvation. That is to say, your amnesia is not a symptom. So you say: Here is the piece of news you have been waiting for, and you tell him. What does Barrett do? He attends in that eager flattering way of his and at the end of it he might even say yes! But he will receive the news from his high seat of transcendence as one more item of psychology, throw it into his immanent meat-grinder, and wait to see if he feels better. (339)

Though it is difficult to say with any certainty, I think that the possibility of faith enters Will's field of vision for the first time here. That possibility had previously been articulated only by Val herself, whom Will instantly disliked. Yet here, as it is expressed in Sutter's sarcastic, hectoring voice, the concept of salvation is put forth by someone whom Will is already inclined to believe. Moreover, Sutter at last gives Will some of the answers that he has sought throughout the novel, offering an explanation for his amnesia and telling him in general terms how he should live. But, of course, Sutter is only providing these answers conditionally, as what Val—not he—might say to Will. Why should Will take them in earnest? Because it is in the nature of internally persuasive discourse that we adapt it to our own ends. Thus, Will takes what he needs from Sutter's utterance—"your trouble is not due to a disorder of the organism but to the human condition . . . your amnesia is not a symptom"—and strips away the rest, the husk of Sutter's argument with Val. In addition, it is important to note that Sutter's words do not by any means convince Will of the reality of salvation; they affect no drastic change in his behavior. Rather, as I asserted above, they only suggest the possibility of salvation, the faint chance that there might indeed be some element of truth to the religious doctrine he has long disregarded.

And yet, not until the climax of the novel, when Will frantically asks Val for help as Jamie lies dying, do we see any evidence that he gives any credence at all to the possibility of salvation. So what, if anything, indicates that he takes Sutter's "answers" here in earnest? (Even Sutter suggests in the casebook that this "news" cannot reach Will's "high seat of transcendence." For Will, Sutter implies, religious faith is only another phenomenon to be studied: a curious psychological condition that afflicts others, not something that speaks to his own predicament.) Admittedly, there is little evidence to suggest that what Will reads here has any effect on him. But if we can say anything about Will's character with any real certainty, it is that his motives are rarely clear and hardly ever consciously articulated by him. Will's true

feelings manifest themselves in his erratic behavior and in the tensions and
contradictions that inhere in his language. Therefore, it is possible that Will
assimilates what he reads at an unconscious level, its impact to be felt only at
that moment of crisis when Jamie is on the brink of death. Then, the "new
and independent words" that have been inspired by Sutter's discourse can be
heard.

The final part of the novel details Will's odyssey in pursuit of Jamie and
Sutter. The journey will take Will back to his childhood home in Mississippi
and end in a hospital room in Santa Fe where Jamie lies dying. But Will's
first stop, after he is separated from Kitty, is at a place that looks like "a lunar
installation": "a raw settlement of surplus army buildings, Quonset huts, and
one geodesic dome" (284) where Val oversees a school for poor black children in rural Alabama. Of course, Will's encounter with Val serves as a tacit
reminder of the responsibility with which she had earlier charged him, to
see to Jamie's baptism. But this scene, which follows immediately the riot at
the university, has another function as well. In contrast to Forney Aiken's
naive liberalism and the southern stoic's despairing withdrawal from involvement in the struggle for civil rights, it suggests an alternative response to the
violence and strife that accompany the end of legal segregation in the South.

Earlier in the novel, when Will and Val first met, she recalled hearing Will's
father "make a speech to the D.A.R. on the subject of *noblesse oblige* and our
duty to the Negro" (199), but although she applauded Ed Barrett's stand, she
disagreed with his reasons for promoting racial tolerance. Why does she feel
this way? Val never explains her disapproval, but its origins can perhaps be
found again in "Stoicism in the South." As noted in chapter 2, Percy asserts
in this crucial essay that the concept of noblesse oblige did not compel upper-
class southerners to defend the rights of blacks "because they were made in
the image of God and were therefore loveable in themselves, but because to
do them an injustice would be to defile the inner fortress which was oneself" (*SSL* 85). By contrast, the Christian rationale for seeking social justice
is quite different. As Percy writes, "What the Stoic sees as the insolence of
his former charge—and this is what he can't tolerate, the Negro's demanding his rights instead of being thankful for the squire's generosity—is in the
Christian scheme the sacred right which must be accorded the individual,
whether deemed insolent or not" (*SSL* 86). If, then, Ed Barrett defended a
black man in a court of law because that action confirmed his sense of himself as a good and honorable man, Val ministers to her pupils because each of
them has been created by God and endowed with a divine spark that must

be respected. Indeed, her work teaching these children who are virtually mute to use language to name the world around them is akin to awakening that spark within them, as they move—according to Percy's theories of language—from mere stimulus-response creatures to talkers and symbol-mongers. As Val says to Will, "When they do suddenly break into language, it is something to see. They are like Adam on the First Day" (289).

But what does all this mean to Will? The answer is suggested by an image that occurs to him as he leaves Val's school. "More than ever," the narrator tells us, "it reminded him of a lunar installation . . . a place of crude and makeshift beginnings on some blasted planet" (290). For Will, despite his misgivings about Val's character, this is a place where life begins again, where one can truly put aside the grievances of the past that have so deeply scored this "blasted planet" and start anew. In contrast to his father's stoic ideology, which, as Percy tells us in "Stoicism in the South," "was based on a particular hierarchical structure and could not survive the change" to a more egalitarian society (*SSL* 85), the Christian ideology that underlies Val's work is far more suited to the world in which Will finds himself. Where the stoic can only mutter darkly about "the insolence of his former charge" and turn his back on the struggle for civil rights, the Christian recognizes "the sacred right which must be accorded the individual" and is empowered by that knowledge, given disposition to act. But if Will senses this difference—as his image of the school as "a place of crude and makeshift beginnings" suggests—he certainly does not yet take it to heart. Even when he leaves, he is as uneasy in Val's presence as ever. "Another hour in this gloomy cancerous wood," he thinks, "and I'd be laid out stiff as a corpse, feet sticking up" (290).

After he leaves Val's school, Will returns at last to his hometown, Ithaca, Mississippi, where he finds his old friend Forney Aiken and several other would-be provocateurs from the North on the wrong side of the law. Once again, Forney's plans have gone awry. One of his colleagues has been arrested, and when the police come after Forney and the others the black man who owns the bar where they are hiding is beaten by Beans Ross, one of the police, who goes on to threaten a woman who is with Forney. This event is all that is needed, though, to awaken the voices of his "honorable and violent family" in Will's consciousness. A black man, a servant of sorts, has been brutalized for no reason, and a white woman's honor is threatened. At last, his family's values pertain to the situation in which he finds himself. The past comes alive, and Will responds instinctively: "For once in his life he had time and position and a good shot, and for once things became as clear as they used to be in the old honorable days. He hit Beans in the root of the neck as hard as he ever hit the sandbag in the West Side Y.M.C.A." (312).

This moment, in which the past and present come together, is of a piece with the sense of déjà vu that assails him as soon as he leaves Kitty and makes his way into the Deep South. Everywhere he looks, he sees something that brings the past to life with such intensity that he cannot distinguish if he has been there or only heard about it in his father's stories: "Once he passed through a town which had a narrow courthouse and an old boarded-up hotel on the square. There were still wrecks of rocking chairs on the gallery. Either I have been here before, he thought, perhaps with my father while he was trying a case, or else it was he with his father and he told me about it" (283). By now, the past has such a hold on him that his voice can merge without irony with the voices of his family. But if Will can remember so much, if he will allow the past such a claim on him, then he must remember everything. And so, inevitably, Will makes his way to his childhood home after his conflict with Beans Ross.

This location, of course, is where the novel's design has been leading all along. As Percy explained in a 1971 interview, "I think Kierkegaard says, 'Every man has to stand in front of the house of his childhood in order to recover himself.' So Barrett is obsessed with . . . his father's suicide. And the whole first two-thirds of the book is going back to [it]" (*Con.* 67). Thus, when Will stands outside his childhood home, he finally remembers what happened on the night his father died. Until now, Will has recalled bits and pieces of that night—the way Ed Barrett walked up and down the sidewalk in front of the house, in the same spot where Will stands now—but the memory always broke off at that moment when his father turned and entered the house. Now, however, Will remembers how his father walked past him on the porch, ignoring his plea to wait, and climbed the stairs to the attic, where he took his own life. At this moment, when Will finally acknowledges the reality of his father's suicide, he takes the first pivotal step in his own ideological becoming.

As his plea to his father, the stark, single word *wait,* echoes in his mind—a word that is "uttered time and time again [in Percy's fiction] by characters reaching out in the deepest need for human contact" (Allen 70)—and as his hands touch an iron hitching post embedded in the coarse bark of an oak tree, Will separates his own voice from his father's.

> *Wait.* While his fingers explored the juncture of iron and bark, his eyes narrowed as if he caught a glimmer of light on the cold iron skull [of

the hitching post]. *Wait.* I think he was wrong and that he was looking in the wrong place. No, not he but the times. The times were wrong and one looked in the wrong place. It wasn't even his fault because that was the way he was and the way the times were, and there was no other place a man could look. It was the worst of times, a time of fake beauty and fake victory. *Wait.* He had missed it! It was not in the Brahms that one looked and not in solitariness and not in the old sad poetry but—he wrung out his ear—but here, under your nose, here in the very curious-ness and drollness and extraness of the iron and the bark that—he shook his head—that— (318–19)

By this point in the novel, the narrator's presence is minimal, reduced to stage directions, so powerful and urgent is the microdialogue of Will's consciousness as he struggles to sort through the voices that echo in his mind. Will is at once child and adult, both himself and his father. The word *wait,* for example, that echoes through the passage is still the cry of the boy on the porch who is about to be orphaned, but it is also Will's message to himself now, as a young man on the verge of an important discovery who needs to articulate what was wrong with his father's beliefs. In much the same way, his father's voice sounds in this passage, too. When Will says "it was the worst of times," he no doubt echoes one of his father's favorite literary allusions, and he seems—for an instant—to concur with his father's judgment of the world in which he lived. But the next phrase is crucial, for suddenly Will's and his father's perspectives diverge once and for all. When Will says that this "worst of times" was "a time of fake beauty and fake victory," he does not attribute this despair to some perceived erosion of values; rather, he points to the inadequacy of those values themselves. And though he cannot yet articulate what he would substitute for his father's "old sad poetry," he is grop-ing for a way of living that does not rely on fortifying the self behind a lofty abstraction called honor.

In "Gentlemen and Fornicators: *The Last Gentleman* and a Bisected Real-ity," Panthea Reid Broughton writes that Ed Barrett "missed the gratuity of the ordinary world and looked for meanings only above and beyond this world. He lived for abstract ideals whose associations with the commonplace had been severed. But Will feels how the old iron hitching post . . . is half covered over by warm bark and knows without words that the two need not be dissociated" (110). Indeed, Will is struggling to fuse the twin poles of tran-scendence and immanence. He dimly perceives that he cannot live for and by a code of abstract ideals that posits—as does his father's stoicism—the refutation of a corrupt and tarnished world. If he is in fact to live in the world, the ideals that guide him must also help him to accept the world in all its flawed beauty. And for Percy, of course, those ideals are the substance of Christianity. In a brief discussion of this scene in "Diagnosing the Modern Malaise," Percy writes, "In terms of traditional metaphysics, [Will] has caught a glimpse of the goodness and gratuitousness of created being," though Will, who is still deeply skeptical of religion, lacks the vocabulary of faith necessary to articulate what he has seen (*SSL* 221).

Indeed, Will's inability to identify such ideals or even to put this knowledge into words is telling. He is certainly onto something here, but the revelation is tenuous, ephemeral. Not until he returns in Percy's fifth novel, *The Second Coming,* will he at last lay to rest his father's ghost and permanently refute his father's beliefs. What does happen here, however, is that Will—in effect—awakens to ideological life. As Bakhtin writes in "Discourse in the Novel,"

> consciousness awakens to independent ideological life precisely in a
> world of alien discourse surrounding it, and from which it cannot
> initially separate itself; the process of distinguishing between one's own
> and another's discourse, between one's own and another's thought, is
> activated late in development. When thought begins to work in an
> independent, experimenting, and discriminating way, what first occurs is
> a separation between internally persuasive discourse and authoritarian
> enforced discourse, along with a rejection of those congeries of dis-
> courses that do not matter to us, that do not touch us. (345)

In that moment when Will separates his voice from his father's Will recognizes that his father's words, though infused with all the authority of his family's storied past, are not internally persuasive for him. He can no longer simply mimic his father's voice and take for granted that his father's expressions are adequate to embody his own intentions and values. If Will does not yet know exactly what he himself believes, he knows what he does not believe, and in this disavowal of his father's beliefs he begins to find himself.

What happens next makes clear the broader consequences of Will's struggle with his father's voice and values. For as he stands under the water oaks in front of his house, in the same place that his father stood, he sees a black man—"a young man his own age" (319)—coming up the sidewalk toward him, in the same manner that others used to come to his father to seek counsel or charity.

Entering the darkness of the water oaks, the Negro did not at first see him (though it had been his, the Negro's, business, until now, to see him first), then did see him two yards away and stopped for a long half second. They looked at each other. There was nothing to say. Their fathers would have had much to say: "In the end, Sam, it comes down to a question of character." "Yes suh, Lawyer Barrett, you right about that. Like I was saying to the wife only this evening—" But the sons had nothing to say. The engineer looked at the other as the half second wore on. You may be in a fix and I know that but what you don't know and won't believe and must find out for yourself is that I'm in a fix too and you got to get where I am before you even know what I'm talking about and I know that and that's why there is nothing to say now. Meanwhile I wish you well. (319)

Although some of Percy's critics, including Martin Luschei in *The Sovereign Wayfarer* and John Edward Hardy in *The Fiction of Walker Percy,* have interpreted this scene as a kind of muted denunciation of the civil rights movement for damaging communication between blacks and whites, I think it has another purpose altogether. This scene shows that in rejecting his father's values Will also has renounced his aristocratic prerogatives. He can no longer presume that the black man will recognize him first. Though there are moments when events configure in such a way that the old relationships seem possible—as when Will faces up to Beans Ross or when he visits his uncle, Fannin Barrett, whose relationship with his black servant Merriam is based on a comfortable, old paternalism—the old racial hierarchy is gone. And though Will insists that "there is nothing to say now," the passage belies that statement. It is not that there is nothing to say, only that neither Will nor the other young man can speak in his father's voice. The paternalistic homilies of another generation and the reflexive, vaguely submissive affirmations that accompanied them sound remote here, archaic. Instead, the sons must forge a new language and a new compact, both of which Will cautiously attempts at the end of the passage. When he thinks "you may be in a fix . . . and I'm in a fix too," he lays the foundation for perhaps the most important kind of relationship in Percy's fiction, one that proceeds from a shared recognition of homelessness, of alienation. Earlier even, Will had hinted at that mutuality in his tacit identification with David Ross and his assertion—inspired by his exasperation with David's "innocence"—that "I should have been born a Negro, for then my upsidedownness would be right side up" (189). Yet Will only recognizes the foundation for a new understanding. Just as he could not say what he would substitute for his father's "old sad poetry," he cannot express aloud the dim sense of identification he feels. Even when he tentatively assimilates the other's dialect—"you got to get to where I am before you even know what I'm talking about"—it is only to explain why he will not explain himself.

The conclusion of the novel finds Will at last in Santa Fe, where he has caught up with Jamie and Sutter. Will's reunion with Sutter is characterized by the same kind of intellectual hide-and-seek that informed their conversations at the Vaught home in Alabama. Once again, Will tries to extract Sutter's advice—this time on whether Will should settle down with Kitty and take a job in Mr. Vaught's car dealership—and once again Sutter refuses to sanction Will's plans. But their interaction here has a darker, graver tone to it that stems from one simple fact: the nearness of death. When Will arrives in Santa Fe, Jamie's condition has become much worse. He is hospitalized now and his face is marked with "purpura," "splotches of horrid color like oil slicks" (347). (As a trained physician, Percy is mercilessly accurate in describing the rigors of Jamie's illness. His prose has never been more exact and powerful than in those scenes in which we see the final decay of Jamie's body.) Not only Jamie's death hangs over the novel's final chapters. When Will talks to Sutter about returning to Alabama after Jamie has died, Sutter bluntly tells him, "If I do outlive Jamie . . . it will not be by more than two hours. What in Christ's name do you think I'm doing out here? Do you think I'm staying? Do you think I'm going back?" (374).

This declaration, we are told, astonishes Will, so much so that he is jarred out of the detached, watchful state in which he has existed for so long. As the narrator, suddenly returning to dominate the text again, explains, this moment "marked the beginning for the engineer of what is called normal life. From that time forward it was possible to meet him and after a few minutes form a clear notion of what sort of fellow he was and how he would spend the rest of his life" (374). Of course, we are meant to believe that the shock of Sutter's threat has transformed Will—though, as usual, the evidence of that transformation is exceedingly subtle—but it is equally important to note that Will is in fact "astonished" by Sutter's threat. After all, Sutter has given many indications before now that he is capable of taking his own life. The last entry in his casebook told of his attempt at suicide following his diagnosis of Jamie's illness—"shot myself, missed my brain, carried away cheek"—and ended with an ominous prediction: "I won't miss next time"

(358). So why is Will so startled? Because the same instinct that enabled him to repress the memory of his father's suicide for years has also shielded him from the evidence of Sutter's self-destructiveness. Will burnt the casebook immediately after he finished reading it and then let his own unreliable memory do the rest; once again, his amnesia disposed of what he did not want to remember. "What was that last sentence?" Will wondered, a few moments after burning the casebook. "It had a bearing" (360).

All these events come to a head immediately after Sutter makes his threat, when Will returns to the vigil he has been keeping at the hospital and finds Jamie on the brink of death. Confronted by the one thing he has feared most, to find himself alone at this moment, Will responds without thinking and calls Val rather than Sutter or Jamie's parents. This is surely a decisive action, but it is also a surprising one given Will's unease with Val and her "Catholic monkey business" (203). Why does he turn to her at this moment of crisis? Perhaps because Sutter's suicidal intentions have shown the failure of his ideology; all he can bring to Jamie's death is Sutter's own death as well. But Will's particular need for Val is also suggested by the thoughts that occupy him as he waits for the long-distance connection to come through: "It was the shame of it, the bare-faced embarrassment of getting worse and dying which took him by surprise and caught his breath in his throat. How is this matter to be set right? Were there no officials to deal with the shame of dying, to make suitable recompense?" (375). Whether he will admit it, Will has formulated at least a tentative answer to his questions.

Typically, though, he attempts to conceal his motives, both from Val and himself. When she answers the phone, Will makes an excuse that he is calling because Jamie has asked him to have Val send him a book on entropy. And, in fact, this is true—Jamie did request the book earlier—but to suggest that the book is the foremost of Will's concerns is ludicrous. Once again, Will's actions betray his assertions. He has scoffed at Val's beliefs and resented her request that he see to Jamie's baptism; however, when he is faced with the immediacy of Jamie's death and the apparent senselessness of it, the cracks in his facade of skepticism show themselves. What he read in Sutter's casebook and what he saw at Val's school certainly have an effect on Will here, but he, as usual, suggests that effect in a sidelong manner, by the preposterousness of the motive he gives for calling Val. There is a self-conscious flimsiness to his excuse that he is calling about the book on entropy. And even what he tells himself when Val forces him to admit that Jamie is dying suggests the subterfuge that conceals his real motives. When Val tells him that she will fly out to

Santa Fe immediately, Will consoles himself that he has set things right by having a woman come to help him attend to Jamie. "It came over him suddenly: there was another use for women after all, especially Southern women. They knew how to minister to the dying!" (376). But if this is what he wanted, why did he call Val and not Mrs. Vaught? Surely, Jamie's mother, a traditional southern woman, would be the more appropriate choice. In the face of this evidence, we must conclude that Will calls Val because he believes—even though he will not consciously acknowledge it—that the only "officials" equipped "to deal with the shame of dying, to make suitable recompense" are those who are empowered by their faith. If Will does not assimilate Val's religious voice here—and his evasions would indicate that he does not—he at least privileges that voice, accords it a weight and significance that the other voices that sound in his consciousness lack. Now, perhaps, Sutter's hypothetical argument in his casebook for the good news of Christianity has its effect on Will. Now, perhaps, we see that Sutter's words were internally persuasive.

It is characteristic, though, that when Val tells Will that he must attend to Jamie's baptism if his condition worsens before she arrives, Will is infuriated by the request. His own core of belief—not even belief, really, but hope—is far too tenuous and fragile to survive unprotected by a shell of derision. Nevertheless, Will reluctantly accepts Val's commission, and the scene that follows, Jamie's baptism on his deathbed, is perhaps the finest moment in all of Percy's fiction.[4] In his essay "Notes for a Novel about the End of the World," Percy suggests that it is extraordinarily difficult to write about religious events because the "old words of grace are worn smooth as poker chips" (MB 116). "How can one possibly write of baptism as an event of immense significance," he writes, "when baptism is already accepted but accepted by and large as a minor tribal rite somewhat secondary in importance to taking the kids to see Santa at the department store?" (MB 118). Percy's solution here is twofold. First, rather than attempting to glorify the ceremony, Percy emphasizes its ordinariness. Jamie's baptism is a rote, haphazard affair, with a workaday priest named Father Boomer who sprinkles water on Jamie's brow from "a clouded plastic glass," while Jamie drifts in and out of his delirium, unable even to control his bowels (389). Curiously, though, these details do not degrade the ritual itself. By stripping away any hint of grandeur, Percy forces us to concentrate on the purpose of the ceremony instead of its trappings. As Jamie signals his assent when the priest asks him if he desires the faith to believe in the truths of Christianity, those truths—which are the essence of authoritarian discourse—become internally persuasive for Jamie.

But the second part of Percy's solution is perhaps most important to us, for the ceremony itself is in a very real sense a dialogic event. Even as Will helps to facilitate the baptism by training his radar on Jamie and acting as a kind of interpreter, mediating between the priest's ceremonial questions and Jamie's feeble, almost incomprehensible responses (an ironic role for someone as uncertain as Will), Will is acutely conscious of Sutter's perspective on this ritual, as he stands a few feet behind Will, a pistol loosely concealed in a coat pocket. Of course, this is in itself an amazing tableau, a testament to Percy's sense of drama and power of invention. But more is on display here than a novelist's ability to orchestrate the movements of his characters. Percy also enables us to hear a kind of unspoken dialogue between Will and Sutter over the significance of the baptism. As Will notes each of Sutter's reactions—the exaggerated courtesy with which he treats Father Boomer, his restless movements during the ceremony itself—Will not only sees the baptism from his own perspective, as a frightened and confused participant of sorts, but also perceives how Sutter sees it as well. Because each of Sutter's actions conveys his usual ironic skepticism, Will knows that Sutter views the baptism from a detached perspective, from his own "high seat of transcendence" (339). In contrast to Will's involvement, all of Sutter's actions are blatantly intended to communicate to Will—who is by now well versed in Sutter's gestural language—that Sutter remains aloof, above it all. Though it may be, as Percy insisted in several interviews, that Sutter understands how the baptism redeems Jamie's death, that understanding has no particular significance for Sutter's own life.[5] It does not speak to Sutter's despair, and it will not deter his suicide. There is a sharp contrast, though, to the baptism's effect on Will. Even if he does not understand exactly what is going on, his involvement in the ritual as the link between Jamie and Father Boomer does not allow for a similar detachment. Will knows something important is going on, as his first subsequent question to Sutter indicates: "What happened back there?" (391). The question is not dismissive but indicates that something has happened that cannot be placed in the usual categories that Will uses to classify experience. It was not merely "one more item of psychology," as Sutter in his casebook claimed that the news of Christianity would appear to Will (331). In contrast to Sutter's irony and detachment, Will at least dimly senses the power and mystery of the baptism, and the dialogic tension between their perspectives underscores the drama of this event.

In the novel's final scene, Will makes one last, desperate attempt to prevent Sutter's suicide. After asking what he thought of the baptism—to which Sutter replies, "Do you have to know what I think before you know what you think?" (391)—Will casts aside all of his usual indirection and uses his own name for the second time in the novel, as a kind of guarantee of his own sincerity: "'Dr. Vaught, I need you. I, Will Barrett'—and he actually pointed to himself lest there be a mistake,—'need you and want you to come back [to Alabama]. I need you more than Jamie. Jamie had Val too'" (393). Of course, as many of Percy's critics have asserted, Will's ability to refer to himself by his own name rather than some coy term like "the engineer" represents a resolution of Will's own confusion over who he is and how he shall live his life.[6] Tentatively at least, he has achieved a fragile sense of his own identity. By accepting his own name rather than a more general descriptive label, Will in effect seals himself off from some of the possibilities that had once seemed open to him. Equally important, his voice, in this one statement at least, is purged of all echoes. Will does not mimic Sutter or Dr. Gamow or his father; he speaks as himself in an integrated voice that is commensurate with his own identity. Sutter's response to Will's plea is ambiguous, however. He tells Will that he will think about it and begins to leave until "a final question" occurs to Will, who calls out to Sutter to wait, repeating here the word that he used to try to prevent his father's suicide (393).

What is Will's "final question?" It ultimately does not matter because it is not in any sense a last question. What is important is that the dialogue between Will and Sutter will continue, as is made clear as Sutter's car pulls to a stop on the last page of the novel and Will runs toward it "with great joyous ten-foot antelope bounds" (393) (an action that contrasts sharply with his passive, supine posture at the beginning of the novel). Will will always have one more question for Sutter because Will finds himself within that dialogue, that field of interaction. For this reason, he needs Sutter—not because Sutter has the answers to Will's questions, but because Sutter in a sense validates Will's uncertainty. Sutter does not offer a solution to Will's predicament, but Sutter at least confirms the reality of that predicament. And in this accomplishment, in acknowledging along with Will how difficult it is to live fully in the world and to live meaningfully, the anomie and alienation to which Will could so easily fall victim are held at bay—just as Will helps hold off Sutter's suicidal despair by acknowledging his alienation as well. For as Percy argues so often throughout his writings, to recognize one's dilemma, to name it, and to have that recognition shared with another is itself a restorative of one's well-being.[7] In the end, then, Sutter serves as a touchstone for Will. As Kate Cutrer does for Binx, Sutter helps Will locate himself in the world. Whatever self he has is contained, stabilized in his interaction with Sutter.

Though some critics have complained that the end of the novel is ambiguous, that we do not know what will become of Will or Sutter—if, for example, Will will go back to Alabama and marry Kitty, as he seemingly intends—I think the end of the novel finds Will in the same position that Bakhtin sees many of Dostoevsky's characters: "on the threshold." In *Problems of Dostoevsky's Poetics,* Bakhtin writes, "Dostoevsky always represents a person *on the threshold* of a final decision, at a moment of crisis, at an unfinalizable—and *unpredeterminable*—turning point for his soul" (61). Through this technique, Bakhtin asserts, Dostoevsky avoids reducing a character to a limited psychological type and allowing a novel itself to be reduced to a monologic work, one that is merely the didactic expression of the author's own ideology. In much the same way, Percy in *The Last Gentleman* refuses to give us any final sense of Will's fate. He does not affect some miraculous conversion or plunge Will into an inalterable state of despair. Rather, he leaves Will almost literally in midair, poised on the threshold of an unknowable future.

The Last Gentleman is a worthy successor to *The Moviegoer* that rivals and in some ways surpasses the earlier novel's achievements. Though not as tightly focused and controlled as Percy's first novel, *The Last Gentleman* is more expansive and dramatic. In *The Last Gentleman,* far more than *The Moviegoer,* Percy depicts the historical currents that shape his protagonist's consciousness. And he creates here one of his most memorable characters, the acerbic Sutter Vaught, whose voice and perspective—though far different from Percy's own—are allowed free expression.

Perhaps most important, though, in *The Last Gentleman* Percy seamlessly weaves his religious and moral convictions into the novel's fabric of voices. Percy often spoke in interviews and essays of his fear of being didactic. "[N]othing would be worse," he said in a 1974 interview, "than a so-called philosophical or religious novel which simply used a story and a plot and characters in order to get over a certain idea" (*Con.* 89). Yet if his later fiction—as we will see—sometimes seems far more overt in its philosophical or moral project, his second novel is always subtle and indirect. The emissaries of religion in *The Last Gentleman,* Valentine Vaught and the stolid Father Boomer, are accorded no special privileges in the novel's dialogue of voices and perspectives. Indeed, Percy seems to go out of his way to emphasize

their mundane or unpleasant qualities: Father Boomer is described as looking like "a baseball umpire" (382), and Val herself confesses to Will a disquieting capacity for hatred (289). Both characters in fact fail to make much of a
case for their beliefs in their interactions with Will; ironically, Percy leaves
that to Sutter, a suicidal agnostic (at best), who offers in his casebook the
only sustained argument for the saving grace of faith. But these touches are
only examples of Percy's deviousness as a novelist. For by dispersing his own
beliefs among these characters and not creating a single, authoritative voice
to hand down his convictions like Moses bearing God's law, he achieves a
careful balance between morality and art. *The Last Gentleman* does not insist
that Will—or, by extension, its readers—embrace the same beliefs that Jamie
does as he is baptized on his deathbed. If anything, the novel only leads us to
consider how those beliefs stand in relation to the other values and convictions expressed in the novel's dialogue of voices. And at the end of *The Last
Gentleman,* we too are left "on the threshold," to choose, if we will, among
the many voices echoing in our hearts and minds.

FOUR

The Moralist's Voice:
Love in the Ruins
and *Lancelot*

To enter the world of Percy's third novel, *Love in the Ruins,* after a careful reading of his earlier fiction, is to experience a strange, lingering disappointment. It is not that Percy has lost his ability to engage our interest. The first sentence of the novel is at once allusive and coy, teasing our curiosity in the manner of the best storytelling: "Now in these dread latter days of the old violent beloved U.S.A. and of the Christ-forgetting Christ-haunted death-dealing Western World I came to myself in a grove of young pines and the question came to me: has it happened at last?" (3). The language here is at once apocalyptic in its concerns ("in these dread latter days") and Faulknerian in its sound and beat ("the Christ-forgetting Christ-haunted death-dealing Western World"), and Percy effortlessly draws us into his narrative with the question at the end of the sentence. (What is the narrator afraid of? What does "it" refer to?) Nor has Percy lost the ability to craft a complex narrative voice in which we can hear a microdialogue of voices and beliefs. Dr. Thomas More, the narrator and protagonist of *Love in the Ruins,* is a man torn between science and faith, between a belief in himself that is almost grandiose and a keen sense of his own failings, and the language in which he recounts his experiences reflects these conflicts. He can seem at times like a latter-day prophet, sounding the day of judgment for his decaying society— "Principalities and powers are everywhere victorious. Wickedness flourishes in high places" (5)—or he can speak in the studied, detached voice of a typical scientist: "I know now that the heavy ions have different effects on dif-

ferent brain centers" (27). Tom's narrative even contains echoes of the same
popular culture that sounds in Binx Bolling's voice: "I am something like
old Doc in Western movies: if you catch old Doc sober, he's all right, etcet-
era" (11).

But despite Percy's narrative skill and verbal pyrotechnics, there is something disquieting about the opening pages of *Love in the Ruins*. At the most
basic level, the novel seems dated. *Love in the Ruins* is ostensibly science fiction, but Percy's futuristic world—a decaying America in 1983, complete
with vines sprouting through the pavement and sleek "bubbletop" cars
(37)—strongly reflects the discord of the late 1960s, when the novel was
written. Tom's world is polarized between many factions: conservatives and
liberals, white segregationists and black radicals, suburban parents and hippie
children. This vision of the future was conceived in all its particulars by
meditating on the stormy conditions of the present. And as a consequence,
because many of the novel's external conflicts were deliberately conceived
to comment on the social and political conflicts of the late 1960s, *Love in the
Ruins* feels bound to its period in a way that Percy's earlier work does not.
Though the culture of the 1950s forms the backdrop of *The Moviegoer*,
though Will Barrett's predicament in *The Last Gentleman* is heightened by
the civil rights struggles of the early 1960s, neither book is so wholly a product of its time as *Love in the Ruins*. The world of 1983 that Percy envisions
was wholly formed in the crucible of the late 1960s.

At a more fundamental level, though, the opening pages of *Love in the
Ruins*—and much of the rest of the novel—lack the dialogic tension of
Percy's earlier work. Despite the elements of a microdialogue that we can
hear in Tom's narrative voice, that voice never enters into any sustained
interaction with another point of view. In contrast to the opening of *The
Moviegoer*, where we are made aware immediately of the tension between
Binx's and his aunt's perspectives when we hear traces of her voice sound
within his own, no living voice—with the possible exception of Father
Rinaldo Smith, as we will see—seems to have made an impact on Tom's
consciousness. As Gary Ciuba has observed in *Walker Percy: Books of Revelations*, "Although consciousness, for Percy, depends on a knowing with, on a
dialogue of heart, mind, and soul, Tom has no central confidant in whose
intimacy he can really become himself by talking out his identity" (135).
Why this lack? First, it certainly exists because Percy must fulfill a narrative
obligation. To situate us in this dystopian culture, he devotes much of the
first chapter to a description of Tom's world and an account of its recent

history; the author's attention is necessarily focused on the external reality
of Tom's surroundings. But there is another reason too, one that speaks more
to a change in Percy's intentions than the particular difficulties of writing
speculative fiction. For as we read the first chapter of *Love in the Ruins,* we
ultimately realize—with a start, perhaps—that there are no characters of any
depth or complexity besides Tom himself. In short, there is no one for him
to interact with. All of the people around him are sociological profiles, easily
summed up and endlessly predictable.

Consider, for example, Ted Tennis, one of Tom's patients: "a well-educated,
somewhat abstracted graduate student who suffered from massive free-
floating terror, identity crisis, and sexual impotence" (32). Ted is not a character but a case study. As Tom says, "Every psychiatrist knows the type: the
well-spoken slender young man who recites his symptoms with precision
and objectivity—so objective that they seem to be somebody else's symptoms—and above all with that eagerness, don't you know, as if nothing could
please him more than that his symptom, his dream, should turn out to be
interesting, a textbook case. *Allow me to have a proper disease, Doctor,* he all but
tells me" (33). Tom's initial comment on Tennis is telling: "Every psychiatrist
knows the type." This offhand remark makes clear why More could never
engage in a true dialogue with Ted Tennis, for he is not seen as an individual—someone inherently unique, unclassifiable—but as a type. And Tennis is all too representative of many characters in the novel. As Thomas
LeClair writes in his essay, "Walker Percy's Devil," "In *Love in the Ruins,* many
of the minor characters become the abstractions that Percy warned himself
against—exemplary figures of various social, political, philosophical, or
scientific persuasions" (166).

What accounts for this style of characterization? In a sense, it represents
Tom's way of seeing himself and others. As a scientist, he is trained to see not
what is unique about his patients' problems but what is common to them. A
symptom or behavior can only be understood through the principle of clas-
sification: how is it like other symptoms? Equally important, though, is Tom's
sense of himself as a troubled genius "who sees into the hidden causes of
things and erects simple hypotheses to account for the glut of everyday
events" (11). At least at the beginning of *Love in the Ruins,* Tom has no small
opinion of his own abilities, as is made clear by the comparisons that spring
to mind when he tries to separate his achievements as a scientist from his
weaknesses as a man. "After all, van Gogh was depressed and Beethoven
had a poor time of it," More reasons. "The prophet Hosea, if you will recall,

had a bad home life" (11). Can a man who casually places himself in the company of such giants have much traffic with ordinary mortals? He looks down on them from a very great height, indeed. No wonder, then, that Tom's perception of the people around him is often so reductive, so quick and summary in its assumptions. No wonder that he refuses to descend from the Olympian heights where he dwells to engage people in dialogue.

Ultimately, however, the fact that Tom's world is peopled with types rather than individuals follows from Percy's intention to write a work of satire. As the tensions over race relations and the war in Vietnam escalated in the late 1960s, the moral concerns that underlay the philosophical quests of Binx Bolling and Will Barrett in Percy's first two novels expanded to the political realm. At heart a social conservative, Percy was disturbed by the rising extremism on both the Right and Left that characterized public life in the 1960s. As Jay Tolson writes in *Pilgrim in the Ruins*, "In Percy's eyes, the level of political discourse seemed to be declining daily, along with the clarity of fundamental political labels—conservative, liberal, and moderate. All in all, the state of the nation was enough to inspire despair—or, in Percy's case, satire" (336). And so his third novel broadly echoed—and parodied—the ideological divisions of the day.

But a work of satire like *Love in the Ruins* also requires a different kind of artistic vision than that of Percy's first two novels. In *The Fiction of Walker Percy*, John Edward Hardy defines—and defends—satire as "a purposive mode in which all sorts of exaggerations, distortions, oversimplifications, outrageous inventions in the way of events, institutions, and even geography, are traditionally acceptable. Most of the characters are types of one sort and another—representatives of social and professional classes, absurd mouthpieces for prejudices and pernicious ideologies—rather than fully individualized human beings. But that is what characters in satire are supposed to be" (111). All these contentions are true enough, of course. Because satire is specifically intended to communicate a particular moral statement—surely what Hardy identifies as its "purposive" qualities—a work of satire must inevitably limit the open-endedness and the ambiguity that the dialogic novelist embraces.

In Bakhtin's terms, then, satire is monologic. Rather than a diversity of voices engaged in complex interaction, it privileges a single voice and perspective that expresses the author's moral or philosophical position. And at a concrete level, the monologic nature of satire is manifest in the presentation of character. In a dialogic work, as Bakhtin insists, the characters must remain "unfinalized" (*Dostoevsky* 58–59). That is, they must resist any tendency to sum up or conclusively define their identities, because to do so would be to objectify them and transform the "I-thou" relationship that is a prerequisite of true dialogue into an "I-it" relationship. But in satire the opposite necessarily occurs. The open-endedness of a dialogic work, its stubborn resistance to the reification of its characters, must be limited so that the same characters can be firmly identified with the various "prejudices and pernicious ideologies" to which Hardy refers. In essence, the characters must surrender their individuality to become the "exemplary figures" of different political or philosophical persuasions that LeClair describes—or, in the term used by both Hardy and Dr. Thomas More, "types."

What shall we make of this work, then? Is it fair to criticize Percy, to express disappointment, simply because he bowed to the demands of the form he had chosen? In this case, however, when we consider not only *Love in the Ruins* itself but also the shadow it casts on Percy's subsequent work, there are no simple answers. On the one hand, who are we to quibble with the choice Percy seems to have made to deliberately restrict his vision to achieve his satiric purposes? As no less an authority than Henry James insists in "The Art of Fiction," we must grant the author his or her *donée,* the particular subject and approach that he or she has chosen, and then criticize the work on its own terms (17). But what if that choice is not as clear-cut as it seems? Hardy argues that "this book is obviously not primarily concerned with the personal life of the hero" and, therefore, we do not find in *Love in the Ruins* a "depiction of [the hero's] involvement with other characters developed in considerable depth, characters who engage our sustained interest to some extent in their own right, not as types but as individuals" (108–9). But the primary concern of *Love in the Ruins* is far from clear. Like several of Percy's subsequent novels, there are internal stresses built deep in the work that muddle its intent, so that what emerges is a curiously divided fiction that is neither clearly and unequivocally a satire nor clearly and unequivocally the story of its hero's philosophical search.

Those stresses in *Love in the Ruins*—the tug-of-war between Percy's satirical intent and the dialogic quality of his earlier novels—continued throughout his career as a novelist. In many ways, in fact, those tensions had always been there. There is certainly an obvious satiric component to both *The Moviegoer* and *The Last Gentleman*—most notably in Percy's merciless skewering of northern liberals in the form of Forney Aiken. And as early as 1962, frustrated by what he felt were misunderstandings of his first novel,

Percy had declared in a letter to his friend and mentor, Caroline Gordon, that he was more interested in moral issues than in art: "Actually I do not consider myself a novelist but a moralist or propagandist. My spiritual father is Pascal (and/or Kierkegaard). And if I also kneel before the altar of Lawrence and Joyce and Flaubert, it is not because I wish to do what they did, even if I could. What I really want to do is to tell people *what they must do and what they must believe if they want to live* (qtd. in Tolson, *Pilgrim* 300).

Perhaps the greatest difficulty in coming to terms with Percy's achievement is to recognize the delicate balance in his work between his moral concerns and his art. It is hard not to take Percy at his word in that letter to Gordon or in the many interviews over the course of his career in which he described himself as "a polemicist and a moralist" or "a satirical novelist" (*Con.* 89; *More Con.* 154). Indeed, in *Walker Percy: The Last Catholic Novelist*, Kieran Quinlan flatly declares that "a Percy novel will turn out to have an agenda—more or less explicit—and be intended to lead to a definite conclusion every bit as much as one of his philosophical essays" (90). Quinlan argues that "Percy's Catholicism had a strong ideological flavor" that shapes and determines his fiction (8). Moreover, Quinlan suggests that Percy specifically responded to the "authoritarian" aspects of Catholicism, finding in his new faith a source of authority to replace the failed gods of stoicism and science (32–33)—a suggestion that is echoed by Bertram Wyatt-Brown in *The House of Percy*: "Part of Walker Percy's understanding of the Christian message remained tied to Will Percy's vision of agonized moral struggle. Moreover, he found in his guardian's severe and morally demanding code an authoritarian undertone which could be translated into the hierarchy and rule of Catholicism" (309).

Of course, the authoritarian quality of Percy's faith and of his stoic heritage—which he never completely renounced: in a 1985 interview he praised the ethical component of stoicism and insisted, "I don't see Christianity and Stoicism as antithetical" (*More Con.* 106)—argue for the primacy of Percy's ethics over his aesthetics.[1] And yet in many of the same interviews in which he spoke of the polemical or satirical qualities of his fiction, Percy was careful to warn against merely being didactic. Despite his own beliefs and the very real desire to communicate those beliefs to his readers, Percy made clear that he also understood that a work of fiction that aspires to art is by its nature fluid and ambiguous; in some essential way, it is always open-ended, polyphonic. In the same 1974 interview in which he called himself "a polemicist and a moralist," for example, he went on to say, only a few sentences later, that "nothing would be worse than a so-called philosophical or religious novel which simply used a story and a plot and characters in order to get over a certain idea" (*Con.* 89). But perhaps Percy's most revealing comments came in an 1981 interview when he was asked about the work of Flannery O'Connor:

> Her Catholicism was never far from her mind, I think; she was very polemical in her writings. And that's a question I've never been quite clear about, to tell you the truth. She would tell you, and has said, that she was very much aware of certain periods in her short stories where she means that the reader is supposed to understand that an action of grace has occurred, a supervention of grace. . . . Well I'm not sure you really see that. . . . She sees her fiction in much more univocal, theological terms than I would see it. I think it works without that rather simple theological reading, and I think it had *better* work without that or otherwise, if you have to share that feeling of grace with her to understand her fiction, I think she's in trouble. (*Con.* 233)

How can we not hear Percy's own worries about his own work in these remarks? When he says that O'Connor's "Catholicism was never far from her mind," he reminds us of his own admission in his 1989 essay "The Holiness of the Ordinary" that "there is hardly a moment in my writing when I am not aware of where my main character. . . stands vis-à-vis the Catholic faith" (*SSL* 368). When he claims that O'Connor "was very polemical in her writings," we recall his own desire to tell his readers "what they must do and what they must believe if they want to live." And, similarly, when he says, referring to O'Connor's polemical intent, "that's a question I've never been quite clear about," he seems to acknowledge the ambivalence about his own aims that surfaces in his scorn for "a so-called philosophical or religious novel which simply used a story and a plot and characters in order to get over a certain idea." We can almost hear him warning himself here to shun the univocal terms in which devout Catholics like O'Connor—and himself—are tempted to see their fiction. When he says that her fiction "had *better* work" "without that rather simple theological reading," he sounds like he is talking to himself.

And perhaps also to one other as well. For statements like this one also clearly reflect what Tolson has called Percy's "long-running quarrel" with "his oldest and closest friend," the novelist and Civil War historian Shelby Foote (*Pilgrim* 491). From the earliest beginnings of Percy's career as a novelist, Foote had urged his friend not to impose his own religious and moral beliefs on his fiction. As Foote wrote in a 1951 letter to Percy,

> You seem to think the novelist is some exalted kind of pamphleteer, and whats more you seem to think that his "meaning" is preferably derived from some standard body of thought his mind has discovered and accepted as a duty to pass on to others—seeking converts to his discovery. As a matter of fact, as I have said before, the best novelists have all been doubters; their only firm conviction, the only one that is never shaken, is that absolute devotion and belief in the sanctity of art which results in further seeking, not a sense of having found. That part of any writer's book which says "Look: here I've found the answer" is always the weakest. The search is always better done; the discovery is invariably a letdown. (Tolson, *Correspondence* 60–61)

Even if Percy would ultimately reject his friend's insistence on "the sanctity of art" above all else—as Tolson argues in *Pilgrim in the Ruins,* when he calls Percy's hard-won faith "the enabling condition of his art" (493)—Percy's evident qualms about a type of fiction that is univocal and dependent on a "rather simple, theological reading" also powerfully suggest that he could never entirely reject his friend's voice in the microdialogue of his own consciousness. It is as if we can hear in many of Percy's statements what Bakhtin calls a "word with a sideward glance," a type of language in Dostoevsky's fiction in which the "most important confessional self-utterances are permeated with an intense sensitivity toward the anticipated words of others about them, and with others' reactions to their own words about themselves" (*Dostoevsky* 205). When Percy seems to retreat from and hedge his proclamations about the religious and moral aspects of his work, he seems to be looking back over his shoulder at Foote and engaging him again in their lifelong dialogue over their art.

The central struggle of Percy's artistic life was ultimately his effort to balance the demands of the "spiritual fathers" that he cited in his 1962 letter to Gordon—Pascal, Kierkegaard, and others—with those of his literary masters. Like Jacob wrestling with God's messenger, the artist in Percy, that part of himself that bowed down before the altar of his literary idols, was locked in a perpetual struggle with the saving angel of his religious convictions. And in *Love in the Ruins,* with its broad satire, with its cast of types clinging to their various "prejudices and pernicious ideologies," that struggle comes to the forefront for the first time, as we hear, somewhere above and behind the novel's antic energies, a new voice in Percy's fiction whose satiric wit only loosely disguises an increasing moral urgency. This voice reflects the authoritarian certitude of his stoic legacy and his Catholic faith, and it tends necessarily toward monologue rather than dialogue. Yet this voice is also itself a participant in the larger dialogue of Percy's fiction. As we will see—most notably in *Lancelot* and *The Second Coming*—Percy repeatedly, perhaps unintentionally, questions and subverts the certainty of the moralist's voice, so that we feel throughout his fiction a struggle that is something like the endless, undecidable contest that Bakhtin envisions between centripetal and centrifugal forces in nature and human existence. Like those forces in life, in culture, and in language that would standardize meaning and expression, the moralist in Percy—that part of himself that gratefully admitted the authority of his faith and was heir to the ethical rigor of the patrician South's stoic culture—cannot help but try to control his fiction, to impose on it a specific shape and set of values. But like those forces that delight in difference and incongruity, that break a single language into many dialects and acknowledge multiplicity as the only truth, another part of himself—the one, perhaps, that knelt "before the altar of Lawrence and Joyce and Flaubert"—resists the heavy hand of the moralist.

On and off throughout his long correspondence with Foote, Percy spoke of his ambition to write what he called in 1967 "the BIG ONE," a work of fiction that would be "bigger than Don Quixote, Moby Dick et al."—though he also realized that such devouring ambition leads potentially "to grandiosity of spirit, flatulence of the creative powers and perdition in general" (Tolson, *Correspondence* 129). As Patrick Samway observes in his biography of Percy, Percy first mentions the work in progress that would become *Love in the Ruins* in the same 1967 letter (257). Percy's third novel was clearly an attempt at "the BIG ONE," an encompassing statement that, in his own words, "was about everything" (*Con.* 46).

Our guide through the busy and densely peopled world of *Love in the Ruins* is Dr. Thomas More, a middle-aged, somewhat seedy physician whose personal life and family history are every bit as complicated as those of Percy's earlier protagonists. At the beginning of the novel, we find Tom at the end of "twenty years of silence and decline" (24). After a promising start to his career that was capped by what he calls "an extraordinary medical discovery," when he deduced the effects of radioactive fallout on psychological states—a discovery crucial to the plot of the novel—his life fell into disarray after the death of his daughter (24). As Tom explains, "My daughter, Samantha, died; my wife ran off with a heathen Englishman . . . and I left off research, left off eating Christ in Communion, and took to sipping Early Times instead and seeking the company of the fair sex, as they used to say" (24). This succinct statement of Tom's decline is critical to our understanding of the novel, for the real focus of the book concerns Tom's efforts to right the shaky course of his life. It is no accident that the climactic moment occurs when Tom reaffirms at least some of what he used to live by.

The importance of Tom's personal struggle is also suggested by the complexity and detail of his heritage. Like Binx Bolling and Will Barrett, he is deeply aware of his ancestry. "[W]e are one of that rare breed," Tom says, "Anglo-Saxon Catholics who were Catholic from the beginning and stayed Catholic," and he even claims his namesake Sir Thomas More as "a collateral ancestor" (22). But as Tom goes on to explain, the family's "illustrious" history was obscured after it settled in Louisiana, "where religious and ethnic confusion is sufficiently widespread and good-natured that no one keeps track of such matters" (22). Indeed, that "religious and ethnic confusion" is manifest in Tom's voice as he details their life in Louisiana: "My forefathers donned Knights of Columbus robes, wore swords and plumed hats, attended French shrimp boils and Irish wakes, made retreats with Germans, were pallbearers at Italian funerals. Like the French and Germans here, we became easygoing Louisianians and didn't think twice about our origins. We fought with Beauregard next to old blue-light Presbyterian Stonewall Jackson and it seemed natural enough. My father was only a third-degree Knight of Columbus, but he too went regularly to Holy Name shrimp boils and Lady of the Lake barbecues and was right content" (22). We can literally hear the creolization of Tom's family in the "southernisms" that dot this speech, as when he calls Jackson an "old blue-light Presbyterian" and speaks of his father being "right content." But these heteroglot traces in Tom's narrative voice are not just details designed to ornament the larger game of Percy's political satire. As we will see, Tom's confused relations to his "illustrious" origins are both reflective of his world and critical to the novel's resolution.

Tom himself, though, is not an entirely reliable guide to his fractured world. From the start, he acknowledges that his vision is limited. Stricken by an allergy to the gin fizzes that one of his many paramours prepares for him and that he nevertheless consumes in spite of their effect on him, he can barely see at the beginning of the novel: "My field of vision is narrowing from top to bottom. The world looks as if it were seen through the slit of a gun turret" (21). Of course, Tom's restricted vision suggests the deliberate distortions of the satirist's art, as if Percy was offering his readers a kind of tacit mea culpa at the start of the book to prepare them for its curiously flattened world. But Tom's narrow field of vision also alerts us to the questionable nature of his perceptions. He is often affected in the novel by drink or fatigue or the mind-altering capabilities of the invention that drives much of the plot, his lapsometer. Indeed, as William Leigh Godshalk notes in "*Love in the Ruins:* Thomas More's Distorted Vision," Tom's narrative is filled with the deliberate contradictions of an unreliable narrator; he confuses countless small details of his immediate situation, like the room numbers in the ruined Howard Johnson's motel where he has hidden his various loves, and minor facts of the chronology of his world (138–39). Even the baseline reality of the main events of his narrative may be in doubt if we accept the suggestion of Lewis Lawson in "*Love in the Ruins:* Sequel to Arrowsmith" that virtually everything in the novel after a prologue on 4 July 1983 "represent[s] his dreamwork during a ten-minute nap" (*Following* 168).

Whatever the ultimate truth of his narrative, though, the world that Tom presents to us is deeply fragmented. America, as Percy envisions it in 1983, is a union in name only, with feuding cities and individual states establishing diplomatic relations with foreign countries, a condition of disunity paralleled by Tom's immediate environs. Tom's community is divided into discrete zones inhabited by different factions of his shattered society. There is the town, a haven for the hard right wing: retired military officers, evangelicals, and the like; Happy Hollow, where most blacks live; Honey Island Swamp, a refuge for hippies and "Bantus," young black radicals who plot revolution and make guerrilla raids on "outlying subdivisions and shopping plazas"; and, most important of all, there is Paradise Estates, the suburb between the town and the swamp where Tom lives and where most of the action of the novel takes place (15–16).

Paradise Estates is, as Tom tells us, "an oasis of concord in a troubled land," where "heathen and Christian, Jew and Gentile, Northerner and Southerner, liberal and conservative"—but not black and white—live more or less amicably alongside one another (17, 16). But Tom's Paradise is at once everything it appears to be and not quite what it seems. On the one hand, despite the general disrepair of Tom's society, with its broken-down automobiles and vines cracking through the pavement, Paradise Estates is not all that different from Binx Bolling's home in Gentilly; as Percy once said of Gentilly and all the places like it, "there are many beauties there" (*Con.* 28). And so Tom can wax lyrical on the "[p]retty cubes and loaves of new houses . . . strewn among the pines like sugar lumps" (12). He can celebrate the suburban lifestyle that brings together both liberal scientists and conservative businessmen as "good fathers and husbands who work hard all day, come home at five-thirty to their pretty homes, kiss their wives, toss their rosy babies in the air, light up their charcoal briquets, or perhaps mount their tiny tractor mowers" (15).

But just as Tom's language in this encomium to suburban life is forced and a little tired with its paeans to "pretty homes" and "rosy babies," so too is the general peace and welfare of Paradise Estates dependent on a kind of collective inauthenticity. We see this fakery most obviously in the northerners who have relocated here. As Tom explains, in a passage that recalls some of the worst excesses of Will Barrett's exaggerated nostalgia for the southern past, "they, the Northerners, have taken to Southern ways like ducks to water. They drink toddies and mint juleps and hold fish fries with hush puppies. Little black jockeys fish from mirrors in their front yards. Life-size mammy dolls preside over their patios" (16–17). For all the liberal convictions of these northerners—who will typically argue with their conservative neighbors that crime is a consequence of poverty and racism—they have surrounded themselves with the trappings of a sentimentalized antebellum past and settled comfortably enough in an all-white neighborhood, where the only people of color are the servants: "faithful black mammies who take care of our children as if they were their own, dignified gardeners who work and doff their caps in the old style" (17). Nor are the southerners any better. The "showplace of Paradise," admired by all apparently, is Tara, a replica of the plantation house in *Gone With the Wind* (75). This "preposterous fake house on a fake hill" (181) is a copy of a copy, twice removed from any historical reality, and its designation as the defining architectural monument of Paradise Estates, the "showplace" of the neighborhood, suggests how deeply the false historical consciousness that it represents lies at the heart of the "oasis of concord" that is Tom's Paradise. Just as Tom himself has only the vaguest connection any more to his "illustrious" origins, proclaiming his Catholic beliefs repeatedly but not acting on them, so has everyone around him become disconnected from the real truths of history, embracing instead a distorted, sanitized vision of a serene antebellum past that is as spurious as the "great plastered columns [of Tara], artificially flaked to show patches of brickwork" (279).

Indeed, this disconnect with history and the inauthenticity it spawns pervades virtually every aspect of Tom's world, infecting even his most intimate relationships. A kind of rumpled Don Juan, Tom is romantically involved with at least three different women in the novel, and all of them blithely transfigure and distort the past. Moira Schaffner, a technician at the Love Clinic, a sexual research center in Fedville, the immense government research complex devoted to behaviorist experiments, is "a romanticist" who "lives for what she considers rare perfect moments" (130). Consequently, her consciousness is almost ahistorical, transfiguring her surroundings to fit the romantic myth that she wants to embrace. When she meets Tom for a tryst at the ruined Howard Johnson's, she imagines the motel as "the haunt of salesmen and flappers of the Roaring Twenties. Whereas," More ruefully explains, "it was far more likely that it was the salesman and his wife and kids and station wagon who put up here in the sixties and seventies" (134). Similarly, Lola Rhodes, the mistress of Tara, envisions herself—fittingly enough— as a latter-day Scarlett O'Hara. "When all is said and done, the only thing we can be sure of is the land," she says, as if her home actually fronted a plantation rather than "six acres of Saint Augustine Grass" (279). Even Ellen Oglethorpe, More's nurse and a bastion of Presbyterian virtue, is somehow cut off from history and therefore less than she seems. A "strict churchgoer and a moral girl [who] does not believe in God" (157), Ellen exemplifies the incoherence of the modern view of humanity that Percy decries in "The Delta Factor," the first essay in *The Message in the Bottle*. Ellen distorts history in her own way as badly as Moira and Lola, by severing the ethical component of the Judeo-Christian tradition from its theological moorings.

But all these willful misrememberings and distortions of the past have deeper consequences than merely inauthentic personal relationships, because—for Tom at least—the current troubles of the nation are rooted in history. As he explains, in a long meditation on history early in the novel:

> Was it the nigger business from the beginning? What a bad joke: God saying, here it is, the new Eden, and it is yours because you're the apple of my eye; because you the lordly Westerners, the fierce Caucasian-Gentile-Visigoths, believed in me and in the outlandish Jewish Event even though you were nowhere near it and had to hear the news of it from strangers. But you believed and so I gave it all to you, gave you Israel and Greece and science and art and the lordship of the earth, and finally even gave you the new world that I blessed for you. And all you had to do was pass one little test, which was surely child's play for you

because you had already passed the big one. One little test: here's a helpless man in Africa, all you have to do is not violate him. That's all.

One little test: you flunk!

God, was it always the nigger business, now, just as in 1883, 1783, 1683, and hasn't it always been that ever since the first tough God-believing Christ-haunted cunning violent rapacious Visigoth-Western-Gentile first set foot here with the first black man, the one willing to risk everything, take all or lose all, the other willing just to wait and outlast because once he was violated all he had to do was wait because sooner or later the first would wake up and know that he had flunked, been proved a liar where he lived, and no man can live with that. And sooner or later the lordly Visigoth-Western-Gentile-Christian-Americans would have to falter, fall out, turn upon themselves like scorpions in a bottle. (57)

This extraordinary passage unites Percy's theological convictions with a Faulknerian vision of history in an appropriately borrowed Faulknerian voice, with the same piling-on of clauses and adjectival phrases. When Tom speaks of "the outlandish Jewish Event" that "the lordly Westerners" only heard "the news" of secondhand, "from strangers," he echoes the terms of Percy's essay "The Message in the Bottle" (*MB* 119–49), terms that were themselves derived from Kierkegaard. But more to the point is "the test" that in Tom's vision God set for "the lordly Westerners." Their failure to not "violate" "a helpless man in Africa" and the subsequent consequences of that failure, when "the lordly Visigoth-Western-Gentile-Christian-Americans would have to . . . turn upon themselves like scorpions in a bottle" is a kind of curse, like the one that Isaac McCaslin envisions in Faulkner's *The Bear*. Though it may well be true, as Hardy argues, that this vision of history is riddled with fallacies, its errors and exaggerations are characteristic not only of Tom's particular vision of history but also of his creator's patrician heritage. When Hardy asks "Who are 'we' . . . that we should assume the 'helpless man in Africa' is or ever was helpless, was created simply to test our worthiness?" (114), he does not hear the echo of Percy's stoic legacy in that claim. Behind this passage, with its insistence on the fate of the "helpless man in Africa" as a test of "the lordly Westerners," lies what Percy has described as the stoic's "stern inner summons to man's full estate, to duty, to honor, to generosity toward his fellow man and above all to his inferiors" (*SSL* 85). Implicit in the gap between "the lordly Westerners" and the helpless Africans are the same class divisions—and subsequent obligations—that define the relations between Percy's patrician class and those whom he casually identifies as their "inferiors."

Within the specific context of *Love in the Ruins,* however, Tom's question—"was it always the nigger business, now, just as in 1883, 1783, 1683"— suggests that the real conflicts in his society are not the differing views over the long-simmering war in Ecuador or the cultural conflicts on religion and sexuality that divide the conservative Knotheads from the liberal Leftpapas. In the end, all we will ever see of those conflicts are shouting matches between liberals and conservatives. No, the real issue that corrupts and rends his society is race. As a result, conservatives and liberals can live side by side happily in the segregated utopia of Paradise Estates as long as everyone tacitly agrees to forget or abridge the real history of America's racial troubles. In addition, the only real threat of violent upheaval in the novel comes from the Bantus, who rioted five and a half years earlier and who now may be planning an armed revolution. For all that the novel's cultural and political divisions parallel the conflicts of the 1960s, the deeper threat of racial violence echoes the worries that Percy expressed in a 1966 letter written to his daughter, Mary Pratt, who was attending college in Washington, D.C. Even the insistent capitalization of his warning emphasizes its urgency: "WE LIVE IN UNSETTLED REVOLUTIONARY TIMES. A LARGE SEGMENT OF THE NEGRO POPULATION IS SO ALIENATED FROM THIS AFFLUENT SOCIETY THAT THEY ARE VERGING ON MASS CRIMINALITY. FOR GOD'S SAKE, TAKE NO CHANCES AT ALL" (qtd. in Samway 247).

In the novel, these fears are manifest in Tom's worries about an armed revolution by the Bantus. His fears are initially spurred when a sniper shoots at him as he sits at his breakfast table on the patio of his home. Later, as he makes his way into town, all the while trying to dodge the sniper who he thinks may be following him, he takes cover on the overgrown golf course of the Paradise Estates Country Club and overhears a conversation involving three black men: Willard Amadie, once a career soldier in Ecuador and now a waiter at the country club; Victor Charles, an older black man who once worked as a laborer for Tom's father and is now a caretaker at the animal shelter; and a man Tom doesn't know, referred to by the others as Uru. The conversation suggests that the Bantus will try to kidnap both the Christian Kaydettes, Paradise Estates' champion league of young female baton twirlers, and many of the doctors from Fedville, who will then be forced to serve as teachers at a school in Honey Island Swamp. After Tom is captured by the Bantus about three-quarters of the way through the novel, we learn that their plan is to seize the outlying houses of Paradise Estates—including Tom's—to get control of the local television tower and that the shots fired at him were meant to scare him out of his house. The Christian Kaydettes will be used as insurance, and the transmitter apparently will enable the Bantus to broadcast revolutionary propaganda to the other blacks—the loyal servants of Paradise Estates, no doubt—who live in Happy Hollow. Though the plan itself is never fully detailed, its final aim seems to be the armed takeover of Paradise Estates. When Tom directly asks Victor and Uru, "Are you all taking over Paradise Estates?" Uru's denial is immediately followed by Victor's more qualified statement, "Not in the beginning, Doc" (298).

Neither Victor nor Uru, however, ever has the opportunity to explain at length what they are doing and why they are doing it. We know from an earlier exchange in the novel between Tom and Victor that Victor, after returning to the South following two years working in the North, has been denied housing in Paradise Estates five times. Indeed, when Victor reminisces about the shrimp jubilees and other local customs that seem to have drawn him back home, it's clear from Tom's reaction that race relations have only gotten worse in the community. Victor happily remembers attending the shrimp jubilees alongside Tom and another friend, a white southerner named Leroy Ledbetter, but Tom remarks that "Leroy Ledbetter wouldn't be next to you now" and notes that as a member of the city council, Leroy has voted repeatedly to deny housing to Victor (148). These actions in fact seem to be the crucial forces that have radicalized Victor, who is older and more traditional than Uru and Willard, and driven Victor to join the Bantu revolution. A Baptist deacon and in his own way a proud southerner, Victor is still enough of a traditionalist to beseech Tom's help—"Do you think you could speak to Mr. Leroy?" he asks (149)—in exactly the same way that poor blacks sought the help of Ed Barrett in *The Last Gentleman* or others in Greenville, Mississippi, in the 1930s sought the help of William Alexander Percy. But because Victor has been radicalized in the fragmented future of *Love in the Ruins,* he quickly tells Tom, "Never mind. It's too late." Instead, Victor ruefully observes what are perhaps the deepest consequences of Tom's dark vision of history, "You would think people with that much in common would want to save what they have. . . . Now everything's got to go and everybody loses" (149).

By contrast, Uru's explanations are grounded in the militant rhetoric of the Black Power movement of the late 1960s. As Uru explains to Tom after his capture, "You chucks had your turn and you didn't do it right. You did bad, Doc, and now you're through. It's our turn now and we are going to show you" (298–99). Uru envisions creating "a new society right here" (300). But for all his outward display of militancy, his rejection of "Jew-Christian names" and his habit of clothing himself in the ceremonial African garb of an herbalist, Uru is not very different from the other northerners in Paradise Estates who have reimagined themselves as southerners (300). Like them, Uru—the former Elijah Washington, a pro football player from Detroit who went on to receive a Ph.D. in political science—has taken on the trappings of a new identity. And like those northerners who have embraced a myth of a genteel southern past, Uru's question to Tom—"What would you do about the four hundred years?" (301)—embraces a defining myth of victimization, which in its single-minded vision of unending oppression is also a distortion of history. Like almost everyone else in the novel, Uru refuses to see the past clearly and, therefore, is caught up in violence and discord. Just as the whites of Paradise Estates cannot redress past injustices because they insist on obscuring them with a sentimentalized vision of southern history, so too, Percy seems to argue, will blacks like Uru fail to overcome those injustices—to "get on with it" in Tom's words (301)—because the injustices are all they see of the past.

Ultimately, however, it is hard to gauge even the clarity of Tom's vision of the past. Though he is obviously a man of compassion, willing to treat anyone, from Victor Charles's dying "auntee" to ailing Bantu guerrillas appearing surreptitiously at his door, his own racial attitudes sometimes seem as much a part of the mythical Old South as the mammy dolls of his neighbors in Paradise Estates (297). When, for example, he wanders through Happy Hollow, his vision of the residents' life there recalls what Wyatt-Brown in *The House of Percy* cites as William Alexander Percy's conception of blacks as "happy Pan-like beings living only in the present" (266). Though Tom notes the "bare ground" that "never dries out" and the harsh sunlight of Happy Hollow, he goes on to claim that "people seem happy here. Happy pot-bellied picaninnies play in the alley. Old folk rock on porches. The unhappy young men are gone. The kindly old folk doff their caps politely" (141). Except for the visible absence of "the unhappy young men," the scene Tom describes seems lifted out of an earlier time when blacks allegedly meekly and happily accepted the forced constraints on their lives. Even his use of the word *picaninnies* seems wholly uncritical, as if Tom here has assimilated the voice and values of the antebellum past. Later, too, when Tom is captured by the Bantus and spots Lola Rhoades, one of his various loves, following them from a distance, he worries that she is "apt to get herself caught or killed or worse" (304). But what is worse than being killed? If Tom means rape, then we catch an ugly whiff here of the old taboo of miscegenation. In fact, though Tom at times speaks with great feeling of the evil of racism, the deep "fault in the soul's terrain" (152) that it reveals, he is susceptible—like his neighbors in Paradise Estates—to an uncritical embrace of older, even distorted values of the southern past.

Perhaps this somewhat muddled vision also enables Tom to see himself as his country's savior, the man who will lift his troubled nation out of the ruins of its history. "I hit on something, made a breakthrough, came on a discovery!" he proclaims, immediately after detailing his vision of the downfall of "the lordly Visigoth-Western-Gentile-Christian-Americans." "I can save the terrible God-blessed Americans from themselves!" (58). Indeed, the core plot of *Love in the Ruins*—in the midst of much activity concerning Tom's complicated love life and his efforts to head off the Bantu revolution—centers on his quest to build on his earlier breakthrough, when he discovered the effects of radioactive fallout from heavy sodium on human psychology. Now, Tom seeks to perfect a device capable, in his words, of "measuring and treating the deep perturbations of the soul" (29). Tom believes that the divisions that rend his society merely reflect the divisions within the soul that trouble the individual. If he can restore the wholeness of the individual, then perhaps he can restore his society, too.

As Lawson notes in "Tom More: Cartesian Physician," Tom's vision of "the deep perturbations of the soul" is rooted in the philosophy of René Descartes: "Refusing to accept alienation as a condition inherent in human consciousness, Tom believes it has developed only as a result of the triumph of Descartes' philosophy" (*Following* 151). Descartes' philosophy is based on a fundamental separation between subject and object. Seeking a core of unequivocal truth in his philosophical explorations, Descartes ultimately finds that bedrock certainty in his own consciousness and therefore splits off his consciousness from the whole world of phenomena to be examined and classified. As Lawson writes, "everything in the Cartesian system rests on the subject/object relationship, the observer and the observed, *res cogitans* and *res extensa*. By such a magnificently simple process, Descartes removed man (and God) from the world, so that man could study it objectively: thus was born the scientific method" (*Following* 152). In Tom's eyes, the dominance of Cartesian thought, of the rigid separation between the observing consciousness and the physical world in which it must live, has had ruinous results:

"Only in man does the self miss itself, *fall* from itself (hence *laps*ometer!). Suppose—! Suppose I could hit on the right dosage and weld the broken self whole! What if man could reenter paradise, so to speak, and live there both as man and spirit, whole and intact man-spirit, as solid flesh as a speckled trout, a dappled thing, yet aware of itself as self!" (36).

There are, however, any number of problems with this idea—not least of which is the link on which Tom (and by extension Percy) insists between individual alienation and social division. Simply put, there is precious little evidence in the novel that restoring the wholeness of the individual will also repair the society's political and racial divisions.[2] Tom's declaration that his invention "can save the terrible God-blessed Americans from themselves" seems instead a measure of his own overweening hubris. And, perhaps, it is also a measure of the "grandiosity of spirit" that Percy feared in his effort to write "the BIG ONE," for the two main elements of the plot, Tom's scientific ambition and the social turmoil around him—especially his fears of the Bantu revolution—seem pasted together, occurring on largely separate lines of action within the novel. If there is in fact any connection between these elements, it is that both proceed from a profound confusion about the past— his society's unwillingness to confront its troubled history and Tom's own tenuous connection to his "illustrious" origins.

Tom's scientific ambitions are also problematic because they conflict with the faith in which he says he still believes. Despite the fact that he no longer practices his religion and readily identifies himself as a "bad" Catholic, he still affirms—albeit tentatively—his faith: "I believe in God and the whole business but I love women best, music and science next, whiskey next, God fourth, and my fellowman hardly at all" (6). No doubt it is because God comes in fourth on Tom's list of allegiances, behind science, that Tom can brush aside the obvious conflicts between his ambitions and his faith. For religion insists on a metaphysical dimension of existence, a divine spark that is not susceptible to the snares of any technology like Tom's invention, but Tom—perhaps because of the distance between himself and the clear convictions of his ancestor and namesake—seems oblivious to the obvious contradictions.

No doubt, also, this conflict between Tom's science and his faith is the reason why the language in which he expresses his ambitions is so confused. When he speaks of "measuring and treating the deep perturbations of the soul," his language is rooted in metaphysics and theology (29). But when he explains that his invention "will measure the electrical activity of the separate centers of the brain," he uses the terminology of science (28). Indeed, though he criticizes his colleagues for their refusal to admit the existence of the soul—"Unfortunately, there still persists in the medical profession the quaint superstition that only that which is visible is real. Thus the soul is not real" (29)—when he tries to explain how his invention works, his only recourse is to talk about its effects on various parts of the brain. We see this linguistic confusion most clearly when he explains the conclusions of twenty years of work: "I know now that the heavy ions have different effects on different brain centers. For example, Heavy Sodium radiation stimulates Brodmann Area 32, the center of abstractive activity or tendencies toward angelism, while Heavy Chloride stimulates the thalamus, which promotes adjustment to the environment, or, as I call it without prejudice, bestialism" (27). The language here is manifestly technical, grounded in a material universe in which all the diverse facets of human personality are hardwired in the physiological reality of the brain, but the grand terms that Tom applies to his theory, *angelism* and *bestialism,* preserve at least vestigial traces of his religious faith.

Tom's ambition to create technology that can "weld the broken self whole" certainly shows only that he is not terribly different, in his methods at least, from the other scientists in the novel who work in Fedville, an immense government research facility. These men are all committed to behaviorist principles, to a mechanistic view of humanity. In a typical division at Fedville, "the Geriatrics Rehabilitation Center," for example, depressed senior citizens are reconditioned with electrodes implanted in their skulls. But though Tom is clearly uneasy with this behavioristic approach, his own invention, "More's Quantitative-Qualitative Ontological Lapsometer," is not very different from the electrodes and "Skinner Boxes" of his behaviorist colleagues. Indeed, after the lapsometer is modified to stimulate certain segments of the brain, it is only a more sophisticated version of the electrodes favored by the technicians of the Geriatrics Rehabilitation Center.

This contradiction between the religious view of humanity to which Tom claims to subscribe and the mechanistic view that governs his research sounds throughout his narrative. At times, he clearly echoes his religious teachings and speaks in the formal language of the church, like a good Communion boy reciting a lesson. When, for example, he has a conversation with Max Gottlieb, his colleague and occasional therapist, about the guilt that follows his various sexual adventures, Tom describes his activities as "sinful," much to Gottlieb's confusion.

"If it is sinful, why do you do it?"

"It is a great pleasure."

"I understand. Then, since it is 'sinful,' guilt feelings follow, even though it is a pleasure."

"No, they don't follow."

"Then what worries you, if you don't feel guilty?"

"That's what worries me, not feeling guilty."

"Why does that worry you?"

"Because if I felt guilty, I could get rid of it."

"How?"

"By the sacrament of penance."

"I'm trying to see it as you see it."

"I know you are."

"What I don't see is that if there is no guilt after *une affaire,* what is the problem?"

"The problem is that if there is not guilt, contrition, and a purpose of amendment, the sin cannot be forgiven."

"What does that mean operationally speaking?"

"It means that you don't have life in you." (117)

Tom's sense of his own conduct is entirely at odds with the more equivocal view of his behavior that for Gottlieb is grounded in his own behaviorist theories. For Gottlieb, such actions bring either pleasure or pain and should be adjusted only if their consequences are unpleasant. But for Tom sexual behavior cannot be separated from the ethical and spiritual realm in which he, as a believing Catholic, tries to live. Indeed, the two men do not even speak the same language. Though Gottlieb says, "I am trying to see it as you see it," the gap between his professional jargon—"operationally speaking"—and Tom's religious nomenclature is too wide to allow for real dialogue.

Tom's quiescent devotion to his faith is also suggested by his interaction with Father Rinaldo Smith, one of the few characters in the novel whose voice clearly sounds in Tom's consciousness. Though Father Smith is, like Tom, prone to depression, his difficulties do not undermine his credibility as a representative of his faith but somehow seem to add to his authority. In fact, virtually the only time in the novel when Tom clearly assimilates some-one else's language, it is a phrase of Father Smith's, an apocalyptic portent that Tom remembers the priest muttering during a psychological examina-tion after being temporarily committed, alongside Tom, in the acute wing of a mental hospital. When Gottlieb asked Father Smith why he could not complete the ten o'clock mass that day, Father Smith replied, "They're jamming the air waves," and the following dialogue ensued:

> "They?" asks Max. "Who are they?"
> "They've won and we've lost," says Father Smith.
> "Who are they, Father?"
> "The principalities and powers." (185)

This exchange suggests at least a possibility of an intersubjective bond between Father Smith and Tom. For Tom, who occupied the next bed in the acute wing, Father Smith's apocalyptic warning coincided with his own eschatological musings. This is made clear when we realize that Tom's ominous declaration as he surveys the ruins of his society in the first few pages of the novel—"Principalities and powers are everywhere victorious. Wickedness flourishes in high places" (5)—is in fact a quotation of something he had heard Father Smith say months earlier. But because the chronology of the novel is scrambled, beginning on 4 July and then moving backward in time, the influence of Father Smith on Tom's own apocalyptic vision is not readily apparent in the opening pages.

By the same token, though, despite the absence of any clear echoes of any particular colleague in his narrative, Tom's scientism is clearly manifest in his forms of expression. Thus, on the day that he perfects the first version of his lapsometer—one that can diagnose the ills of the spirit but not treat them—he sees the world in a way that is not very different from the scientists at Fedville. At once elated and depressed by his success, Tom becomes entranced by "the sight of tiny jewels strung along the glittering web of saliva" (92) in the mouth of Lola Rhoades. And this vision leads to a description of Lola that is informed by his ambition as a scientist: "Her membranes are clear as light, the body fluids like jeweler's oil under a watch crystal. A lovely inorganic girl" (92). Tom uses this mechanical imagery—which itself is based in the clockwork universe of the Enlightenment, the dawning of the scientific consciousness that Tom exemplifies—because his objective of "weld[ing] the broken self whole" necessitates that he conceive humans as "inorganic" creations, susceptible at the deepest level to the intervention of technology.

The conflict between Tom's ambition and faith is ultimately exploited by a character who may or may not be the devil. In an extended play on the legend of Faustus—yet another element in the novel's very busy plot—Tom is tempted by Art Immelmann, a seedy bureaucrat who first appears in a flash of lightning and mysteriously knows of Tom's invention. Immelmann initially offers Tom funding for research on his lapsometer and later provides the technology that enables him to treat—as well as diagnose—the soul's maladies. As LeClair notes, Immelmann's function in the novel is very much like the role of the devil in *The Brothers Karamazov,* a sinister doppelgänger of Ivan Karamazov (160). Throughout *Love in the Ruins,* Immelmann speaks and makes concrete Tom's desires, as in this exchange, when he appears to Tom for the second time and gives him the attachment to his lapsometer that makes it a therapeutic as well as diagnostic tool. But Immelmann is apparently not satisfied fulfilling Tom's ambitions and so attempts to stoke them to a higher pitch:

> "Doc, you have two great potentials: a first-class mind and a heart full of love."
> "Yes."
> "So what do you do with them?"
> "I don't know, what?"
> "Know and love, what else?"
> "Yes."
> "And win at both."
> "Win?"
> "Is there anything wrong with being victorious and happy? With curing patients, advancing science, loving women and making them happy?"
> "No."
> "Use your talents, Doc. What do you know how to do?"
> "I know how to use this." I pick up the lapsometer.
> "What can you do with that?"
> "Make people happy."
> "Who do you love, Doc?"
> "Women, knowing, music, and Early Times."
> "You're all set, Doc." (216)

Here, Immelmann exploits Tom's own angelism-bestialism. Immelmann's injunction to "know and love" appeals both to Tom's discarnate consciousness, the characteristic abstraction of the scientist, and his carnal body. But this exchange is hardly an example of dialogue in the Bakhtinian sense. For Bakhtin, true dialogue requires an interaction of two sovereign selves, each with his or her own point of view. Yet Immelmann in this scene—and elsewhere in the novel as well—really has no point of view. The most dreamlike aspect of the novel, he is only the black hole of Tom's own desires, at best a projection of the conflicting impulses in Tom's consciousness.

Indeed, while Immelmann gives expression to Tom's ambition and desires, his scenes with Tom are flat. Though Immelmann is a good joke at first—a version of Mephistopheles who looks like "the sort of fellow who used to service condom vendors" and who smells too strongly of deodorant (213)—he is the most paper-thin of the novel's types, and he gradually comes to seem more of a plot device trundled onstage to advance the narrative or express an idea than a character in his own right. Even his style of speech, the distinctive linguistic traces that Percy heretofore has used so deftly to define his characters, can be discarded if the need arises. When, for example, Immelmann demonstrates the power of Tom's lapsometer—now enhanced by Immelmann's attachment—to allay the everyday terrors of humanity, his manner of speaking changes completely as he describes the lapsometer's effect on a particular area of the brain, where the "musical-erotic" response is housed. Where Immelmann had previously sounded like a traveling salesman or a bureaucrat, he now sounds like a philosophy textbook (and only like a philosophy textbook; those traces of other warring voices that typically make the voices of Percy's characters so rich and complex are absent here): "Here the abstract is experienced concretely and the concrete abstractly. Take women, for example. Here one neither loves a woman individually, for herself and no other, faithfully; nor does one love a woman organically as a dog loves a bitch. No, one loves a woman both in herself and insofar as she is a woman, a member of the class women. Conversely, one loves women not in the abstract but in a particular example, this woman. Loves her truly, moreover. One loves faithlessly but truly" (213).

Of course, within the terms of Percy's Faustian allegory, Immelmann's protean nature is true to his diabolic character; the devil has traditionally been portrayed as a quick-change artist who can become whatever his mark wants him to be. And since Percy needs to show us at this moment in the novel how Tom's abstraction leads him astray, why not suddenly confer upon Immelmann these theoretical insights? But in having Immelmann voice these ideas, Percy succumbs to exactly the sort of narrative determinism against which he often warned in interviews: the use of "a story and a plot and characters in order to get over a certain idea" (*Con.* 89). We can almost hear the grinding of the novel's thematic gears over the voices of its characters in this scene.

Immelmann's machinations ultimately drive the plot of the novel to its dramatic conclusion. Immelmann provides Tom with the adjustment to the lapsometer that can treat as well as diagnose the soul's ills. Immelmann shows Tom how the newly empowered lapsometer can release people from their inhibitions. And then Immelmann steals a carton full of lapsometers and distributes them throughout Tom's fractured society, where they can unleash everyone's hidden demons, like gasoline on the fire of their political passions. Finally, after many extravagant episodes, including Tom's capture and escape from the Bantus (he slides out of an air-conditioning duct in the abandoned church where he is imprisoned in a symbolic rebirth that prefigures his renascent faith), the various threads of the novel's plot culminate at the Paradise Estates Pro-Am Golf Tournament, where the stolen lapsometers cause the sand traps to smoke in a heavy sodium reaction that will loose a cloud of noxious particles capable of sweeping away inhibitions like a massive charge from the lapsometer.

Yet this seeming fulfillment of the apocalypse that Tom had predicted at the beginning of the novel proves false. Though the cloud descends on the spectators at the golf course, its only apparent result is to unleash familiar hostilities among the crowd's conservatives and liberals, who abuse one another with old insults and empty gestures. Instead of an apocalypse, the scene devolves into a final hallucinatory confrontation with Immelmann, who appears out of the smoke to reprise his temptation of Tom. Once again, Immelmann exploits Tom's angelism-bestialism, telling him, "Develop your genius," and urging him to enjoy the pleasures of his various lovers (364). But Immelmann's voice is countered by another from Tom's memory, as his despair at Immelmann's apparent triumph recalls the despair caused by his daughter's death and his subsequent loss of faith.

Indeed, just as Immelmann is about to escape to Denmark with Tom's lapsometer and his nurse (and true love), Ellen Oglethorpe, another voice of a particular individual finally registers in Tom's consciousness. Confronted by the fruits of his genius on the golf course, by the consequences of his scientism, Tom hears again the voice of his dead daughter, Samantha, another precocious, doomed child in Percy's fiction, who, like Lonnie Smith in *The Moviegoer,* is afflicted by a mortal illness that is tempered by her faith. Her voice echoing in Tom's consciousness warns him not to commit "the sin against grace": "If God gives you the grace to believe in him and love him and you refuse, the sin will not be forgiven you" (374). But as Tom hears Samantha's voice in his mind, he also realizes that he has committed this sin by refusing to take her to Lourdes, as his ex-wife Doris had wished, in the hope of a miracle cure. Instead of trying to believe, Tom allowed himself to revel in despair over Samantha's fate, to indulge in the license for depravity that tragedy provides and, in his own words, "feast on death" (374). Yet this realization, so long delayed, somehow strengthens Tom and provides the faith to mumble a haphazard prayer to his ancestor Sir Thomas More that at last drives off Immelmann in a cloud of smoke.

Tom's act of praying aloud—which surprises even him—represents his ideological becoming. Pressed by circumstances to choose between science and faith, Tom reaches back into his past, beyond his southern heritage, beyond his upbringing as another "easygoing" Louisianian, connecting finally to his own "illustrious" origins (22), as he embraces the faith manifest in Samantha's memory and embodied in the image of his ancestor and in his own truest history. Why does he ultimately make this choice? For one reason, because Immelmann, acting out Tom's own ambitions, has shown him the consequences of unbridled abstraction. The scientific knowledge that Immelmann embodies, which is "neutral morally, abstractive, and godlike" (214), leads first to the euthanasia center at Fedville and then to the mock apocalypse on the Paradise Estates golf course. But the Judeo-Christian tradition, which Tom tentatively embraces with his prayer, rejects the mechanistic notion of humanity that is intrinsic to the work at Fedville and the healing powers of the lapsometer.

Moreover, faith is a tonic for Tom's hubris; it is a way of reconciling himself to and seeing the beauty in ordinary life. When Tom makes confession at the end of the novel—an act that Ciuba calls "a Percyan sacrament of dialogue" (168)—Father Smith, whose voice has also echoed in his consciousness, counsels Tom that faith compels one to temper ambition and concentrate instead on small acts of kindness: "like doing our jobs, you being a better doctor, I being a better priest, showing a bit of ordinary kindness to people, particularly our own families . . . doing what we can for our poor unhappy country—things which, please forgive me, sometimes seem more important than dwelling on a few middle-aged daydreams" (399). Of course, the "daydreams" to which Father Smith refers are more than the lusts to which Tom confesses just prior to this response: they are also the fruits of Tom's abstraction, his grandiose schemes for his lapsometer. Only by adopting the kind of faith that Father Smith articulates can Tom ever see the folly in such schemes (which he does not completely do, even at the end of the novel—in the epilogue he is still committed to perfecting the lapsometer).

In fact, as Tom himself recalls as he lies on the golf course wanly trying to beat back Immelmann's temptation, religion once had the power to save him from his own abstraction. When he and Doris toured the country in the early years of their marriage, he would delight in taking Communion at the small churches in the towns through which they passed. For Tom, the Communion ritual figuratively brought him back to earth: "it took religion to save me from the spirit world, from orbiting the earth like Lucifer and the angels . . . it took nothing less than touching the thread off the misty interstates and eating Christ himself to make me mortal man again and let me inhabit my own flesh and love [Doris] in the morning" (254). As Ciuba notes in *Walker Percy: Books of Revelations,* Tom's memory of the salvational quality of this ritual "is expressed in language bluntly physical that avoids such euphemism as 'receiving communion' for the starker image of feeding on God" (156). Indeed, the concreteness of this language is analogous to the power of faith to ground Tom in this world and thus to dispel the abstraction that Immelmann exploited.

But however moving, the conclusion of *Love in the Ruins* makes clear that the novel's real focus is the violent clash in Tom's soul, not the polarization of his society. The pivotal moment in the last chapter, after all, is not a bloody Götterdämmerung as Tom's world explodes into factional conflict but a turning back in his consciousness on the moment that he lost his way and abandoned his faith. Indeed, the last chapter is striking for its lack of action. In a novel punctuated by random attacks from snipers and Tom's edgy cat-and-mouse game with the Bantus, the climax is curiously peaceful. A series of minor characters yell slogans at one another as faces from his past appear in the heavy sodium mist before an exhausted and largely passive Tom. Even the Bantu uprising does not come to much. Though a state trooper tells Tom that the Bantus have carried out some vandalism in Paradise Estates, in the epilogue that carries the story forward five years, Tom explains that the Bantus' revolution "was a flop; they got beat in the troubles five years ago and pulled back to the swamp" (385).

It is striking—and a clear measure of the novel's internal stresses—that Percy virtually abandons the subplot of the Bantu revolution at the end of the book, allowing tensions developed throughout the course of the novel to be resolved offstage. Percy's genuine concern for the state of the nation that apparently drove him to begin *Love in the Ruins* is almost shrugged off at the end, for by the time we have reached the dramatic climax of the book he has practically changed the subject. Tom virtually admits as much when

Uru appears to him in the heavy sodium mist on the golf course. When Uru declares that the Bantus will "Take what we need, destroy what we don't, and live in peace and brotherhood," all Tom can offer in reply are his reasons why they can't really engage one another in dialogue. "We're not talking about the same thing. We're talking about different kinds of trouble," he says (372), and his admission is telling. The forces over which Tom ultimately must prevail in the novel, the devils that really interest Percy, are "different kinds of trouble" than the political struggle in which Uru and Victor are engaged. No doubt for this reason, Percy ultimately relies on a deus ex machina, the sudden discovery of oil in Honey Island Swamp, to resolve the novel's racial and political conflicts. Rather than attempt to show the "better things and harder things to do" to which Tom refers when he rejects Uru's rhetoric of destruction—as Percy did in *The Last Gentleman,* with Valentine Vaught's school in rural Alabama—Percy, like a kind of benevolent deity, simply bestows wealth on the Bantus and allows them to buy Paradise Estates (373). While this development is an entertaining comic turn, allowing for all kinds of economic and social reversals in the new society that it spawns, it hints at a failure of nerve on Percy's part, an unwillingness to look too hard at the long history of racial strife that he had once identified as the diseased heart of his nation's troubles.

And yet, even if the real focus of the novel is the fragmentation in Tom's soul rather than in his society, *Love in the Ruins* still seems to come up short. For in contrast to the searches of Binx Bolling and Will Barrett, Tom's spiritual turmoil lacks resonance because there is virtually no one else in the novel's gallery of types who could mirror it or understand it. Over the course of the novel, only a handful of other characters ever seem to rise above Percy's satiric vision and, briefly at least, engage in a dialogic interaction with Tom. There is Samantha, of course, whose voice echoes in his memory so powerfully at the end, and Father Smith, whose explicitly religious language seems to give structure and meaning to the apocalyptic portents that More details in the opening chapter of the novel. Indeed, the shared recognition of these signs is itself the ground of an intersubjective union between Tom and Father Smith; like Binx Bolling and his half brother, Lonnie, like Will Barrett and Sutter Vaught, Tom and Father Smith see something that those around them do not, thereby creating the potential at least for a more profound interaction. But Percy does not really explore this possibility in *Love in the Ruins.* Only in his last novel, *The Thanatos Syndrome,* which is a sequel to *Love in the Ruins,* does this more extended and complex interaction occur.

Surprisingly, virtually the only other character who engages Tom in a dialogic interaction is his friend, Leroy Ledbetter, the owner of the Little Napoleon, where Tom goes to drink, and the man who turned down Victor Charles's request for housing in Paradise Estates. Although Leroy is by no means a pivotal character, he is someone with whom Tom identifies. They are kinsmen of a sort, with similar origins that extend back for generations: both southerners—"seventh-generation Anglo-Saxon American" (152)—who prefer the "peaceable gloom" of the Little Napoleon to "the lounges of the suburbs, the nifty refrigerated windowless sealed-up Muzaked hideaways" (151). At times, they even speak alike. When Tom describes Leroy as "the sort of fellow, don't you know, who if you run in a ditch or have a flat tire shows up to help you," he adopts something of Leroy's ambling, casual syntax (152). Indeed, Leroy serves as a kind of touchstone for Tom. Their relationship embodies Bakhtin's belief that we look to others, through dialogue, to help us see ourselves. Thus, Tom depends on Leroy for self-perception, Tom's sense of himself as a good and capable man: "Leroy believes that doctors do wonders, transplant hearts, that's the way of it, right? Isn't that what doctors are supposed to do? He knows about my lapsometer, believes it will do what I say it will do—fathom the deep abscess in the soul of Western man—yes, that's what doctors do, so what? Then do it" (153). Here, even as Tom props up his sense of himself with Leroy's view of him, their voices seem to merge. The rhetorical questions, the offhanded tone that quietly scolds, all come from Leroy, all mimic his reply when Tom earlier insisted that he would not see patients on Saturday afternoons. "You're a doctor, aren't you" Leroy had asked, both mystified and indignant that Tom would refuse his professional duty (153). In the passage above, we can hear a synthesis of Tom's and Leroy's voices. Tom's vast ambition—his dream of "fathom[ing] the deep abscess in the soul of Western man"—becomes entwined with Leroy's laconic, matter-of-fact manner of speaking.

Indeed, precisely because Tom subtly identifies with Leroy, Tom becomes so disturbed in what is arguably the most powerful scene in the novel, when Victor Charles helps Tom into the Little Napoleon after he has wandered into Happy Hollow and nearly passed out from a combination of stress, drink, and heat.[3] Tom's entrance with Victor violates the decorum of his racially polarized society and briefly upsets Leroy. The incident is "a near

breach," Tom says, that is quickly resolved when Leroy realizes that Victor
has only come into the bar to help Tom. But Tom's anxiety is heightened
when he remembers one of the events that set off the Bantu riot five years
earlier, Leroy's brutality to a black couple in a bowling alley that he and Tom
had bought together as a business venture:

> Where did the terror come from? Not from violence; violence gives
> release from terror. Not from Leroy's wrongness, for if he were alto-
> gether wrong, an evil man, the matter would be simple and no cause for
> terror. No, it comes from Leroy's goodness, that he is a decent, sweet-
> natured man who would help you if you needed help, go out of his way
> and bind up a stranger's wounds. No, the terror comes from the good-
> ness and what lies beneath, some fault in the soul's terrain so deep that
> all is well on top, evil grins like good, but something shears and tears
> deep down and the very ground stirs beneath one's feet. (152)

Although this passage seems purely reflective, a meditation on the problem
of evil, Tom's tacit identification with Leroy gives it a dialogic thrust. For by
understanding how Leroy's fundamental decency can be intermingled with
an irrational cruelty, Tom might also understand his own flawed nature—the
hubris of which he is dimly aware and the carnality to which he is so liable.
No doubt for this reason, the quality of Tom's attention differs markedly here
from his other encounters with friends and neighbors. In contrast to the
detached, objective summation of Ted Tennis's neuroses quoted at the beginning of this chapter, Tom is far more engaged in this section, so much so
that his observations shift back and forth from the incongruity in Leroy's
character to the "terror" that it inspires in Tom. He clearly does not view
Leroy from the same abstracted heights from which Tom looks down on his
patients' difficulties. Because the divisions in Leroy mirror the divisions in
Tom himself, what he sees in the other touches him deeply and speaks to his
own confusion.

In fact, precisely because of Leroy's ambiguous nature, he provides a far
more unsettling reflection of Tom than does Immelmann, Percy's devil.
Though Immelmann expresses Tom's dark side, the way in which those evils
are concentrated in Immelmann makes him less threatening, a caricature of
evil. Indeed, one of Tom's comments about Leroy inadvertently points to
the reason for Immelmann's failure as a character: "if he were altogether
wrong, an evil man, the matter would be simple and no cause for terror."

The simple, black-and-white terms in which Immelmann's villainy is portrayed are unconvincing. But because the evil in Leroy is so thoroughly blended with his sweetness and decency, he offers a far more disturbing reflection for a divided man like Tom. As a result, Tom's reaction, when he considers the latent violence in Leroy's character, is immediate and visceral: "something shears and tears deep down and the very ground stirs beneath one's feet."

That fault line deep in Leroy's soul is perhaps the most obvious manifestation of the curse that Tom sees as the cause of his nation's current troubles. After all, it is in response to Leroy's racism that Victor Charles says, "You would think people with that much in common would want to save what they have. . . . Now everything's got to go and everybody loses" (149). But Percy does not linger long enough to look very deeply into that "fault in the soul's terrain" where Leroy's blind hatred is located. For the most part, this brief glimpse is all we see of Leroy in the book, and all of the other bigots in the novel—both white and black—are cardboard characters with no real depths to probe. It is tempting, though, to imagine what Percy might have done if Tom and Leroy's dialogue occupied more of the novel. What then might Percy, our preeminent literary diagnostician, have revealed of the virulent, seemingly ineradicable pathology of racism? In fact, just as Leroy reflects Tom's flaws in a more disturbing way than does Immelmann, so too do the subtle tensions that follow from Victor Charles's incursion into the white preserve of the Little Napoleon seem far more real than other aspects of Percy's satire of the political and racial polarization that gripped America in the 1960s. For all the humor of Percy's satire, it does not do much beyond paint in broad terms the same arguments that filled countless editorial pages. But because Percy was a child of the South, a gifted observer steeped in the folkways and beliefs of what was "above all a society of manners" (*SSL* 86), his depiction of the way that racial tensions are mingled with the forms of southern life is much more acute than his political satire. Percy understood all too well the knife-edge of custom that his characters must walk. So it should be no surprise that his vision of racial polarization is most convincing when it is inscribed in the language of manners. Indeed, nothing else in *Love in the Ruins* is as disturbing or fully imagined as this mistake in etiquette, this "near-infraction of zoning" (152).[4]

Ultimately, *Love in the Ruins* is a flawed, uneven novel that seems, in the end, to succumb to the "grandiosity of spirit" that Percy feared in any attempt to write "the BIG ONE." Though the divisions in Tom More himself are evoked with all of the novelist's masterful control of nuance and shading, the flat, cartoonish world in which Tom is set down is clearly a product of the moralist's stark vision. And, consequently, many of the characters in Percy's third novel are denied their individuality, transformed into representative figures running through their paces in an authorial scheme. An oddly unbalanced work, *Love in the Ruins* frustrates the reader, and the complexities of the protagonist's voice sound in a vacuum, searching for an answering note. In Percy's next novel at least, the protagonist will find one.

Though the first words of Percy's fourth novel, *Lancelot,* purport to be the opening of a dialogue—"Come into my cell. Make yourself at home" (3)—what emerges over the course of the novel is a terrifying picture of human isolation. It is not only that we first encounter the narrator of the novel, Lancelot Andrewes Lamar, confined in a cell in what he calls "the nuthouse" for reasons he cannot remember, or that for Lancelot ordinary human relations have been so drained of meaning that "true communication" consists of tapping out simple messages in code to the woman in the cell next to his who is recovering from being brutally gang-raped and "won't speak to anybody" (3, 12). No, Lancelot's isolation is most dramatically represented in the way that the implied dialogue of the novel's opening quickly becomes overwhelmed by the force and insistence of his monologue as he theorizes, rants, and struggles to recount the reasons for his confinement. As Robert H. Brinkmeyer has suggested in his Bakhtinian reading of the novel, "Walker Percy's *Lancelot:* Discovery through Dialogue," Lancelot "closes himself off within what Bakhtin would call a monologic consciousness—a consciousness that sees itself as self-sufficient, whole, and finalized" (36). Consequently, even Lancelot's listener is reduced to a kind of instrumentality, as his presence functions for Lancelot as "a kind of catalyst," "the occasion of my remembering" (13). The perspective of Lancelot's addressee emerges only gradually in the interstices of Lancelot's monologue to question his vision and draw him reluctantly into dialogue.

Although the voice of Lancelot's listener is entirely omitted from the text of the novel until its conclusion, we come to know him indirectly through Lancelot's responses to him.[5] A childhood friend, Harry, the man Lancelot calls Percival, is now, in Lancelot's words, "a priest-physician. Which is to say, a screwed-up priest or half-assed physician. Or both" (10). We gradually learn that Percival is in fact suffering a crisis of faith. After leaving New

Orleans twenty years earlier to perform missionary work in Biafra, he has returned a changed, perhaps disenchanted man. As Lancelot observes early in the novel, the listener does not wear a priest's traditional dress but "phony casuals" (5). And he will not comply with a woman's request that he say a prayer for the dead when he passes through the cemetery across the street from the hospital where Lancelot is interned—an action that prompts Lancelot to remark, "So something went wrong with you too" (11).

In many ways, this statement is characteristic of their relationship, for the lives of these men often paralleled one another. Both sons of "honorable families," they were "classmates, fraternity brothers, and later best of friends" (14). And though there were always differences between them—Lancelot was more gregarious, a football star in college, while his friend was introverted, a bookish loner occasionally given to dramatic, sometimes self-destructive gestures—they seemed to recognize in each other a shared sensibility. This aspect of their relationship is clear from their first meeting in the hospital, when Lancelot sees in his friend "an abstracted look in which I recognize a certain kinship of spirit" (5). As Lancelot says, when he recalls his first sight of the other after twenty years, "when I saw you yesterday, it was like seeing myself. I had a sense of being overtaken by something, by the past, by myself" (5).[6]

Indeed, the complex bond between the two men is crucial to Lancelot. It is his compass in his effort to negotiate the murky terrain of his past; he insists that only by talking to his friend can he understand what has happened to him. "Christ, why is it that I could never talk to anybody but you?" Lancelot asks at one point. "Well, you're here now and I can use you. I've discovered that I can talk to you and get closer to it, the secret I know yet don't know" (62). Over and over again, Lancelot refers to a "secret" buried in his past that he will only discover when he tells it to his friend. "It is as if I knew that the clue was buried somewhere in the rubble," he says, "and that I have to spend days kicking through the rubble to find it. I couldn't do that alone. But we could do it" (106). As Brinkmeyer notes, Lancelot's need to talk suggests that even at the beginning of the book his vision of himself is not as secure as it seems:

> His extensive interchange with Percival reveals that a part of Lance will not permit him to close himself off with the shell of his self-image and its system of belief and judgment. If Lance were as strong as he characteristically makes himself out to be, he would have no need to talk with

Percival and to respond to his judgments. Any justification that Lance felt he needed for his actions would have to be self-justification. Such a state of affairs is precisely what Lance has strived for, but upon his reunion with Percival he instinctively senses that only through dialogue with his old friend will he be able to discover what mysteriously bothers him. (39)

But to enlist his friend in this search, Lancelot must remake him, a feat he accomplishes through the act of naming. Though his friend's given name is Harry, and though he has taken on the religious name of John on entering the priesthood, Lancelot insists now on calling him *Percival*—one among the many nicknames by which he was once known.[7] As Lancelot explains,

> We knew each other by several names depending on the oblique and obscure circumstances of our lives—and our readings. . . . To begin with, you were simply Harry, when you lived at Northumberland close to us on the River Road and we went to school together. Later you were known variously as Harry Hotspur, a misnomer because though you were pugnacious you were not much of a fighter. Also as Prince Hal, because you seemed happy only in whorehouses. Also as Northumberland, after the house you lived in. Also as Percival and Parsifal, who found the Grail and brought life to a dead land. Also by several cheerful obscene nicknames in the D.K.E. fraternity of which the least objectionable was Pussy. (9–10)

It is curious, though, that Lancelot chooses the fourth—and in some ways the least clearly derived—of these nicknames to summon up his old bond with his friend. Though Lancelot suggests how each of his friend's other nicknames was connected to some fact of his life or character, Lancelot does not explain the origin of his friend's identification with the Percival of Arthurian legend or why he himself now insists on using that name. In fact, there is a willfulness to this act that points to a deep need on Lancelot's part to enlist the other man in Lancelot's fantasy. For as we will see, Lancelot will characterize the events that led to his internment as "a quest for evil," and to maintain this interpretation he must see himself as a kind of knight-errant (138). The Arthurian associations that he evokes by calling the other man *Percival* are a way of making reality conform to his desired vision of himself. Ultimately, though, the principal dialogic tension in the novel arises from the conflict between the heroic interpretation that Lancelot struggles to impose on his actions and alternate interpretations that encroach on his field of vision.

As Lancelot notes, though, Percival bestowed on him his own ironic name, *Sir Lancelot,* after Lancelot was discharged from the army because of a persistent case of diarrhea (28). In many ways, in fact, the ironic disjunction between Lancelot's heroic name and the real facts of his military career characterized much of his life before the events that led to his incarceration. As we learn gradually over the course of Lancelot's narrative, the grand expectations of his youth never rose beyond a single feat, his performance on the football field in college, when at age twenty-one he achieved "the longest punt return in history" (15). The closest he came to duplicating this achievement was his involvement as a lawyer in the civil rights movement, but when what he calls "the happy strife of the sixties" (59) was over, he abandoned his legal practice and settled down to give tours of his family estate, Belle Isle, and write historical articles about the Civil War.

What emerges most clearly from Lancelot's account of the first half of his life are the contradictions and evasions that characterized it. For one thing, we see that despite Lancelot's participation in the civil rights movement, his motives were more ambiguous than a simple desire for justice. "It was a question of boredom," he says at one point (58). Later he explains that "We basked in our own sense of virtue and in what we took to be *their* gratitude" (91). In fact, Lancelot's own racial views are considerably more ambivalent than his public stance in the civil rights movement would suggest. At several points in his narrative, his words and actions evoke an older form of paternalism, even a sense of ownership, that echoes uncomfortably of the relation between master and slave. When, for example, Lancelot's servant, Ellis Buell, was threatened by the local Klan for letting civil rights organizers meet at his church, Lancelot told the Grand Kleagle—an old football buddy from college—that the "uppity nigger" he'd targeted was "my nigger" (93). In a similar fashion, years later, when Lancelot enlists Ellis's son, Elgin, in a scheme to spy on Lancelot's wife, their manner suggests a recurrence of the past. Lancelot gives his orders to Elgin from behind a "plantation desk," while Elgin sits "in [a] slave chair, made by slaves for slaves" (43). Indeed, even though Elgin—with Lancelot's help—has won a scholarship to MIT, Lancelot insists that the past cannot really be transcended. "[N]othing really changes," he muses when Elgin accepts another of Lancelot's tasks, "not even Elgin going from pickaninny to M.I.T. smart boy. For you see . . . he was still in a sense 'my nigger'" (142). (Elgin is also unable to resist the pull of these old roles. In the first report to Lancelot on the results of the initial attempts to spy on his family, Elgin refers to Lancelot's older daughter, Lucy, as "Miss Lucy" [124], a figure of speech that prompts Lancelot to muse over the way that Elgin too retreats to the past when it suits him. As Lancelot thinks, "*Miss Lucy?* He had never called her that. I saw that he felt a need to put a distance between himself and this business. . . . In his nervousness he had put the greatest distance he could think of: he had retreated to being an old-time servant" [124].)

And yet, even as Lancelot seems to reenact the southern past, we are also aware of a kind of artifice, for everything around him in Belle Isle has been restored, packaged for public consumption by tourists and historical societies. Lancelot's plantation desk, the slave chairs, the carefully restored walls of slave brick in the study-cum-pigeonnier where he meets with Elgin—these are all the results of Lancelot's second wife Margot's efforts to remake Belle Isle into a perfect replica of what it had been a hundred years earlier. As Lancelot says of Margot, "even me and herself she transformed: to take an old neglected abused thing, save it, restore it, put it to new and charming use. She loved to drink, laugh, and make love, but almost as well, better maybe, and orgasmically too, she liked cleaning away a hundred years of pigeon shit and finding lovely oiled-with-guano cypress underneath, turning a dovecote into a study, me into Jefferson Davis writing his memoirs. She was a Texas magician" (81–82).

Such illusions, though, are fragile constructs. The story that Lancelot tells Percival about the terrible events of a year ago is ultimately the story of how that construct came undone. For Lancelot, the illusion began to shatter on an ordinary October afternoon in his pigeonnier when he looked down at his daughter Siobahn's application for a riding camp on his desk and noticed that her blood type did not match his own. Until that moment he had lived happily enough in the "transformed" world that Margot had created for him. As Lancelot says of his condition before this observation, "There I sat in my pigeonnier, happy as could be, master of Belle Isle, the loveliest house on the River Road, gentleman and even a bit of a scholar (Civil War, of course), married to a beautiful rich loving (I thought) wife, and father (I thought) to a lovely little girl; a moderate reader, moderate liberal, moderate drinker (I thought), moderate music lover, moderate hunter and fisherman, and past president of the United Way. I moderately opposed segregation. I was moderately happy" (24).

We can literally hear in this passage the tensions and evasions in Lancelot's life rising to the surface, as the vaguely sardonic voice that is heard in the parenthetical statements continually interrupts and undermines the seemingly bucolic tone of the main narrative (so much so that Lancelot is driven at the end of the passage to modify his initial claim that he was "happy as could be"). Over the course of the novel, the tensions in Lancelot's narrative will become even more extreme as he comes closer to the violence that killed his wife and several others, destroyed his ancestral home, and led to his incarceration in the "nuthouse." Because he genuinely does not know how he feels about his actions (he desperately wants to believe they were justified, but the contradictions and uncertainty in his narrative signal his doubt) because he does not really even know what sort of man he is (a jealous husband, a moralist lashing out on principle, or another anonymous failure in a world of broken men), the voice that recounts Lancelot's story is more conflicted and volatile than the voices that we hear in Percy's other novels. Lancelot's narrative, the microdialogue of his consciousness, is characterized by extreme and sudden shifts in voice and tone. And though this microdialogue is filled with echoes, like the fragmented consciousnesses of Percy's other protagonists, his relation to these echoes is even more troubled; the irony that Binx Bolling or Will Barrett sometimes uses to distance himself from a voice or perspective that he cannot comfortably assimilate becomes overpowering and corrosive here. Most of all, perhaps, Lancelot's hold on reality is questionable. There is a disjunction between the elaborate interpretation he tries to impose on his actions and his own muffled awareness of the insufficiency of that vision. And as Lancelot's heroic image of himself begins to give way in the face of Percival's increasingly wary reaction to everything Lancelot recounts, the voice that dominates the novel becomes even more erratic.

These extreme shifts in voice and perspective that characterize Lancelot's narrative are evident as he reacts to the realization that Siobahn's blood type forces on him: Margot has been unfaithful. Though he tries to react with an analytical equanimity—"Why is it such an unspeakable thing for one creature to obtrude a small portion of its body into the body of another creature?" he asks in the voice of a man conditioned by the scientism of his culture—he cannot help but envision Margot's infidelity in the most intimate, most personal terms: "Isn't it unspeakable to me to imagine Margot lying under another man, her head turning to and fro in a way I knew only too well, her lips stretched, a little mew-cry escaping her lips?" (16). Lancelot cannot view his wife's infidelity from the posture of objectivity because, as

Lawson has observed in "The Fall of the House of Lamar," his ideas on
sexuality parallel those of Sutter Vaught in *The Last Gentleman* (228). For
Lancelot, sexual love is, as Sutter called it, "the sacrament of the dispossessed"
(*LG* 269). In a secular, scientific world where the only truth is that which
can be grasped empirically, sexual love is the only way that one can—temporarily at least—transcend the quotidian reality of existence. As Lancelot
tells Percival in the second of their five meetings, "sex is not a category at
all. It is not merely an item on a list of human needs like food, shelter, air,
but it is rather a unique ecstasy, ek-stasis, which is a kind of possession" (21).
Or as he says later, twisting Percival's religious language to his own ends,
"The orgasm is the only earthly infinity" (140). But what is one to do if this
sacrament is lost—as Lancelot eventually admits, "lately I had trouble making love to Margot" (66)—or worse, if it is corrupted by a kind of violation?
For Lancelot, then, everything comes asunder: possessiveness, security, love,
the underpinnings of his being.

Yet the discovery of Margot's infidelity is also disturbing to him because
it suggests the artifice that has characterized so much of his life. In fact, the
extent of Lancelot's illusory world is underscored by his environment at the
moment he makes his discovery. As he looks down at Siobahn's application
and sees her blood type, he hears thunder rumbling outside his window. But
what in another, more melodramatic work would simply be a signal of ominous portent is here profoundly ironic. For the clap of thunder that punctu-
ates Lancelot's initial discovery of the lie at the center of his life is itself artificial, the creation of a film company that is making a movie at Belle Isle,
and Percy's staging emphasizes the tension between illusion and reality that
confounds Lancelot. As he confesses to Percival later, "There I was in early
middle age and I couldn't answer the most fundamental question of all. What
question? This: Are people as nice as they make out and in fact appear to be,
or is it all buggery once the door is closed?" (131).

This question is particularly troubling because it is connected for Lancelot
to uneasy memories from his childhood. Increasingly, his narration of the
events surrounding his discovery of Margot's infidelity becomes entwined
with his memories of another, earlier revelation:

> I can only compare it to the time I discovered my father was a crook. It
> was a long time ago. I was a child. My mother was going shopping and
> had sent me up to swipe some of his pocket money from his sock
> drawer. For a couple of years he had had a political appointment with

the insurance commission with a "reform" administration. He had been
accused of being in charge of parceling out the state's insurance business
and taking kickbacks from local agencies. Of course we knew that could
not be true. We were an honorable family. We had nothing to do with
the Longs. We may have lost our money, Belle Isle was half in ruins, but
we were an honorable family with an honorable name. Much talk of
dirty politics. Maury, I *told* you not to get into it! (my mother). The usual
story of the honorable man besmirched by dirty politicians. The honor
of the family won out and even the opposition gave up. So I opened the
sock drawer and found not ten dollars but ten thousand dollars stuck
carelessly under some argyle socks. (41–42)

As this passage clearly shows, Lancelot is as haunted by the past as Will
Barrett in *The Last Gentleman,* another son of an "honorable family." And like
Will, Lancelot's consciousness echoes with the voices of his family. We can
hear their outraged dignity when he begins his litany: "We were an honorable family." Indeed, the more he talks, the more their voices rise in his own,
until his mother literally speaks through him. But there is a tension in this
microdialogue that was not in Will's, a veiled anger that reflects Lancelot's
more extreme confusion. For though Will gradually comes to realize that
what those voices have to say to him is inadequate for the world in which
he finds himself, Lancelot knows that their claims are lies. No doubt as a
result, he seems to deliberately overemphasize their protestations through
repetition and, in the end, he offers a kind of dismissive summation: "The
usual story of the honorable man besmirched by dirty politicians." It is as if
Lancelot is trying to hold himself apart from what he says, quoting his
family's claims but not identifying with them, for to do so would be to step
into that world of artifice in which they—and Margot—seem to dwell.

But the tension between his family's "honor" and their actions becomes
even more severe when Lancelot later confronts another phantom from his
childhood: the possibility that his mother had an affair with her distant
cousin, Harry Wills, "a handsome beefy Schenley salesman, ex-Realsilk salesman, who was always in and out of Belle Isle when I was a child" (96). As
Lancelot explains to Percival, "Uncle Harry would come roaring up in his
Buick convertible and holler out: I'm taking everybody joyriding to False
River. My father would insist that Mother go: she needed the air.... And off
they'd go, we'd go—I sometimes but not always—'joyriding.' Christ, joyriding! Jesus, do you really imagine that—? Of course the question is not why

but why not. Ha ha, what a laugh in a way. Because we were such an honorable family. And of course here is the most intriguing question of all: Did my father know all along?" (96). In this passage, the tensions in Lancelot's voice become almost unbearable, so powerful is the disjunction here between the quaint, archaic vocabulary that he has inherited from his family and the truth that those words are intended to conceal. Lancelot's horror at the possibility of his mother's infidelity is manifested in the way this utterance degenerates into a jumble of fragmentary, unfinished thoughts. We can hear his bitterness too in the way he toys with "Uncle Harry's" euphemism, *joyriding,* as if to feel the lie in his own mouth. But Lancelot's anger is nowhere more powerful than it is when he explains that he is laughing—a harsh, forced laughter—"because we were such an honorable family." The word *such* exudes irony and contempt like an open sore.

Ultimately, however, what troubles Lancelot even more than his mother's betrayal or the apparent hypocrisy of his family's "honorable" reputation is his father's passivity. As Lancelot tells Percival, that is "the most intriguing question of all": did his father knowingly acquiesce to his mother's infidelity? Although Lancelot will never know the answer to that question, it hardly seems to matter, for—knowing or not—his father created the conditions for his own betrayal. Cursed with a pathological fear of failure, condemned to live in the shadow of his forefathers' accomplishments (like the men in the Bolling family and the Barrett family), Lancelot's father "didn't, couldn't, try anything for fear the world would come to an end if he failed. So he became editor of the second best of the two weekly newspapers in a county parish, suffered from 'weak lungs' whatever that is, not tuberculosis, but a 'tendency' toward it, and was a semi-invalid, spending his days writing poems and little historical vignettes" (95–96). Of course, the father's fate is often rehearsal for the son's, and we cannot help but see how much Lancelot's life resembles his father's. After an undistinguished career in law, he too became a "semi-invalid"—through drinking, though, not some supposed illness—and began writing his little articles on Civil War history. Most glaring of all, Lancelot too has been cuckolded by his wife, an event for which he perhaps bears some responsibility because of the sexual debility that is almost certainly a consequence of his alcoholism.

Lancelot never comments on these similarities, though, in his conversations with Percival. Like Binx Bolling and Will Barrett, he resists identifying with his father. Because he does not want to acknowledge any responsibility for Margot's infidelity, he must reject his father's life as a model for his own.

Instead, Lancelot reaches further back in time and family history to find a suitable reflection for himself. He first alludes to this model for his actions when he asks Percival if he remembers the bowie knife they found as boys in his pigeonnier. The knife belonged to an "ancestor" who "did know Bowie," Lancelot says, "even had a part in the notorious Vidalia sand-bar duel in which Bowie actually carved a fellow from limb to limb" (18). That ancestor who strode into Lancelot's youthful consciousness out of the world of legend was his great-great-grandfather, Manson Maury Lamar, a Civil War hero, who, as Lancelot later tells Percival, also fought a duel to defend his mother's honor, "a fight to the death with fists and knives just like Jim Bowie, in fact on the same sand bar" (154). It is notable, however, that his ancestor's legend changes the second time Lancelot mentions it. Now, instead of being a secondary figure in Jim Bowie's duel, Manson Maury Lamar is a principal in one of his own. This shift suggests both the apocryphal nature of the story and Lancelot's need to reassemble its basic components to provide the right example for his own actions. Thus, he now emphasizes how his great-great-grandfather responded to an insult—a suggestion that his mother had had a black lover—with deadly force. In stark contrast to Lancelot's father, whose passivity and apparent lack of concern for his wife's virtue were themselves failures of honor, Manson Maury Lamar offers Lancelot a simpler model to emulate, one that is untainted by any maddening inconsistencies between word and deed. As Lancelot tells Percival, "I could live that way, crude as it was, though I do not think that men should butcher each other like animals" (155).

Indeed, Lancelot's identification with Manson Maury Lamar is the lifeline that he grips amid his confusion and despair. More than anything, Lancelot wants to see himself as a man of honor like his ancestor. If he can do so, then all the rest makes sense: the modern world in which he is set down is faithless and corrupt, his parents were weak (it is not that their values were wrong, only that they could not live up to their beliefs), and Margot's infidelity is a blot on his honor that had to be erased. In essence, this is Lancelot's project over the course of his narrative: to convince Percival—and himself—that these are the right terms in which to see the story.

Toward that end, Lancelot buttresses his tentative identification with his ancestor by embracing Manson Maury Lamar's values and making them the center of a vague plan to impose a new moral order on the squalor that Lancelot sees everywhere in his society. Immediately after telling Percival of Manson Maury Lamar's bloody duel and announcing (with a characteristic

note of uncertainty), "I could live that way," Lancelot suddenly turns pro-
phetic and envisions "a new order of things" that will be triggered by the
actions of one just man: "what if one sober, reasonable, and honorable man
should act, and act with perfect sobriety, reason, and honor? Then you have
the beginning of a new age" (156). Of course, though he does not say as
much, Lancelot is casting himself here as the harbinger of this new order.
The moral scheme he is about to unveil for Percival depends on a vision of
himself as a man who acted with "sobriety, reason, and honor." But what is
most striking about Lancelot's "new order" is its resemblance to the one that
shaped his great-great-grandfather's actions. When Lancelot explains the
guiding principles of this secular reformation, he adopts a voice that is
steeped in the courtly values of the Old South:

> Who are we? We will not even be a secret society as you know such
> things. Its members will know each other without signs or passwords.
> No speeches, rallies, political parties. There will be no need of such
> things. One man will act. Another man will act. We will know each
> other as gentlemen used to know each other—no, not gentlemen in the
> old sense—I'm not talking about social classes. I'm talking about
> something held in common by men, Gentile, Jew, Greek, Roman, slave,
> freeman, black, white, and so recognized between them: a stern code, a
> gentleness toward women and an intolerance of swinishness, a counsel
> kept, and above all a readiness to act, and act alone if necessary. (156–57)

The "stern code" that Lancelot describes in such lofty, sweeping terms is, of
course, the stoic code of Manson Maury Lamar's patrician class, as is clear
from its stark, simple morality—there is no doubt in Lancelot's vision that
"swinishness" is easily recognized—its taciturn quality, and its latent violence. Indeed, as Lancelot elaborates on his new order later in the same conversation, his comments about women recall the distinction drawn by another stoic, Ed Barrett in *The Last Gentleman,* between "ladies and whores."
"There will be virtuous women who are proud of their virtue," Lancelot
declares, "and there will be women of the street who are there to be fucked
and everyone will know which is which" (178).

Over the course of the novel, Lancelot returns several times to the subject
of his new order, but his purpose in doing so is not so much to prophesy as
it is to inveigh. Though Lancelot's plans for what he calls the "third revolution" are vague, he is explicit in his condemnation of the sexual decadence
of contemporary life, the false piety of the South, and the corruption and

hypocrisy of America's political culture (157). And in articulating this rage, Lancelot becomes the dark apotheosis of Percy's own satiric impulse; he is the voice of the moralist in Percy with—literally—a vengeance. As Tolson notes, "Lancelot in all his fury and anger against the modern world was temperamentally and intellectually what Percy would have been were it not for one all-important difference: his faith" (*Pilgrim* 413). Indeed, the wish that Percy once expressed to Gordon, "to tell people what they must do and what they must believe if they want to live," is taken here to its hellish extreme (qtd. in Tolson, *Pilgrim* 300). Stripped of the faith that tempered Percy's own anger (a faith that is embodied, of course, in his namesake, Percival), Lancelot's moralizing verges on fascism. "We are going to set it out for you," he tells Percival, "what is good and what is bad, and no Jew-Christian waffling bullshit about it" (177).

But if Lancelot's elaborate vision of a new order is a way of joining hands with his ancestor across the abyss of time, his immediate reaction to the discovery of Margot's infidelity mitigates that link. For though he admires above all Manson Maury Lamar's "readiness to act" in the face of dishonor—so much so, in fact, that he enshrines this quality as the moral center of his "third revolution"—when Lancelot first discovers evidence of Margot's betrayal he does not act. Rather, like Hamlet, he hesitates, and, as William Rodney Allen notes, "he adopts [Hamlet's] device—the play within the play—to gain the certain proof he seeks" (116). Instead of confronting Margot with what he knows, Lancelot embarks on a complicated plan to catch her in the act by arranging for Elgin to secretly videotape her when she visits the Holiday Inn where the film crew working at Belle Isle is staying.

In the simplest sense, Lancelot sets this trap because he believes Margot is having an affair with Robert Merlin, one of the codirectors of the film, and he wants proof of the identity of her lover.[8] But Lancelot's obsession with seeing his wife betray him also becomes, in his own twisted version of these events, "a quest for evil" (138) whose implicit purpose is to flush God out of hiding. All too affected by the scientism of his culture, Lancelot believes that the only empirical evidence of God's existence in a scientific age is sin, "a purely evil deed, an intolerable deed for which there is no explanation" (52). "If there is such a thing as sin, evil, a living malignant force, there must be a God!" he reasons when he first tentatively broaches this subject (52). Therefore, if Lancelot can see with his own eyes what is for him "a purely evil deed," he will be like Robinson Crusoe stumbling on Friday's footprint, no longer marooned and alone in a godless universe. But Lancelot's quest is—at the very least—problematic, because the condition of his search for God, its scientific insistence on objective proof of his existence, is inimical to the inherently religious concept of sin. For when seen through the prism of scientific values, what appears to be evil is only sickness. As Lancelot himself notes, even the most extreme example of evil breaks down this way. "What about Hitler, the gas ovens, and so forth?" Lancelot asks. "What about them? As everyone knows and says, Hitler was a madman. And it seems nobody else was responsible. Everyone was following orders" (138).

Lancelot's quest for what he calls "the Unholy Grail" of sin ultimately becomes the controlling metaphor of his narrative (138). In his need to rise above the sordid reality of the events at Belle Isle—infidelity, voyeurism, and violent retribution—Lancelot seizes on his and Percival's boyhood fascination with Arthurian legend and applies that mythic vision to his own narrative, as if it were an alchemical solution that could transform a base metal into something finer, more heroic. And so, on the third day of his conversations with Percival, just before he brings up Manson Maury Lamar's famous duel and the "new order" that will be modeled on the ancestor's values, Lancelot erects an elaborate metaphorical structure that insists on a parallel between his own actions and the events narrated by Sir Thomas Malory and others. "We've spoken of the Knights of the Holy Grail, Percival," he says, calling on his friend to remember their past and reviving old associations by once again addressing the other as *Percival*. "Do you know what I was? The Knight of the Unholy Grail" (138). In this symbolic version of the events at Belle Isle, Lancelot not only is able to distance himself from the seamy truth but also reinforces his tentative belief that he acted in accord with the strict code of values inherited from his great-great-grandfather by draping himself in the chivalric legends that in a large measure inspired those values. And, of course, by transforming himself in his narrative into a heroic figure on a quest for sin, Lancelot resolves any moral ambiguities—such as his own inadvertent complicity in Margot's infidelity—into the kind of stark, black-and-white dichotomy that accords with his ancestor's stern morality.

It is important to remember, however, that Lancelot's vision of himself as the "Knight of the Unholy Grail" is an afterthought, an interpretation imposed on his actions in retrospect. There is no evidence that he ever thinks of himself in these terms at the time of the events that he narrates, as he relentlessly stalks proof of Margot's infidelity. Only a year later, as he struggles to come to grips with what he has done, does he reach back to a boyhood fancy, to the chivalric values of the Old South, and find in those sources an image of himself that seems to justify his actions. Indeed, Lancelot acknowledges this perspective—and the desperation that underlies this vision of himself—the first time he refers to his search for photographic proof of his wife's betrayal as "a quest." As he says to Percival, "I think I see now what I am doing. I am reliving with you my quest. That's the only way I can bear to think about it" (137). Though Lancelot's casual reference to his "quest" suggests that this interpretation is nothing new—despite the fact that he has not used this term previously in his narration—his last admission here is critical. When he says "That's the only way I can bear to think about it," he implicitly points to the gap, the metaphorical space, between his vision of "a quest" and the reality of what took place at Belle Isle. Further, he admits how much he needs to close that gap; he can only stand to remember these events when they are dressed in a medieval finery.

But although Lancelot's quest for evil is intended as a kind of exculpatory fiction to dress up a series of painful acts, the metaphor of the search for the "Unholy Grail" has a powerful resonance that goes far beyond the ameliorating effects that Lancelot intends. For there is indeed a quest for evil in the book. That quest occurs though in Lancelot's narration to Percival, in the outer frame of the novel, not in his narrative itself, the inner frame. By his "reliving" these events with Percival, by their "kicking through the rubble" of Belle Isle in the long sessions in which Lancelot tells his story, both men undertake a quest for evil (106). Yet it is a quest that in reality leads through Lancelot's tortured consciousness, not the bedrooms of Belle Isle or the anonymous rooms of the Holiday Inn.

In the end, what happens in those hotel rooms is made all too clear on Elgin's videotapes. Though the tapes turn out poorly, a combination of blurry images and bad sound, they nevertheless show Margot having sex with Janos Jacoby, Robert Merlin's codirector of the film being made at Belle Isle. (The tapes also show Lancelot's daughter by his first marriage, Lucy, engaged in a ménage à trois with two actors in the film, Raine Robinette and Troy Dana.) Outwardly detached—watching the videotapes "as gravely as I used to watch afternoon reruns of *Gunsmoke*" (185)—Lancelot is at last moved to decisive action. He quickly procures the supplies he needs to open the well of natural gas on top of which Belle Isle was built—in effect, turning the estate into a huge bomb—and then, citing a real hurricane that is bearing down on them, he sends away everyone whom he will spare from his revenge: Siobahn; Margot's father, Tex; Lucy; Elgin and his parents; and, most surprising, Robert Merlin. (Although the dialogue on Elgin's videotapes confirms that Merlin was once Margot's lover, Lancelot seems to feel a faint kinship with Merlin since he too has been cast off by Margot in favor of Jacoby.)

Before Lancelot takes his revenge, though, he experiences a hallucination that makes absolutely clear how his pain and anger over Margot's infidelity are linked to his confused feelings about his parents' dishonor. After taking a drug offered by Robinette, he retreats to the pigeonnier, briefly falls asleep, and awakens to see a strange woman standing before him wearing a camellia pinned to her dress. This woman—whom he mockingly calls "Our Lady of the Camellias" (211)—resembles a dimly remembered acquaintance from his youth, a woman with a tarnished reputation. Claiming to be a friend of the family, she confirms for Lancelot that his mother indeed had an affair with Harry Wills and that his father knew and acquiesced. Subsequently, however, she seems to become his mother, and she places his great-great-grandfather's bowie knife—which heretofore had decorated Lancelot's study—in his hand, as if enjoining him to do what his father failed to do and redress her dishonor. (It is in keeping with Lancelot's symbolic interpretation of these events that he initially refers to the bowie knife in this scene as a "sword" [226].)

When Lancelot leaves his pigeonnier, then, bowie knife in hand, his objective is both to avenge his own betrayal and to restore his mother's honor. With the hurricane shrieking around him, the lights at Belle Isle extinguished by the storm, and the atmosphere of the house saturated with methane gas, past and present come together. But Lancelot is not merely reliving his parents' dishonor. As he stalks the corridors of Belle Isle with his great-great-grandfather's knife in his hand, he embraces a part of the past that is even further removed, a time when men readily fought duels with "fists and knives" to defend their honor (154). In a sense, Lancelot attempts to achieve his ideological becoming through this act. When he takes up his ancestor's knife, he chooses among the voices echoing in his mind and knowingly, determinedly assimilates Manson Maury Lamar's ethos and perspective.

In the final, nightmarish scenes of Lancelot's narrative, he acts in deadly accord with his great-great-grandfather's code. First, he proves his masculinity by having sex with Raine, a woman whom his ancestor would consider a "whore" rather than a "lady" and therefore suitable to use in this way. Though Lancelot has apparently been impotent for a long time, his debility is cured by the hate that stirs in him when the sight of Lucy's ring on Raine's hand reminds him of his daughter's seduction. And in the most basic symbolic terms, his phallus becomes an extension of the knife here, a weapon to use against Raine in a struggle for dominance. Indeed, his hatred of her, his desire for power rather than pleasure, is embodied by his posture during intercourse: "I was alone, far above her, upright and smiling in the darkness" (235). This act is only a prelude, though. When he leaves Raine, he finds Margot and Jacoby in bed together and stands on the threshold of his vengeance. Now, Lancelot can reenact his great-great-grandfather's duel. After briefly, almost comically struggling with Jacoby, Lancelot pulls the other man's head back and cuts his throat in the same manner in which Manson Maury Lamar killed his opponent in the duel fought a century earlier.

In recounting this event to Percival, however, Lancelot focuses on the disjunction he felt at that moment, the gap between the action and his expectations. "What I remember better than the cutting," he says, "was the sense I had of casting about for an appropriate feeling to match the deed. Weren't we raised to believe that 'great deeds' were performed with great feelings—anger, joy, revenge, and so on? I remember casting about for the feeling and not finding one" (242). In the simplest sense, his confusion here is the result of his failure to perceive that cutting the throat of a smaller, weaker, and more vulnerable man is not a heroic act. But Lancelot's confusion is also a consequence of the self-consciousness with which he performs this act. Unlike his great-great-grandfather, who simply reacted to his immediate circumstances, to the fact of the insult, Lancelot is also conscious of the historical tradition of which he wants to be a part. When he refers to Jacoby's murder as the "deed," Lancelot implicitly suggests that it too is the stuff of stories, a piece of family lore to accompany Manson Maury Lamar's famous duel. Yet, of course, Lancelot's self-consciousness and the sordid reality of what he is doing combine to thwart his ambitions. He cannot seamlessly assimilate the voice and perspective of his great-great-grandfather or evoke the "great feelings" that history has assigned to his ancestor (whatever the reality might have been). And so, the second time Lancelot speaks of doing "great deeds," he places that phrase in quotation marks, as if to indicate that the idea of "great deeds" is itself imperiled, difficult to sustain under such circumstances.

Indeed, the final moments of Lancelot's revenge are consumed by a lingering disappointment that, in his words, "there are no longer any great historical events" (240). As Lancelot and Margot succumb to a delirium caused by methane poisoning, they talk listlessly, inconclusively about old resentments and the possibility of starting anew. Even Jacoby's murder does not seem to reach Margot. In Lancelot's view, her sole feeling is "dismay that things had gotten out of hand" (243). His emotional numbness is pierced only when he attempts to light a gas lamp and the house explodes as the methane ignites. As he is literally blown out of the house, he thinks, "Ah then ... there are still great moments" (246).

As Lancelot's narrative comes closer to its violent climax, however, his listener is profoundly affected by what he hears. After Lancelot first speaks of his "new order" on the third day of their talks, he describes his listener as being "pale as a ghost" (160). And the following day, Percival appears in Lancelot's cell dressed in a priest's traditional raiment. Indeed, as Lancelot himself observes in their final talk, Percival has been transformed by this encounter. In the most obvious sense, he has regained his faith; in addition to again wearing his collar, Percival is seen at the end of the novel praying for the dead in the cemetery across from Lancelot's cell, an act Percival had been unable or unwilling to do at the beginning. As Lancelot says, "I have the feeling that while I was talking and changing, you were listening and changing" (254).

Of course, the kind of interaction that Lancelot describes is in fact dialogic. By Lancelot opening himself to the other and steadily bearing all, and by Percival listening, listening actively, the lunatic solipsism and monomania of Lancelot's monologue have been subtly undermined. Monologue, rather, has been transformed into the kind of dialogic encounter that Bakhtin finds so often in Dostoevsky's work: "Two characters are always introduced by Dostoevsky in such a way that each of them is intimately linked with the internal voice of the other. . . . In their dialogue, therefore, the rejoinders of the one touch and even partially coincide with the rejoinders of the other's internal dialogue. A deep essential bond or partial coincidence between the borrowed words of one hero and the internal and secret discourse of another hero—this is the indispensable element of all Dostoevsky's crucial dialogues" (*Dostoevsky* 254–55).

Lancelot's "borrowed words," his angry assimilation of Manson Maury Lamar's stoic values, have of course left their mark on Percival's "internal and secret discourse." As Lancelot rages at Margot and the corruption he sees around him, as he rejects Percival's entreaties for forgiveness and Christian love—"Don't talk to me of love until we shovel out the shit," he responds (179)—Percival's faith and sense of purpose are clearly reawakened. Though we do not know what experiences in Biafra or elsewhere previously shook that faith, his beliefs now clearly give him the strength to confront Lancelot's hatred and anger. Even Lancelot seems to recognize this change and implies as much when Percival appears in his cell on the fourth day wearing his collar. "Are you girding for battle or dressed up like Lee for the surrender?" Lancelot quips (163). But nothing as clearly indicates the profound effect of Lancelot's "borrowed words" on Percival as his plans at the end of the novel. In sharp contrast to Lancelot's grand scheme of establishing a "new order," Percival's intentions are determinedly mundane. He will become an ordinary parish priest. In Lancelot's words, "So you plan to take a little church in Alabama, Father, preach the gospel, turn bread into flesh, forgive the sins of Buick dealers, administer communion to suburban housewives?" (256). Where Lancelot wants to sweep away the corruption around him, to burn it down and build a "new order" on its ashes, Percival, by ministering to others, will work to slowly transform it.[9]

But how, beyond providing the opportunity to recount his story, has this dialogue changed Lancelot? That question is complicated, for Lancelot—like so many of Percy's characters—lacks a coherent sense of self. In the simplest terms, he does not know who he is. Is he an ordinary man—moderately happy, moderately successful—whose life has now been marred by tragedy? Is he a weak, naive husband, a man so foolish and so sheltered that he still does not know if all in life is "niceness or buggery" (137)? Or is he a heroic figure like his ancestor, quick to recognize evil and quick to strike out at it? By telling his story to Percival, Lancelot tries to insist that the third version is correct. And so, over the course of his narrative, he portrays himself as the "Knight of the Unholy Grail," a chivalric figure for the twentieth century, and he tentatively offers this vision to Percival for validation. Like Will Barrett desperately beseeching Sutter Vaught for advice and approval, like Tom More seeking himself in the perception of Leroy Ledbetter, Lancelot looks to Percival to find out who he is, perhaps to see this vision of himself reflected in the other's eyes.

But he does not succeed, of course. Rather, Lancelot sees himself—if at all—as the evil he sought. When he beckons Percival to stand with him and look out from the single, narrow window of his cell, the other man's reaction is telling. "Why so wary?" Lancelot asks. "You act as if I were Satan showing you the kingdoms of the world from the pinnacle of the temple" (254). Indeed, far from being the redeemer of the squalor and decadence he sees around him, Lancelot is its avatar. And the quest that he and Percival undertook in the telling and receiving of his story proves to be successful, albeit in an ironic manner. For as Percival's reactions indicate, Lancelot—

who committed adultery with Raine Robinette and who murdered Jacoby, Margot, Raine, and Dana—embodies the evil he sought. As William J. Dowie writes in "*Lancelot* and the Search for Sin," "So taken up with his search for sexual sin in others, Lancelot misses the sinfulness of his own acts, sexual and violent" (254).

Does Lancelot have any awareness, though, of the true nature of himself and his actions? Perhaps. His ability to sustain his vision of himself as a heroic figure is threatened by Percival's wariness toward him and his own disenchantment with his quest. As Brinkmeyer notes, Lancelot "is finally unable to keep his vision of himself whole and unsullied by the judgment of others; Percival's presence has penetrated Lance's consciousness, influencing his thoughts and words. Even when Percival merely listens, Lance is influenced by the traces of his already spoken words and by the anticipated responses. Lance, in other words, alters the shape of his vision—though he would be the last to admit it—to take account of Percival's judgments" (41). Surely, then, as a result, when Lancelot finally voices "the secret" he hoped to find by telling his story to Percival, it is only that there was no secret. As Lancelot says, "Why did I discover nothing at the heart of evil? There was no 'secret' after all, no discovery, no flickering of interest, nothing at all, not even any evil" (253). Though his refusal to assess his own actions is evidenced again by his final assertion, this utterance also shows us that his vision of undertaking "a quest for evil" is itself embattled. Just as the murder of Jacoby did not feel like a "great deed," his "quest" was disturbingly anticlimactic.

That Lancelot cannot easily sustain this heroic vision of his actions is evidence of how his encounter with Percival has changed him. By telling his story aloud, by having to explain his elaborate interpretation of his actions to another, and by seeing the other's response—his skepticism and bewilderment—the essential fallacy of Lancelot's interpretation is exposed. Surely for this reason, Lancelot's tone in the final chapter is extremely erratic. As he talks to Percival in their last meeting, Lancelot's voice changes dramatically. He exults over the fact that he will soon be released from the hospital (at least he claims he will be released), and then he begs Percival to help him understand why he does not feel anything at all; he acknowledges his confusion over the anticlimactic nature of his quest, and then he blusters again about his grand scheme for a "new order." These dramatic shifts in rhetoric and tone suggest a sense of desperation, as if all of the tensions that we have heard in Lancelot's voice throughout his narrative are no longer supportable. It is as if his personality fragments at last, whatever fragile unity it had com-

ing undone, as he veers back and forth between admissions of his own uncertainty and overwrought attempts to compensate for it.

At the end of the novel, Lancelot is as isolated as he was at the beginning.
Though he has insisted to Percival that his tapping on the wall with Anna,
the woman in the next cell, comprised a dialogue, "true communication,"
their ultimate face-to-face encounter is, at best, inconclusive (12). For when
Lancelot suggested to her that she had suffered "the worst violation a woman
can suffer" and so was qualified to join him "as the new Adam and Eve of
the new world," Anna was—not surprisingly—offended by his characterization (251). In keeping with his attempt to remake Percival to fit his own preferred interpretation of his past, Lancelot sought to remake Anna to fit his
preferred vision of his future. But he could only see her as the New Woman
of his new world—a sort of fascist pastoral in the Shenandoah Valley—if he
ignored the real woman. And so we see that what Lancelot considered "true
communication" in reality amounted to little more than a crude stimulus-
response exchange: simple signals answered by other signals. Just as his vision
of himself as the "Knight of the Unholy Grail" breaks down in the final
pages of the novel, so too does his vision of a possible life with Anna.

I do not believe, though, that Lancelot as yet recognizes the full extent of
his own delusion. Rather, as Percival's voice is at last heard on the final pages
of the novel, the single-mindedness of Lancelot's vision begins to give way,
just as the absolute dominance of his dramatic monologue is ended. Like
Will Barrett at the conclusion of *The Last Gentleman*, Lancelot stands, in
Bakhtin's words, "*on the threshold* of a final decision, at a moment of *crisis,* at
an unfinalizable—and *unpredeterminable*—turning point for his soul" (*Dostoevsky* 61). The scales do not fall from his eyes; nor are they fastened so tightly
that they will never be removed. It is as if a curtain lifts for a moment and a
different view of the world is momentarily revealed. We do not know if
Lancelot will ever embrace that view or if he will ultimately turn away from
it, only that he seems to see it, to know it is out there.

In many ways, *Lancelot* is Percy's most complicated book. With its dual
structure and its devious, unstable narrator, the experience of reading *Lancelot*
is something like that of entering a labyrinth. And in many ways, *Lancelot* is
Percy's most profoundly dialogic book, for the core of the novel, its central
event, is not Lancelot's discovery of Margot's infidelity or his terrible revenge but the long encounter between Lancelot and Percival as they talk
about those things. Yet *Lancelot,* like *Love in the Ruins,* is also a problematic
work, for it shares some of its predecessor's flaws.

As in *Love in the Ruins,* only one voice, that of Lancelot himself, is truly allowed free expression. Only Lancelot's voice is really compelling, for the secondary characters in *Lancelot,* like those in *Love in the Ruins,* often seem like caricatures, representative figures cobbled together to satirize various mores and attitudes of which Percy disapproved. As Joyce Carol Oates has written, the novel's secondary characters "are curiously flat and vaporous, hardly more than assemblages of shrewdly noted details" (64). To take only one example, consider this description of Raine:

> She was amazingly pretty, with a pure heart-shaped face and violet-cobalt eyes which seemed to look from her depths into yours, a trick I came to learn, that steady violet gaze, chin resting on the back of her bent hand. Her depths were vacant.... Her single enthusiasm, besides her niceness, was her absorption with a California Cult called I.P.D., or something like that—Ideo-Personal-Dynamics maybe. She told me of it at length. I remember very little except that she said it was more scientific than astrology, being based not merely on the influence of the stars but on evidence of magnetic fields surrounding people. The existence of these fields or auras had been proved, she said, by special photography. (112)

We can see here the shrewd eye for detail that Oates finds in Percy's work. Percy's ability to evoke Raine's studied poise, to describe a character's manner and to suggest at the same time the hint of artifice contained in that manner, is masterful. Yet for all that Raine is vividly seen, Percy also hastily disposes of her. What we are offered is ultimately a stereotype: a flaky actor whose essential vacuity is epitomized by her belief in special photography that can show one's aura. Raine is almost completely objectified, and though Percy's point may be that such glittering creatures are inevitably shallow—as Lancelot says, "Her depths were vacant"—that point itself suggests a failure of sympathy. Percy does not want to understand Raine or to humanize her but to judge her.

Yet in dealing with such a complex, devious work as *Lancelot,* we must be careful in offering our own judgments. For Raine, though a creature of Percy's imagination, is also seen through the distorted optic of Lancelot's narrative, and this fact raises a fundamental question: how much of Raine's portrayal should we ascribe to Percy's satiric intentions, and how much is a consequence of Lancelot's judgmental, misogynistic vision? Certainly, we know that Lancelot sees the world and the people around him in the most

extreme terms. In *Walker Percy: A Southern Wayfarer,* Allen speaks of Lancelot's
" 'either-or' thinking": "a woman is either a lady or a whore, a man is a master or a slave, and his friend should decide whether he is a doctor or a priest"
(106). Even Margot recognizes this kind of thinking in Lancelot in the final,
delirious moments before her death: "With you I had to be either—or—but
never a—uh—woman," she says (245). Given this tendency, then, is it not
possible that Raine and many of the other characters in the novel are transformed by Lancelot's distorted vision? That they are not Percy's stereotypes
but Lancelot's?

Because *Lancelot* is constructed like a Chinese box, it is almost impossible
to answer this question with any finality. For at yet another level of this almost maddeningly complicated novel, Percy seems aware of its limitations.
It is as if he set out to embody in *Lancelot* the conflict in his own writing between the dialogic novelist and the moralist. As I suggested earlier, Lancelot
himself exemplifies Percy's moralistic temper; he is, in Allen's words, "the
voice through which [Percy] lets loose his self-professed desire 'to attack
things in our culture'" (111). Yet not only does Lancelot embody Percy's polemical impulses, but his shrill tone and murderous anger also illustrate the
dangers of moral zeal. As Dowie suggests, "Percy seems at once to be ex-
pressing his own outrage and, at the same time, parodying it" (249).[10] Even
the shallow portrayal of the novel's secondary characters can be taken as an
implicit comment on the limits of the moralist's vision. After all, Lancelot is
not only a violent avenger ready to act on his principles but also a storyteller
whose convictions play no small part in shaping his narrative. In a sense,
Lancelot's tyrannical refusal to depict Raine or Jacoby or even Margot as
anything more than carriers of the corruption that his "new order" would
eradicate recalls Percy's refusal to present the secondary figures in *Love in the
Ruins* as anything more than representative figures of various bankrupt ideologies. Consciously or not, Percy seems to be satirizing himself here, using
Lancelot to expose the weaknesses of the moralist when he seeks to embody
his principles in stories.

Lancelot, then, can also be read as a self-referential fiction, a comment on
Percy's own conflicting intentions as a writer. In it, through the voice of his
protagonist, he allows his moral concerns free rein and pursues them to their
most outrageous extremes. Yet the moralist in Percy is also checked in his
fourth novel. For the dialogic writer, the man intent on evoking "a quality
of consciousness" in his fiction, is also present in the work, in the form of
Percy's namesake, whose quiet manner and repeated queries to Lancelot

continually force him to abandon his tirades and return to the task at hand, the exploration of his own consciousness. And in contrast to the people we see in Lancelot's narrative—who are almost uniformly objectified and presented in shallow, stereotyped terms as representative figures—Percival's silence leaves him, in Bakhtin's term, "unfinalized." No matter how Lancelot tries, Percival cannot be summed up. His silence suggests hidden depths that either Lancelot cannot see or Percival himself will not express, and his presence therefore anchors the book in a more complex and changeable reality, outside the limitations of the moralist's field of vision. Thus, though this tour de force is dominated by Lancelot's anger, it is ultimately redeemed by the presence of his friend and listener, Percival, who continually draws both Lancelot and Percy himself away from the simple truths of satire and polemic. As Percival speaks at the conclusion of the novel, we seem to enter a different realm, where the course of our lives is always a mystery and anything is possible.

FIVE

Brave New World:

The Second Coming and

The Thanatos Syndrome

Like *The Sound and the Fury,* William Faulkner's classic novel of the decline of the Old South, Percy's fifth novel, *The Second Coming,* begins on a golf course. But though Faulkner's voice—as we will see—infuses an important part of the book, the world that Percy depicts is radically different from Faulkner's. Where in *The Sound and the Fury* the golf course is an alien world, separated from Faulkner's characters by a chain-link fence and their inherent suspicion of the encroachments of modern culture, for Will Barrett and his friends "the immaculate emerald fairway" (6) is a lush and welcoming paradise, as familiar and companionable as their suburban homes and their foreign cars. Rather than representing a break with the past, as in *The Sound and the Fury,* where land passed down from one generation of the Compson family to another is sold off and converted to a golf course, in the New South of *The Second Coming,* the well-trimmed green is the triumphal preserve of successful businessmen and professionals. Indeed, only when Will is struck by an intense memory of his childhood and falls down on the golf course does he actually begin to recover his own past.

At the beginning of the novel Will seems to have forgotten his past as thoroughly as he did during any of his "fugue states" in *The Last Gentleman.* This situation is made clear for us when he catches a quick glimpse of "a shadowy stranger" in the side mirror of his Mercedes and doesn't realize initially that this stranger is himself (13). This brief moment of nonrecognition epitomizes Will's condition at the beginning of the novel. Now middle aged, a rich widower living in North Carolina after retiring early from a prosperous career as a Wall Street lawyer, Will has walked through the last thirty years of his life with the dazed attention of an amnesiac. As he gradually realizes, his life until this point was "a long night's dream" (73). Though he had done everything he was supposed to do—married, established a career, raised a daughter—it has all turned to ashes.

The Second Coming is the story of Will's rise, phoenix-like, from the wreckage of his own life. Over the course of the novel, he learns how to live in his own skin at last by rejecting the voice of his father—which has lingered below the surface of his consciousness long after Ed Barrett's violent death by his own hand—and assimilating instead the voice of Allison Huger, the slightly addled daughter of his old flame, Kitty Vaught, who has escaped from a mental institution to live in an abandoned greenhouse into which Will literally crashes in what is perhaps the deftest comedy in all of Percy's novels. More so than anywhere else in Percy's fiction, in *The Second Coming* his character's struggle to sort through the voices that echo in his consciousness is a life-or-death matter. For if Will does not reject his father's voice, he will succumb to the same despair that drove Ed Barrett to suicide.

At the beginning of the novel, in fact, Will is far closer to that point than he realizes—a truth forced on us by a discursive narrator who dominates the opening chapter of the novel and then, as in *The Last Gentleman,* Percy's only other third-person work, recedes into the background. As the narrator explains, life has seemed increasingly "senseless and farcical" to Will "with each passing day" (3), so much so that he has begun to think seriously about killing himself. But the narrator is evasive when it comes to evaluating Will's behavior; in fact, in a lengthy aside, the narrator actively works to subvert any easy judgment of Will:

> What is one to make of such a person?
>
> To begin with: though it was probably the case that he was ill and that it was his illness—depression—which made the world seem farcical, it is impossible to prove the case.
>
> On the one hand, he was depressed.
>
> On the other hand, the world is in fact farcical.
>
> Or at least it is possible to make the case that for some time now life has seemed to become more senseless, even demented, with each passing year.
>
> True, most people he knew seemed reasonably sane and happy. They

played golf, kept busy, drank, talked, laughed, went to church, appeared
to enjoy themselves, and in general were both successful and generous.
Their talk made a sort of sense. They cracked jokes.

On the other hand, perhaps it is possible, especially in strange times
such as these, for an entire people, or at least a majority, to deceive
themselves into believing things are going well when in fact they are
not, when things are in fact farcical. Most Romans worked and played as
usual while Rome fell about their ears. (4)

In many ways, Percy's overarching ambition for *The Second Coming* is en-
capsulated in these paragraphs. The novel ultimately will present Will as a
sort of test case, an example of a man who refuses to deceive himself any
longer "into believing things are going well." Over the course of *The Second
Coming,* he will gradually find a middle course between the self-deception
of those around him and the fury and despair that destroyed his father. But
the narrator's insistence that "the world is in fact farcical" is expressed in the
moralist's voice that we heard in Percy's two previous novels. Though more
restrained, the narrator's tentative recognition "that for some time now life
has seemed to become more senseless, even demented, with each passing
year" echoes Lancelot's rage at the modern world. Even the ominous comparison to the destruction of Rome in the final sentence recalls the first true
moralist who appears in Percy's fiction; such grim tidings could just as easily
have been voiced by Emily Cutrer as she inveighs against the corruption of
her beloved evening land. No doubt, then, because the narrator sympathizes
with Will's perception that life is farcical, the narrator withholds judgment
on Will's self-destructiveness. And as we will see, Will later gives voice in an
extended monologue to the moral argument implied in the narrator's comments here—though in the complications that ensue, we are reminded of
the limits of the moralist's perspective.

The events of *The Second Coming* are precipitated by a series of strange
symptoms of some deeper malaise that are manifest in Will's behavior. Will
begins asking odd questions of his friends, suddenly breaking out of a remote silence to ask if all of the Jews have left North Carolina—though a
skeptic at best, he becomes intermittently obsessed with biblical visions of
the Second Coming—or "if the tendency to suicide is inherited" (10). Then
on the day on which the novel begins, he collapses on the golf course and is
struck by an intense flash of memory. In contrast to the recurrent amnesia
that plagued him in *The Last Gentleman,* Will now is susceptible to fits of re-

membering. Eerily sensitive to familiar scents or sights, he is assaulted by sudden, intense memories of long-forgotten episodes from his past. As J. Gerald Kennedy argues in "The Semiotics of Memory: Suicide in *The Second Coming,*" Will's world in this novel is a tissue of signs, each of which recalls a specific memory from his past (210). For example, "the acrid smell of rabbit tobacco" on a golf course recalls "a weedy stretch of railroad right-of-way in a small Mississippi town" where the same plant grew, and the smell of the tobacco flings him back to his teenage years, when he wandered over that railway ground bemoaning his lust for Ethel Rosenblum, a particularly attractive classmate (8, 7).

But the small things that Will remembers—his unrequited desire for Ethel, the way a particular golf club used to be called "a spoon" (6), the spot where he once stood to catch the subway in New York—are really just harbingers of a more important memory, the rumblings that precede an earthquake. For when Will steps through a barbed wire fence to retrieve a golf ball after he has sliced out of bounds, the manner in which he holds his club becomes another link to the past: "even as he was climbing through, he had shifted his grip on the iron so that the club head was tucked high under his right arm, shaft resting on forearm, right hand holding the shaft steady—as one might carry a shotgun" (44). Will suddenly remembers, for the first time in years, the "hunting accident" in Georgia that nearly killed both his father and him when he was twelve. Though his family always insisted that his father's high blood pressure had made him dizzy and caused him to discharge his shotgun, wounding himself and Will (Will's cheek was grazed and his left eardrum perforated), Will now realizes—or allows himself to realize—that it was no accident. By forcing himself to remember the number of times he heard his father reload and the number of shells that were found afterward, Will finally concludes that his father intended to kill both of them yet for some reason pulled back at the last moment.

But even as Will's memory of the accident is described in the narrative, the voice of the novel changes. As Will struggles with his father's memory, another sort of struggle occurs in the prose itself, as Percy evokes the voice of a writer whose influence he had long disclaimed, Faulkner. We first hear an echo of Faulkner in the way that Will and his father are referred to as the "boy" and the "man," much as Isaac McCaslin is simply referred to the "boy" throughout much of Faulkner's great hunting story, "The Bear." Later, when Percy describes the hunt itself, he duplicates to near perfection the cadences of Faulkner's prose, its intense compression of language and detail: "Didn't he hear it again, the so sudden uproar of stiff wings beating the little drum of bird body and the man swinging toward him in the terrific concentration of keeping gunsight locked on the fat tilt-winged quail and hard upon the little drumbeat the shocking blast rolling away like thunder through the silent woods?" (56).

This overt assimilation of Faulkner's voice is curious, however, in light of Percy's repeated denials throughout his career of Faulkner's influence. That contention was a kind of leitmotif in the ritual of the literary interview that Percy so often obligingly performed. Percy's questioner would dutifully ask about his influences, and Percy would insist that he was more affected by French or Russian writers than Americans. And then, as often as not, he would single out Faulkner as being particularly unimportant to his own development and vision as a novelist: "I'm probably least influenced by him than anyone else," Percy stated in a typical 1971 interview (*Con.* 53).[1]

And yet it is almost impossible to ignore the presence of Faulkner throughout Percy's fiction. Even Percy himself admitted as much in a 1984 interview when, after claiming that the southern history that Faulkner explored "doesn't interest me in the slightest," Percy abruptly stopped and modified his position; the fading traditions and the fatal pull of history about which Faulkner wrote comprised "the backdrop" for the "here-and-now predicament[s]" of Percy's own characters (*Con.* 299).[2] Indeed, a Faulknerian vision of history, expressed in a suitably Faulknerian voice, informs Tom More's understanding of the troubles that plague his country in *Love in the Ruins.* Moreover, *Lancelot,* Percy's next novel, roughly parallels Faulkner's *Absalom, Absalom!* In both works, a conversation between two friends becomes an occasion for remembering and narrating a tale of madness and obsession, as the novel mediates back and forth between the conversation and the narrative itself. In both works, also, the narrator's consciousness clearly attempts to repress or obscure his knowledge of the final horror until his listener's insistent questions draw him out. In fact, as Patrick Samway notes in his biography of Percy, Percy even considered working on "a long term project about . . . Faulkner" in 1977, after the publication of *Lancelot* (336). (Perhaps some carryover from this abortive project even helps explain the Faulknerian presence in the work into which Percy eventually settled, *The Second Coming.*)

Faulkner was thus clearly more important to Percy than he was willing to admit, as a pair of incidents from Percy's life seems to affirm. When Percy and Shelby Foote were traveling through the South before going to college, they stopped at Faulkner's home in Oxford, Mississippi, but Percy could not

bring himself to go in (despite the fact that he could claim a prior acquaintance with Faulkner, who was an occasional guest at William Alexander
Percy's home). As Percy explained in 1981, "My friend stayed two hours with
him, while I slept in the car. They had a wonderful conversation and I missed
it, because of this absurd fear" (*Con.* 245). Also suggestive is what happened
when Percy took his English placement exam as a freshman at the University of North Carolina in 1933. Still under Faulkner's spell from his reading
of *The Sound and the Fury* that summer, Percy deliberately echoed Faulkner's
voice, with disastrous results. As Jay Tolson writes, Percy "quickly dashed off
a convoluted, Faulkner-inspired description of the Mississippi River, a mis-
begotten effort that promptly earned him a place in one of the three sections of 'A' English, the remedial sections that carried no college credits"
(*Pilgrim* 111–12).

   Of course, it is easy enough to play amateur analyst and to read in Percy's
personal and literary history a larger pattern: fearful of Faulkner's influence,
Percy strove through much of his career to, in effect, remain in the car while
other writers entered Faulkner's house. I prefer, though, to see Percy's complex relationship with Faulkner as an ongoing dialogue. For in Bakhtinian
terms, Percy's extensive evocation of Faulkner's voice in *The Second Coming*
is akin to his use of William Alexander Percy's voice in *The Moviegoer.* As I
suggested earlier, Percy embodied his adopted father's voice in the person of
Emily Cutrer so that he could come to terms with the influence of William
Alexander Percy's stoic philosophy. Similarly, Percy's deliberate echo of
Faulkner's style in large sections of *The Second Coming* represents a clear effort to come to terms with the influence of a writer whom Percy once described as "the blessing and curse of all Southern novelists" (*Con.* 276). It is
as if, after years of shunning Faulkner for fear of being overpowered by him,
Percy decided that the only way to come to terms with this most domineering of his literary fathers was to reverse course and deliberately, willfully imi-
tate him.

   But Percy's appropriation of Faulkner's voice does more in *The Second
Coming* than merely parallel—on the level of style—the father-son struggle
that is at its core. For in assimilating Faulkner's voice, Percy also assimilates
the vision of time that is inherent in that voice. As Faulkner once explained,
the long, tortuous structure of his sentences was only a way of encompassing the past's continuous power to shape the present: "to me, no man is himself, he is the sum of his past. There is no such thing as was because the past
is. It is a part of every man, every woman, and every moment. And so a man,

a character in a story at any moment of action is not just himself as he is then, he is all that made him, and the long sentence is an attempt to get his past and possibly his future into the instant in which he does something" (qtd. in Gwynn and Blotner 84). By using the same rhetorical devices and circular syntactic constructions as Faulkner, Percy also emphasizes that the past *is* for Will Barrett, no matter how hard he may try to forget or deny it. Will, too, is the sum of "all that made him"—perhaps most of all the product of his father's bungled attempt to take both their lives.

In many ways, the sudden recurrence of that memory is the initiating event of the novel. It knits together the vague feelings of unease and the sense that life is farcical that have plagued Will up until this point. Those things were only signs, he realizes, semiotic signals of a deeper psychic unease, not important in themselves, except perhaps as evidence that his life is following the course that was determined for it when his father tried to kill him so many years ago (51). Thus, when Will remembers the terrible hunting trip that he had tried to forget for so long, he knows that nothing else that had happened to him really matters: "Only one event had ever happened to him. Everything else that had happened afterwards was a non-event" (52). Indeed, Will is haunted now by what his father told him only moments before the "accident" as they stood in the Georgia woods, one of Ed Barrett's arms wrapped around Will, the other holding a shotgun.

> *You and I are the same,* said the man as if he were speaking to the gun.
> *How?*
> *You are like me. We are two of a kind. I saw it last night.*
> Here came the pats again, hard, regular, slow, like a bell tolling.
> *Saw what?*
> *I saw the way you lay in bed last night and slept or didn't sleep. You're one of us, I'm afraid. You already know too much. It's too bad in a way.*
> *Us? Who's us?*
> *You'd be better off if you were one of them.*
> *Who's them?*
> *The ignorant armies that clash by night.* (55)

Now, years after the "accident" and his father's suicide, this exchange resonates like a curse. As Will himself flirts with the possibility of suicide, he must determine if he is in fact, as his father says, "one of us." And so, Will enters into a kind of ghostly dialogue with his father, both struggling with the traces of his father's voice that linger in his mind and literally talking back to

his ghost—or at least the ghost that Will creates, the shadowy form he sees
flitting through the trees in the woods adjacent to the golf course.

There is a curious ambivalence, though, in Will's responses to his father.
On the one hand, as Will himself realizes, he has tried desperately throughout his life to renounce his father's influence. In a long passage in which
Will's thoughts are incorporated directly into the narration, he bluntly declares, "Ever since your death, all I ever wanted from you was out, out from
you and from the Mississippi twilight, and from the shotguns thundering in
musty attics and racketing through funk-smelling Georgia swamps, out from
the ancient hatreds and allegiances, allegiances unto death and love of war
and rumors of war and under it all death and your secret love of death, yes
that was your secret" (72). But Will's extravagant Faulknerian rhetoric of
course belies his renunciation of his father. It is not only that the stylistic
qualities of the sentence deliberately evoke Percy's literary father's view of
the determining power of the past on the present. In the father-son struggle
within the text, Will's voice in this passage also sounds something like Ed
Barrett's. His invocation of "the ancient hatreds and allegiances, allegiances
unto death" has the same romantic, Wagnerian pitch as his father's grim allusions to "the ignorant armies that clash by night." Moreover, as Will himself
realizes, his attempts to flee from his father's influence were failures. Though
he lived and worked in New York rather than his father's cherished South,
though he cultivated a sort of mild religiosity that his father could not abide,
such efforts were only the frailest stays against the claims of memory. "In two
seconds, he saw that his little Yankee life had not worked after all" (73). Indeed, as Will looks around him at a world that seems increasingly "senseless
and farcical," as he surveys the ruins of his life from middle age, he recognizes in himself the same anger and despair that drove his father. "We're together after all," Will thinks (74).

Perhaps most of all, as Will stands in the woods cradling his golf club like
a shotgun, he shares Ed Barrett's sense of moral outrage at a world gone
wrong. For Ed, of course, that corruption was rooted in the collapse of the
old hierarchy that had given order and stability to the South. Like William
Alexander Percy, who bemoaned the triumph of a new breed of populist in
his autobiography, *Lanterns on the Levee*, Ed could not abide the transformation of the South to a more egalitarian culture in the first decades of the
twentieth century. As class and racial lines gave way, so too did the aristocratic code that drew clear distinctions between right and wrong; for Ed, the
rise of crude, amoral men like Huey Long and James Vardaman was like a

virus that infected his patrician class as well. As he says in *The Last Gentleman,*
"Once they were the fornicators and the bribers and the takers of bribes
and we were not and that was why they hated us. Now we are like them"
(317). Will's outrage, however, stems from the self-deception of those around
him. As in *The Last Gentleman,* his "radar" enables him to quickly see through
the inauthentic selves that the people who surround him construct. When,
for example, Will remembers a poem written by Lewis Peckham, a onetime
English teacher, Vietnam vet, and now "discontent golf pro," he is indignant
at Lewis's pretensions and his failure to achieve a coherent sense of self:
"How could Lewis, who could locate others so well, so misplace himself?
How could he read signs and people so well, yet want to be a third-rate
Rupert Brooke with his rendezvous with death at Khe Sanh? Why would he
even want to be a first-rate Rupert Brooke? On the other hand, what was
Lewis supposed to do? be an Indian scout? goatherd? English teacher? golf
pro? run a Confederate cave? Lewis didn't seem to know" (150–51). Though
there is a mild sympathy near the end of this passage for Lewis's struggle to
weave together the different threads of his life, the outraged tone at the beginning suggests that Will stands in judgment of Lewis. For Will, it seems,
Lewis's inability to find himself is virtually a moral failure; it offends Will.
And Lewis's pretensions are part and parcel of Will's general indictment of
his place and time. In different ways, almost all of the people with whom he
comes in contact are as lost as Lewis. Whether it is a minister's, Jack Curl's,
pathetic attempt to be hip, wearing ill-fitting jumpsuits and peppering his
speech with awkward expressions like "It's not my gig," or Kitty's newfound
faith in astrology, or even his daughter Leslie's severe insistence that true faith
consists of "a personal encounter" with God absent of "church, priests, or
ritual," all Will sees when he looks around him are false self-conceptions and
various forms of spirituality that are equally self-involved (135, 158).

Both Will and his father ultimately see the world in stark, Manichean
terms. For Ed Barrett, the world is divided between "us" and "them": a small,
doomed group clinging futilely to principle and the "ignorant armies" who
have overrun the South. For Will, who in the first half of the novel has
clearly assimilated his father's voice and perspective, the world is similarly
divided between a small bastion of sanity—himself, really—and a rising tide
of madness that sweeps up the faithful and the secular alike. As he explains in
a long letter to his old mentor, Sutter Vaught, a little more than halfway
through the novel, "It has taken me all these years to make the simplest discovery: that I am surrounded by two classes of maniacs. The first are the be-

lievers, who think they know the reason why we find ourselves in this ludicrous predicament yet act for all the world as if they don't. The second are
the unbelievers, who don't know the reason and don't care if they don't"
(190). Though Will's complaint here is not couched in strictly ethical terms—
he does not speak of good and evil but sane and insane—he is as quick to
judge those around him and as severe in his judgments as his father. And so
we see that Will, though a generation removed, is nevertheless touched by
the same moralistic temper that informed the stoic code of his father's South.
If Will does not adopt the stoic's specific vocabulary, a language grounded
in a firm sense of right and wrong, he employs its late-twentieth-century
replacement: a way of speaking about life in which one does not strive to
be honorable but, above all, to be healthy, to be well-adjusted—for self-
fulfillment is perhaps the only moral standard left in Will's America. (Percy
will satirize this same self-help culture, of course, in his next book, *Lost in the
Cosmos.*)

But though Will assimilates his father's sense of moral outrage, Will differs
from Ed Barrett in one key aspect. He abjures what he calls his father's "secret love of death" (at one point, Will imagines his father's suicide as an almost sexual act: "the penetration and union of perfect cold gunmetal into
warm quailing mortal flesh, the coming to end all coming" [149]). In his
own mind at least, Will is more rational; he will not just throw his life away
in a brief, violent paroxysm of rage. Rather, though he is perfectly willing—
eager, in fact—to end his life, he will use his suicide for a larger purpose. As
Will tells his father, in one of the many passages in the novel in which he
speaks both to the memory of his father and to himself, "Father, the difference between you and me is that you were so angry you wanted no part of
the way this life is and yourself in it and me in it too. You aimed only to
make an end and you did. Very well, perhaps you were right. But I aim to
find out. There's the difference. I aim to find out once and for all. I won't
have it otherwise, you settled for too little" (134).

Will's plan is simple; he will descend into a huge cavern nearby and wait
for one of two things to occur: either he will die of starvation and exposure,
or God will appear to him. As Will tells Sutter in the long letter in which he
details his plan, adopting the scientific voice that all of Percy's protagonists
appropriate at one time or another,

> Unless I am mistaken, I've hit on the perfect, the definitive experi-
> ment—as definitive as the famous Michelson-Morley experiment which

asked a question about the nature of space which could only be answered by a yes or a no, no maybes allowed.

We have had five thousand years of maybes and that is enough.

Can you discover a single flaw in this logic?

I've got him!

No more tricks!

No more *deus absconditus!*

Come out, come out, wherever you are, the game's over.

No, I do not mean to joke. What I am doing is asking God with the
utmost respect to break his silence. (192)

Of course, we can see here the roots of Will's own uncertain faith. His insistence on applying the standard of scientific empiricism to the question of
God's existence is self-defeating. Yet Will's reference to "the famous Michelson-
Morley experiment," his Latinism, and his pride in the simple logic of his
plan all show that he is as convinced of the ultimate truth of the scientific
method as he was when he was a young man and thought of himself as the
"engineer." (It is no surprise, then, that the only person Will tells of his experiment is Sutter, who has retired in New Mexico and is only an offstage
presence in *The Second Coming.* Even now, in middle age, Will still seems to
need the other man's validation and approval.)

The outcome of Will's "experiment," however, is one of the most perfectly realized comedic turns in all of Percy's fiction. After hiding in one of
the deepest recesses of the Lost Cove Cave and—with the aid of a bottle of
sleeping pills and other supplies—planning to wait as long as it takes for God
or death to arrive and claim him, Will receives the most ambiguous possible
sign: a toothache so powerful that it feels "like a hot ice pick shoved straight
up into the brain" (213). Though it is of course possible, as the narrator implies, that the toothache is itself "God's doing," Will's pain is so intense that
he literally has no stomach for such questions (213). And so, after several days
in which he alternates between nausea and unconsciousness, he makes his
way out of the cave and literally falls into the hands of Allison Huger, Kitty's
daughter, who has herself escaped from a mental hospital and made her
home in the abandoned greenhouse that is adjacent to the cave.

Allison—or Allie, as she is more often called—is Percy's most fully developed and sympathetic female character since Kate Cutrer in *The Moviegoer.*
Moreover, unlike Kate, Allie is strong enough to command several chapters
of her own in *The Second Coming.* The first eight of the twelve chapters in

the novel alternate between Will's and Allie's points of view—the only time in Percy's fiction that he ever truly departs from the point of view of one of his cool, watchful protagonists. And yet Allie is cut from the same cloth as Percy's heroes. Like them, she sees the world around her from an outsider's perspective. After being committed to a sanatorium for depression from anywhere between two to four years (she cannot remember herself) and subjected to a regular course of electroshock therapy (which has of course scrambled her memory), her view of the world is not clouded by habit or inherited assumptions. In a sense, as if to confirm the theory articulated by Tom More in *Love in the Ruins* and by Percy in his nonfiction, Allie is purified by her ordeal. She is like the only survivor of a recent plane crash, a man whose brush with death had left him not in shock but "in his right mind, as if he had crossed a time warp or gone through a mirror, no, not gone through, come back, yes, the only question being which way he went, from the sane side to the crazy side like Alice or back the other way" (30).

What Allie sees of the world around her raises much the same question. When she leaves the sanatorium, slipping out in a bread truck after she is left untended following a final shock treatment, her mind is close to a blank slate. Consequently, she brings no preconceptions about the behavior of those around her. She sees with uncomfortable clarity the pretensions, false assumptions, and evasions of daily life. When, for example, another woman invites her to a gathering of born-again Christians, Allie is confused by the woman's statement that "a person like yourself might get a lot out of it." "Does that mean you know what I am like?" she asks. But when the woman ignores Allie's question, Allie is struck by what amounts to a kind of bad faith that is implicit in her use of language: "she reflected that people asked questions and answered them differently from her. She took words seriously to mean more or less what they said, but other people seemed to use words as signals in another code they had agreed upon" (33–34). Interestingly, though, Allie withholds judgment on the other's use of words; in contrast to Will, she is reluctant to evaluate or criticize the people with whom she comes in contact. "Such a code, she reflected, may not be bad. Indeed, it seemed to cause people less trouble than words" (34).

Allie herself has much trouble with words, in part because she has simply forgotten many of them after years of shock therapy and self-imposed silence in the sanatorium (when Will first hears her speak, she sounds to him "like a wolf child who had learned to speak from old Victrola records" [76]), and also because she is acutely conscious of how words are deprived of meaning through casual, thoughtless use—as in the exchange above. Consequently, because she does not know the "code" that allows others to spend their words so carelessly, she develops a language all her own, a simple yet highly metaphorical style of speaking that is commensurate with the clarity and freshness of her perceptions of the world around her. When, for example, Allie tries to explain to Will the reasons for her commitment, she rejects the abstract terminology of a classificatory science in favor of a vivid yet simple spatial metaphor that powerfully evokes her struggle to overcome depression: "I was somewhat suspended above me but now I am getting down to me" (108). Similarly, when she tries to articulate the reason why she feels so out of sorts in the late afternoon after she has finished her tasks for the day, she metaphorically conjoins her longing for someone or something else with her heightened awareness of time's slow passage. "This time of day is a longens.... In this longitude longens ensues in a longing if not an unbelonging" (238), she says to a stray dog she adopts, at once delighting in the repetition of sounds and lamenting her loneliness and alienation, her "unbelonging."

Allie ultimately sets out to create a life for herself that is as simple and uncluttered as her vision of the world around her. She takes up residence in an abandoned greenhouse that she inherited from an elderly friend of the family, and gradually—as if to fulfill the postapocalyptic fantasies of Tom More and so many of Percy's characters—clears away some of the debris and makes a home amid the ruins. As William Rodney Allen points out, "Allie's retreat to her mountain greenhouse recalls Thoreau's to Walden Pond. There is much Thoreauvian listing by Allie of exactly how much things cost: her knives, block-and-tackle, clothes. She proclaims her intention 'to live with very few things' (43), and her principal goal is self-reliance" (141).

Will first meets Allie only moments after he finally remembers his fateful hunting trip with his father. As he stands in what he thinks is a hidden vantage point in the woods that abut the golf course, looking on at the greenhouse where his errant golf ball landed, Allie catches him unaware—unnerving, even angering him when she intrudes on his solitude. Of course, this staging by Percy symbolizes the role that Allie will play in Will's life. For when she first comes upon him, he effectively dwells in the same isolated region of the mind where his stoic father spent his last days, that fortress of icy contempt for a fallen world that Percy once called—paraphrasing his own adopted father—"the wintry kingdom of self" (*SSL* 85). Over the course of the novel, Allie will intrude on this spiritual solitude as well, even-

tually drawing Will out of this no-man's-land by offering an alternative to
his father's "secret love of death." (It is no accident that when Will seems to
see his father's ghost in a grove of trees just off the golf course, the shadowy
form obscured by the leaves is actually Allie's.) As Kennedy points out,
Allie's greenhouse and Ed Barrett's Greener shotgun function as "the antipo-
des of [Will's] life-death ambivalence" (218).

Indeed, for reasons that he does not seem to fully understand, Will becomes fascinated with Allie. He visits her at her greenhouse on the day after
she surprises him in the woods, and, at a deeper level, he begins to assimilate
her sensitivity to language and her eccentric speech patterns. "I would hope
that you would go in hope," he tells Jack Curl at one point, adopting Allie's
circular, repetitive syntax (136). Later, too, as he watches his daughter, Leslie,
argue over religion with Jack at a party a few days before her wedding, he
tries to see Leslie through Allie's eyes:

> Looking at her, his daughter, he found himself thinking not about her or
> the wedding or the argument but, strangely enough, about how the girl
> in the woods might see her. In her nutty way with words, she would
> have seen Leslie in her name *Leslie* and now he too could see her, had
> always seen her as a *Leslie,* the two syllables of the name linked and
> hinged and folding just as her legs folded under her and the stems folded
> against her glasses, the whispering of her panty hose and the slight clash
> of the glasses connoted by the *s* in *Les* and the *Leslie* itself with its *s* and
> neuterness signifying both prissiness and masculinity, a secretarial
> primness which indeed Leslie had and which was all the more remark-
> able what with her being born-again. It was impossible to envision her
> personal encounter with Christ as other than a crisp business transaction.
> (159–60)

As Will himself recognizes, he clearly sees Leslie as Allie might, finding
Leslie's self in the seemingly inevitable conjunction of signifier and signified.
But Will does not seem to recognize that Allie's influence on him is tempered by his father's. For as Will's thoughts continue, the act of seeing Leslie,
truly looking at her—as Will probably has not done in years—subtly elides
into the sterner business of judging her. When Will offers his dismissive
evaluation of Leslie's faith at the end of this passage, he places himself again
on the same lonely pinnacle to which his father clung, that vanishing spit of
ground that the moralist occupies as a sea of chicanery and madness ebbs
and flows around him. In a sense, then, this passage constitutes a tacit microdialogue, a tug-of-war in Will's consciousness between Allie's acute yet fun-

damentally innocent perceptions and Ed Barrett's darker vision; if we do not hear specific traces of their voices echoing in the language of the passage, Allie's and Ed's respective influence on what and how Will sees is clear.

It is significant, though, that his father's influence dominates at the end of this passage, for this moment occurs when the legacy of Ed Barrett's anger is its peak, not long before Will concocts his grand plan to kill himself or force God to appear before him. What happens after his plan goes awry, however, is less clear. If Will's consciousness is dominated by his father's voice when he descends into the cave, the balance of power in his heart and mind seems to shift after he falls into Allie's greenhouse from a small vent that opens into a framed hole in her roof. For as Allie nurses Will back to health, the amorphous fascination that she previously held for him becomes something deeper. His father's grim infatuation with death is now countered by a simpler, more earthly love.

In many ways, Will and Allie's romance (seen through Allie's eyes in the last chapter of the novel that is given over to her point of view) is based more on the intimacy engendered by a shared language than it is—for the time being, at least—on physical passion. Though they lie together naked after Allie covers an exhausted Will with her own body in an effort to stop a fit of shivering, they do not make love. Instead, they simply talk, and their exchange of words is for Allie a kind of intercourse that is erotic in itself. "Though he hardly touched her, his words seemed to flow across all parts of her body. Were they meant to? A pleasure she had never known before bloomed deep in her body. Was this a way of making love?" (262). At its core, the pleasure Allie feels is a consequence of what their words reveal in this scene, for Will at last recognizes her unique importance to him. He makes this recognition clear when he tells Allie that he will explain to her what he learned in the cave "because, for one reason, you may be the only person who would understand it" (259). With these words, Will acknowledges the dialogic bond between the two of them, a link that Allie also acknowledges when she asks, "why does it seem I am not only I but also you?" (260). Indeed, their strange affinity is manifest in what Will calls "our new language" (262). As if to celebrate their communion, he deliberately appropriates and echoes her metaphorical speech in their dialogue. When Allie, searching for a way to convey her understanding of the demons that drove Will into the cave, says "I do that. . . . I go round and down to get down to myself," Will takes up her words like a gift and alters them slightly to fit his own experience. "I went down and around to get out of myself," he replies (263). (Curiously, Percy only lets us hear fragments of Will's explanation of what he allegedly learned in the cave. Though Will's ordeal seems to have revealed to him the extent of his own alienation from daily life, his inability to, in his words, "reenter the world" [262], the exclusion of this speech from the narrative suggests that his self-knowledge at this point in the novel is incomplete.)

Will's experience in the cave and his love for Allie ultimately seem to transform him, to give him a new strength and purpose. As Allie tells him, "You seem different. Before, when you climbed through the fence and I saw you, you were standing still a long time as if you were listening. Now you seem to know what to do" (264). Indeed, when he leaves Allie's greenhouse, he is intent, as he declares to her, to do "[w]hat is expected of me. Take care of people who need taking care of" (265). By this statement, he means to fulfill his obligations to Leslie and, also, to take quick legal action to defend Allie from Kitty's attempt to gain control of her inheritance—both the greenhouse and a far more valuable property, an island off the Carolina coast. But though Will's intentions are surely laudable, the way he expresses them is vaguely troubling, for there is a distinct echo in his declaration to Allie of the stoic's traditional injunction "to duty, to honor, to generosity toward his fellow men and above all to his inferiors" (SSL 85). Once again, we seem to hear his father's ghost stirring in his words, and it is clear that—no matter what else has changed—something still remains of Ed Barrett's legacy.

In fact, in an odd way, at the moment in which Will exults in what he believes is his triumph over his father's spirit, he again assimilates the same almost supernal sense of outrage that isolated and ultimately destroyed Ed Barrett. As Will stands in the country club parking lot shortly after leaving Allie, pacing back and forth beside his silver Mercedes, he is struck by a revelation so grand and sweeping in its reach that he does a jig in its honor.

> Ha, there is a secret after all, he said. But to know the secret answer, you must first know the secret question. The question is, who is the enemy?
>
> Not to know the name of the enemy is already to have been killed by him.
>
> *Ha,* he said, dancing, snapping his fingers and laughing and hooting *ha hoo hee,* jumping up and down and socking himself, *but I do know. I know. I know the name of the enemy.*
>
> The name of the enemy is death, he said, grinning and shoving his hands in his pockets. Not the death of the dying but the living death.
>
> The name of this century is the Century of the Love of Death. Death

in this century is not the death people die but the death people live. Men love death because real death is better than the living death. That's why men like wars, of course. Bad as wars are and maybe because they are so bad, thinking of peace during war is better than peace. War is what makes peace desirable. But peace without war is intolerable. Why do men settle so easily for lives which are living deaths? Men either kill each other in war, or in peace walk as docilely into living death as sheep into the slaughterhouse. (271)

It is hard, reading *The Second Coming,* not to be swept along by the joy of Will's epiphany. As he stands in a cold, clammy rain, laughing and dancing and kicking the tires of his Mercedes, his condemnation of the various forms of death—whether the bourgeois pieties of "Christendom," rampant consumerism, astrology and other New Age faiths, or the obligations of marriage and family—and his insistence that there is a third choice open to him, in addition to "death in life" or a shotgun barrel in the mouth, are so impassioned and trenchant that we want to believe in Will's victory over what he calls his own "death genes" (274). And yet, this ostensible moment of triumph is deeply flawed, for Will's resolution, in his words, "to choose life" is short-lived and incomplete (274). Within a few hours, he will seek out again the weapons of death that he had hidden in a closet before descending into the Lost Cove Cave—the Greener shotgun that once scored his cheek, a Luger his father took from a Nazi colonel in World War II—and will set out to return to the Georgia swamp where Ed Barrett once nearly killed him, apparently to accomplish what his father could not. For a reader of *The Second Coming* who had shared the exhilaration of Will's epiphany, this turn of events is puzzling and disappointing.

What accounts for the failure of Will's epiphany? In the most simple terms, it can perhaps be seen as a consequence of Percy's admittedly improvisational method of composition. Percy was not the sort of writer to carefully plan a work before beginning it. He would often start a book with only a vague idea of where he wanted it to go and would trust instead to the course of his imagination, trying to follow the thread of inspiration through the long labyrinth of a novel's composition. As he explained in 1968, "My writing involves many false starts, many blind detours, many blind passages, many goings ahead and backing up where something has been tried and doesn't work. Sometimes, the first half will be all right and the second half doesn't work at all. You don't know why it doesn't work, it doesn't swing, it doesn't cook, it doesn't go; so, you just back up. It's mysterious, this thing of not knowing why it doesn't work. All you know is that when it *does* work, you know it" (*Con.* 32). Given this method of working, it is possible to say that *The Second Coming* simply got away from Percy, that he did not know where to end his novel—so what should be a climactic moment, insight followed by swift and dramatic action, dissolves instead into irresolution. But this explanation implies not only a lack of planning on Percy's part but a general carelessness as well—a carelessness that is belied by the characteristic beauty and precision of his prose. More important, though, this explanation completely ignores the way in which the underlying tensions that shape a writer's vision may be felt in the artistic choices that he or she makes. Even if Percy's improvisational way of writing did unintentionally subvert what was meant to be a climactic moment, that act of subversion surely proceeded from the workings of more powerful forces than simply some failed sense of narrative design. Indeed, the anticlimactic nature of Will's grand revelation is itself a reflection of the ongoing dialogue within Percy's work between the voice that expresses the ethical concerns of his patrician heritage and his Catholic faith, the moralist who says, "this the way the world *ought* to be," and the voice of the artist who eschews didacticism, who insists that "nothing would be worse than a so-called philosophical or religious novel which simply used a story and a plot and characters in order to get over a certain idea" (*Con.* 89).

When Will delivers his jeremiad on the "Century of the Love of Death," he clearly conveys Percy's moral concerns. Will here expands on the narrator's earlier observation that "the world is in fact farcical" (4) and articulates an angry vision of the twentieth century that Percy will echo in his nonfiction. A 1986 essay, "Novel-Writing in an Apocalyptic Time," reprises Will's complaint in strikingly similar language: "no other time has been more life-affirming in its pronouncements, self-fulfilling, creative, autonomous, and so on—and more death-dealing in its actions. It is the century of the love of death. I am not talking just about Verdun or the Holocaust or Dresden or Hiroshima. I am talking about a subtler form of death, a death in life, of people who seem to be living lives which are good by all sociological standards and yet who somehow seem more dead than alive" (*SSL* 162). Percy's words express a key tenet of his moral vision, and their similarity to his character's monologue in *The Second Coming* confirms that when Will too declaims the century of the love of death, we hear again, as we did in *Love in the Ruins* and *Lancelot,* the moralist's voice.

But if Will is a vehicle here, a mouthpiece for the moralist in Percy, the character's his stance at this moment is troubling. For his voice, as he catalogs the various forms of death, is detached, theoretical. When he says, for example, that "Men love death because real death is better than the living death," his insistence on speaking in broad, sweeping terms about men in general recalls the abstraction to which Binx Bolling succumbed in his "search" in *The Moviegoer*. Like a scientist who has stumbled on what Binx once called "the big one, the new key, the secret leverage point" (*MG* 82), Will is aloft in the grip of pure theory as he articulates his thesis on the origins of the malaise of the late twentieth century. More important, though, he is also—within the terms of Percy's own narrative—dangerously close to assimilating his father's perspective. For Will's sweeping denunciation of his times and his insistence that he alone has found a way to escape the fate that entraps virtually everyone else recall yet again his father's preferred self-image: a man alone on Matthew Arnold's "darkling plain," surrounded by confusion and venality yet unwilling to surrender his own tattered standard. Indeed, though Will declares in his monologue his victory over his father —"You gave in to death, old mole, but I will not have it so" (273)—the way in which he proclaims his triumph, setting himself high above the ignorant armies struggling inconclusively below him, transforms it into a Pyrrhic victory. As his subsequent actions demonstrate, Will has not beaten Ed Barrett's spirit. Ironically, even his behavior during this act of renunciation mimics his father. When Will paces beside his Mercedes, condemning the spirit of death that has infected believer and unbeliever alike, his manner is reminiscent of the troubling memories of Ed Barrett in *The Last Gentleman* pacing back and forth in front of the porch, declaiming the moral weakness that corrupts patrician and plebeian alike.

What, then, are we to make of this peculiar, anticlimactic sequence of events that occurs more than three-quarters of the way through *The Second Coming?* On the one hand, when Will chants to himself "the many names of death" (274) in the country club parking lot, his insight into the strange pathology of the twentieth century is indistinguishable from his creator's own diagnosis of our malady. Yet the way in which Will expresses that insight— his abstracted, vaguely self-righteous tone—echoes his father's voice and thus links him again to Ed Barrett's suicidal legacy. It is as if Percy deliberately meant to express his own moral convictions and, at the same time, to expose the flaws inherent in the moralist's position. As in *Lancelot,* we can hear a dialogue in *The Second Coming* over the accomplishments and the dangers that follow from setting oneself up as a moralist. For in both books, the moralist's anger leads to a self-destructive spiritual isolation—whether in the form of Lancelot's madness, Ed Barrett's bitter and ultimately suicidal contempt for his peers' ethical failures, or Will's overweening detachment.

The failure of Will's grand epiphany precipitates the novel's final turn. After he returns to town following his ordeal in the cave and his recovery in Allie's greenhouse, Will retrieves his father's guns, stores them in the trunk of his Mercedes, and promptly drives his car off the side of the road as he heads toward Jack Curl's for a reunion with Leslie. This accident, though, strips away whatever pretense Will had maintained of exorcising his father's ghost. Stunned by a slight concussion, he automatically sets out to return to the woods where Ed Barrett tried to kill him so long ago; he boards a bus for Georgia and tells another passenger that he is on his way to buy a farm, a slang expression for death. Only when he thinks of Allie again, however, does he hesitate on this march to self-destruction. But when he abruptly tries to get off the bus to return to her, a scuffle with the driver leaves him unconscious, and he wakes up twelve hours later in the Linwood hospital surrounded by Leslie, his doctor, and Jack Curl, who persuade him to enter a convalescent home.

Will's experience in what he calls the "old folks home" reprises a key theme of *Love in the Ruins* (314). After being diagnosed as suffering from a hydrogen-ion deficiency, Will's strange *longueurs*—with the notable exception of his desire for Allie—vanish when he is given regular hydrogen supplements. As with Tom More's steadfast belief in the power of his lapsometer to diagnose and heal "the deep perturbations of the soul" (*LR* 29), the chemicals smooth away Will's distress like oil lubricating a car engine. Here, again, as in *Love in the Ruins,* human beings are conceived as little more than complex machines whose emotions and behavior are determined solely by physiology and whose functionings can be altered through the proper application of scientific knowledge. But this conception of human life has, apart from its mechanistic view of humanity in general, dire consequences for Will in particular. Earlier in the novel, in the midst of his epiphany in the country club parking lot, he had declared, "Death in the form of genes shall not prevail over me" (274). Yet if Will conceives of himself as a creature whose behavior, whose whole outlook on the world, can be regulated by the proper balance of chemicals in his system, must not he also accept a kind of genetic determinism? Is his future inscribed in the DNA spirals that he inherited from his father? In many ways, it seems to be, for life in the "old folks home" is, as Will finally realizes, only a more benign form of suicide than his father's:

"I've found a better way than swallowing gun barrels: in short, I can shuffle off among friends and in comfort and Episcopal decorum and with good Christian folk to look after every need" (325).

But if Will's experience in the convalescent home entraps him in a slough of lethargic calm, it also increases his assimilation of Allie's voice and perspective by paralleling her forced confinement in the sanatorium. Here, the drugs that Will is given do the work of the electric shocks that imposed an unnatural calm on Allie. And just as Kitty's concern for Allie's welfare was tainted by more avaricious motives, a desire to control her inheritance, Leslie knows that Will's protracted treatment for his hydrogen-ion deficiency will allow her to keep a firm grip on the family fortune. Indeed, only when Kitty learns of Allie's whereabouts and accosts Will in the nursing home for his involvement with Allie and for keeping his knowledge of Allie from her does Will begin to shake off his lethargy. Kitty's insistence that Allie must be committed for life finally motivates Will to abandon the stultifying comfort of the rest home. After Kitty confronts him, he realizes at last that he has only chosen a more gradual form of self-destruction than his father's. Galvanized by this recognition, he abruptly leaves the convalescent home, finds Allie, hides her from Kitty and the authorities at the local Holiday Inn (the favored refuge and rendezvous of Percy's heroes), and quickly sets in motion the legal procedures necessary to prevent her from being committed against her will.

Will's newfound decisiveness is only made possible, though, by what occurs simultaneous with it: his rejection, once and for all, of his father's ghost. As Allen notes, when Will approaches Allie's greenhouse after leaving the nursing home to save her from Kitty, "he symbolically kicks down the half-rotten fence that had set off his memory of his father's suicide" (149). This is only one step, however, in the process of Will's ultimate renunciation of his father's love of death. The most crucial step occurs as Will lies in bed with Allie at the Holiday Inn. As Allie sleeps with Will nestled around her, he evokes Ed Barrett's voice in his consciousness and literally speaks as his father. (Though we have previously heard traces of Ed's voice in Will's, in this scene, for the first time in the novel, Will's voice merges with his father's.) "Come," Will/Ed thinks, as he reminds himself of the guns that are still locked in the trunk of his Mercedes, "it's the only way, the one quick sure exit of grace and violence and beauty. . . . What other end if you don't make the end? Make your own bright end in the darkness of this dying world" (336–37). But though Will seems to accede to the urgings of his father's voice when he rises from the bed, retrieves the guns, and goes to a deserted lot across from the hotel, he does not kill himself in that remote spot. Instead—in a final, decisive gesture—he throws the Greener and the Luger over the side of a cliff and silences his father's voice at last.

What enables Will to rid himself of his father's voice? His love for Allie is clearly a determining factor. Her physical presence in the bed beside Will as he evokes and argues with Ed Barrett's voice is a powerful counterweight to his father's despair, for the warmth of Allie's skin, the feel of her breath on his arm, save him from the supernal detachment that is the inevitable consequence of the moral outrage that he and his father shared. In the terms that Allie's uncle, Sutter Vaught, had used in his casebook in *The Last Gentleman,* the physicality of Allie's presence—which makes tangible Will's love for her—represents the triumph of immanence (being in the world) over transcendence (orbiting far above it in the posture of a detached observer). But love for Allie is not enough in itself to enable Will to purge his father's despair. If it was, he would not have given in again to his suicidal impulses after his experience in the cave and his subsequent epiphany.

In the end, Will must manifest his father's voice before he can reject it. He must let Ed Barrett speak at length, let him have his say, before Will can renounce his father's dark vision. In a sense, Will must do exactly what Walker Percy needed to do to come to terms with the influence of his adopted father, William Alexander Percy. Just as Walker Percy first embodied his guardian's voice in the person of Emily Cutrer in *The Moviegoer* to cast off what was inadequate about William Alexander Percy's stoic philosophy, Will must deliberately re-create his father's voice to renounce his love of death. For through this process, as Bakhtin notes in "Discourse in the Novel," "a conversation with an internally persuasive word may continue, but it takes on another character; it is questioned, it is put in a new situation in order to expose its weak sides, to get a feel for its boundaries, to experience it physically as an object" (348). For this reason, Will's triumphant rejection of the "Century of the Love of Death" is insufficient in itself. That long exclamation is one-sided; it is an example of Will speaking to his father's ghost, rather than with him. The only way, finally, to exorcise this unquiet spirit is through dialogue. Will cannot drown out his father's voice or block his ears to it; he must evoke Ed Barrett's voice and respond to it. Only then will Will's rejection be complete. Only then will he finally complete the process of ideological becoming that he began when he first tried to separate his voice from his father's as he stood outside his ancestral home in the psychological climax of *The Last Gentleman.*

In the final pages of the novel, Will's perspective changes markedly. Rather than holding himself aloof from others, a stern judge of their actions, Will now sees instead the potential of those around him. This change is made clear when he enlists the services of two of his fellow patients in the convalescent home, Mr. Arnold, an ex-builder who has suffered a debilitating stroke, and Mr. Ryan, an ex-contractor who has lost his legs to diabetes and arteriosclerosis, in a plan to build a community of low-cost log cabins. Though these two old men can be as irrational as any of the characters Will previously labeled as insane—they cannot even hold a conversation without the television on, and they are liable to sudden eruptions of rage, physically striking at each other with fists or crutches—Will sees beyond the peevishness and the juvenile behavior, beyond even their physical disabilities, and recognizes the talent that still exists inside them. In sharp contrast to his cutting evaluations of Lewis Peckham or even Leslie, he does not judge these old men. He observes them carefully, notes their faults, and then studiously appeals to their better natures.

In these actions, we see again the effects on Will of Allie's perspective. For at a concrete level, his decision to build a community of his own and to rehabilitate these cast-off men in the process is only a larger version of Allie's determination to make a new future for herself in her abandoned greenhouse by restoring the discarded remnants of its past. At a deeper level, though, Will's refusal to pass judgment on Mr. Arnold and Mr. Ryan emulates Allie's unwillingness to condemn those around her. As noted earlier, Allie does not judge the people with whom she comes in contact. If she sees their pretensions and self-deceptions, she nevertheless refuses to evaluate them or to label them as good or evil, sane or insane. The worst she will say of them, as she does of Dr. Duk, her Pakistani psychiatrist, who is given to knock-knock jokes and phony accents, is that they are "out-of-focus" (90). In a sense, there is an openness to Allie's vision, a humility toward the mystery of human complexity, that parallels Bakhtin's insistence that we are all ultimately *unfinalized.* As he writes in *Problems of Dostoevsky's Poetics,* in a passage that at once explains Dostoevsky's literary vision and assimilates it into Bakhtin's own emerging philosophy of dialogue and human subjectivity: "*In a human being there is always something that only he himself can reveal, in a free act of self-consciousness and discourse, something that does not submit to an externaliz-*

ing secondhand definition. . . . As long as a person is alive he lives by the fact
that he is not yet finalized, that he has not yet uttered his ultimate word"
(58–59).

We see this same quality of vision most dramatically in *The Second Coming*
in Allie's interaction with Will. Though she immediately perceives his self-
destructive tendencies—the anger in him almost rises up through his skin:
"His eye sockets were too deep, his eyes too light, his mouth too grim, his
skin burned too dark by the sun" (106)—she also sees through the fog of
bitterness that lingers around him. Indeed, as their relationship deepens, her
refusal to sum him up or evaluate him becomes so strong that she resists even
the totalizing effect of his name: "What to call *him?* Mr. Barrett? Mr. Will?
Will Barrett? Bill Barrett? Williston Bibb Barrett? None of the names fit. A
name would give him form once and for all. He would flow into its syllables
and junctures and there take shape forever. She didn't want him named"
(249).

In the final scene of the novel, when Will asks Father Weatherbee, a
wizened former missionary now in the convalescent home, to perform his
wedding to Allie, Will both assimilates this quality of her vision and seems to
recognize—dimly at least—its religious dimension. As with Mr. Arnold and
Mr. Ryan, he sees beyond the old priest's outward eccentricities. (There are
many. Father Weatherbee is almost pathologically timid, he has a childlike
obsession with model railroads, and even his physical features seem to mock
him: one eye has "a white rim and [spins] like a wheel," and a "red bleb"
forms at the corner of his mouth when he speaks [311].) Perhaps because
Father Weatherbee's almost mystical belief in apostolic succession—a priestly
laying on of hands that began with Jesus and the apostles—echoes Will's spo-
radic conviction that the Jews are mysteriously leaving North Carolina in
anticipation of the Second Coming, he turns to Father Weatherbee in much
the same way he did to Sutter Vaught in *The Last Gentleman.* Though Will
insists, "I am not a believer," he also tells the priest what he once told Sutter:
"I have the gift of discerning people and can tell when they know something I don't know. Accordingly, I am willing to be told whatever it is
you seem to know and I will attend carefully to what you say" (358). Of
course, Will makes no promises. He will only "attend carefully" to Father
Weatherbee's words (which are, to say the least, reluctantly offered; Father
Weatherbee literally shrinks in terror at Will's request). But Percy leaves
Will—as he does so many of his heroes—on the threshold of revelation and
of change. In the final sentences of *The Second Coming,* as Will's questions to

Father Weatherbee become more urgent, Will suddenly sees Allie as a potential sign of God's existence. As in the beginning of the novel, his world is a tissue of signs, a semiotic code, but now that code reveals a far different message than the doomed injunctions of his father's uneasy ghost: "Will Barrett thought about Allie in her greenhouse, her wide gray eyes, her lean muscled boy's arms, her strong quick hands. His heart leapt with a secret joy. What is it I want from her and him, he wondered, not only want but must have? Is she a gift and therefore a sign of a giver? Could it be that the Lord is here, masquerading behind this simple silly holy face? Am I crazy to want both, her and Him? Not, not want, must have. And will have" (360).

This is the least equivocal declaration of faith in all of Percy's fiction. Will demands to believe in God in much the same way that Percy insisted on the necessity of faith: "I took it as an intolerable state of affairs to have found myself in this life and in this age, which is a disaster by any calculation, without demanding a gift commensurate with the offense. So I demanded it" (*Con.* 177). Yet Will's tentative recognition that God is "masquerading behind [Father Weatherbee's] simple silly holy face" is also consistent with his recognition of the potential that still exists in Mr. Arnold and Mr. Ryan. For in seeing that these two old men can still prosper and change, Will embraces a vision of human possibility that also allows a timid, sometimes childish, half-blind old priest to briefly assimilate the voice of God. And in this we are reminded that the quality of vision that Will has assimilated from Allie— in which all God's creatures are *unfinalized*—is itself consistent with what Percy describes as a the traditional Judeo-Christian vision of "man as wayfarer": "a creature in trouble, seeking to get out of it, and accordingly on the move . . . a pilgrim whose life is a searching and a finding" (*SSL* 369). Both visions emphasize a certain inevitable incompleteness, an openness to all possibilities. In both, humanity is always "on the move," on a search that will end only at death.

In several essays, Percy argued that this Judeo-Christian view of humanity as wayfarers was "inherently congenial to the novelist." Christian dogma, he wrote, "is a guarantee of the mystery of human existence and for the novelist, for this novelist anyhow, a warrant to explore the mystery" (*SSL* 177, 178). So it is fitting that the dominance of this vision at the end of *The Second Coming* should seem to cap the novelist's triumph over the moralist. For in renouncing his father's voice and perspective and instead assimilating Allie's, Will rejects the moralist's finalizing vision, which labels and judges, in favor of a more open, ambiguous vision. And though *The Second Coming* is in part a product of the moralist's vision—particularly in its depiction of the shallow, venal types who surround Will for much of the novel—its conclusion happily leaves us in a more ambiguous realm of indeterminacy and hope.[3] For it is there that Will and Allie will build their brave new world.

The Thanatos Syndrome envisions a new world too, but Percy's last novel is a cautionary tale about the triumph of scientific abstraction in the late twentieth century. Perhaps because Will's ultimate rejection of his father's voice in The Second Coming so clearly resolved many long-standing themes in Percy's fiction, there is no confusion of motives here. Percy's last novel is clearly designed to articulate an explicit moral statement, and as a consequence the dialogic qualities of his other novels are subdued here. What takes precedence in The Thanatos Syndrome is not the anguished microdialogue of the protagonist—who here is an older and somewhat chastened Tom More—but the careful construction of the plot. Structured as a kind of mystery, The Thanatos Syndrome employs Percy's most intricate narrative architecture as its protagonist's investigations bring him steadily closer to a moral abyss in which the sanctity of the individual is nearly sacrificed to the spirit of scientific abstraction. Over the course of the novel, Tom struggles to discover and ultimately expose a secret medical project that, Percy suggests, is the embodiment of Thanatos, Freud's death instinct. And yet dialogue as a basic condition of human existence remains central to Percy's artistic vision. For it is also possible to see Tom More's efforts in The Thanatos Syndrome as a quest to restore the capacity for dialogue, which has been jeopardized both by the artificial diminution of human faculties and by the bad faith of Tom's antagonists, who willfully use language to deceive and manipulate. Furthermore, the success of Tom's quest is itself dependent on his own ability and willingness to enter into a dialogue of heart and mind that is as intense and meaningful as any in Percy's fiction.

At the beginning of The Thanatos Syndrome, Dr. Thomas More, who seemed destined for better days at the end of Percy's third novel, Love in the Ruins, has just returned to his home in Feliciana Parish in Louisiana after serving a two-year prison sentence for selling amphetamines and sedatives to truckers.[4] Though Tom appeared to be on the verge of prosperity in the epilogue to Love in the Ruins, the domestic peace that seemed to follow his marriage to his nurse Ellen Oglethorpe has foundered on the shoals of Tom's alcoholism, as has his medical practice. His subsequent financial distress drove him to sell drugs as a way of supplementing his failing practice. But prison, as Tom makes clear early in *The Thanatos Syndrome,* was not necessarily a bad experience. It steadied him and helped him find himself. As Tom explains,

> In prison I learned a certain detachment and cultivated a mild low-grade curiosity. At one time I thought the world was going mad and that it was up to me to diagnose the madness and treat it. I became grandiose, even Faustian.
>
> Prison does wonders for megalomania. Instead of striking pacts with the Devil to save the world—yes, I was nuts—I spent two years driving a tractor pulling a gang mower over sunny fairways and at night chatting with my fellow con men and watching reruns of *Barnaby Jones.*
>
> Living a small life gave me leave to notice small things—like certain off-color spots in the St. Augustine grass which I correctly diagnosed as an early sign of chinch bug infestation. Instead of saving the world, I saved the eighteen holes at Fort Pelham and felt surprisingly good about it. (67)

Of course, Tom's reference to his former point of view, which was "grandiose, even Faustian," is an allusion to *Love in the Ruins* and the pact he struck with Art Immelmann, a diabolical figure, to help perfect the lapsometer, a device that Tom hoped would cure the ills of Western civilization. But as Tom makes clear here, he has renounced such "grandiose" dreams; his old ambition now seems like a form of madness, and even the devilish characteristics he once saw in Immelmann now seem delusional, an expression of Tom's "megalomania." Indeed, what is most striking about this passage is its relative serenity. In contrast to the echo-laden voices of Percy's other protagonists—including, of course, the younger Tom of *Love in the Ruins*—the language here is free of tension. We do not hear "a conflict of voices" (Bakhtin, *Dostoevsky* 74) in Tom's expression. His voice in this passage seems thoroughly integrated, virtually univocal.

Yet if Tom is for the most part secure in his professional identity and ethos, his private self is less stable. At home, he is a distant, awkward father whose children regard him warily, "as if," he says, "I were still a drunk, a certain presence in the house which one takes account of, steps around, like a hole in the floor" (38). Then, too, his relationship with Ellen has clearly been weakened by his long absence, so much so that he finds himself drifting into an

affair with his distant cousin, Lucy Lipscomb, an epidemiologist whose help
will be crucial in unraveling the mystery that dominates the novel. Indeed,
as the erotic chaos of Tom's life escalates, he seems less and less like the clear-
headed man who emerged from prison at Fort Pelham and more like an
ancestor from the revolutionary era who supported the British and committed suicide after he was exposed as a bigamist. A victim of "spells of terrible melancholy," Tom's ancestor's conviction "that certain unnamed enemies were after him" presents a disturbing parallel to Tom's own increasing
suspicions of a dangerous conspiracy operating around him (136). And
throughout the novel, a subtle danger exists that Tom will embrace the example of his suicidal forefather while grappling with marital difficulties and
elusive enemies.

Ultimately, though, the attention to "small things" to which Tom refers
above has large consequences in *The Thanatos Syndrome*. It is what causes Tom
to first notice the strange goings-on in his hometown that are at the core of
the novel. When an old patient has suddenly shed the anxiety that once
troubled her; when another patient, a wealthy refugee from El Salvador, has
lost the perpetual rage that once gripped him; when any number of people
in the region demonstrate what Tom calls an "idiot-savant response," an ability "to recall any information they have ever received" (69); and when several women, including Tom's wife, suddenly exhibit a strange loss of sexual
inhibition, he knows that something is seriously wrong.

Perhaps the crucial clue, though, is the change in the speech habits of
these affected people. As Tom notes when he tests the savant-like abilities of
the first two women who seem afflicted by this strange malady, they will respond to any question he asks, no matter how incongruous it is. Neither
objects when Tom asks seemingly irrelevant and obscure factual questions,
such as "what date will Easter fall on next year?" or "Where is Cut-Off,
Louisiana?" (8, 18). Both merely roll their eyes upwards, "as if [they] were
reading a printout," and then provide the information he requests (9). Further, when they speak, they talk in disjointed, almost fragmentary sentences.
As Tom observes, after seeing both women exhibit these and other symptoms, including aggressive sexuality, "The main objective clue so far is language. Neither needs a context to talk or answer. They utter short two-
word sentences. They remind me of the chimp, Lana, who would happily
answer any question any time with a sign or two to get her banana. Both
women will answer a question like Where is Chicago? agreeably and in-

stantly and by consulting, so to speak, their own built-in computer readouts. You wouldn't. You'd want to know why I wanted to know. You'd want to relate the question to your—self" (21–22). Of course, what Tom is getting at is that these women have lost the ability to engage in dialogue—an ability that is, perhaps, the quintessence of what it means to be human. Their utter disregard for "a context to talk or answer" and their lack of concern for any personal connection to the subject in question make dialogue impossible, since both qualities are a prerequisite for dialogue. (In Bakhtin's terms, certainly, both qualities are absolutely necessary for a dialogic interaction. Bakhtin, after all, is not interested in language as an abstract system but in language as it is manifest in "its concrete living totality" [*Dostoevsky* 181]— that is, language as it is used in a specific context to represent the perspective of a specific individual. Stripped of these qualities, Bakhtin suggests, language becomes abstract, lifeless, incapable of participating in dialogue.)

Tom is particularly troubled by this decay in his patients' language facilities because his orientation on the world and on his profession has changed radically since *Love in the Ruins*. We see this shift first in the opening scene of the novel, a consultation with one of his old patients, whom Tom will see for the first time since his release from prison. Mickey LaFaye, a wealthy but bored housewife who used to complain to Tom of a nameless terror that perpetually afflicted her, has been referred to Tom again by another doctor, Bob Comeaux, after Mickey inexplicably went on a rampage, shooting several of her own prize stallions and making sexual overtures to a teenaged stable boy. Mickey's behavior and her odd demeanor during this consultation will be Tom's first sign of the mysterious syndrome that has affected his hometown. But Tom's thoughts, as he waits to see Mickey and reviews their previous interaction, are also the first sign for us that his professional ideology is very different than it was before. As he considers the "terror" to which Mickey is prone, Tom casually remarks, "I seldom give anxious people drugs. If you do, they may feel better for a while, but they'll never find out what the terror is trying to tell them" (6). It is curious, though, that Tom does not remark on the stark change in perspective that these words indicate, because in *Love in the Ruins* he was only too willing to assuage his patients' terrors with artificial means, by exposing them briefly to heavy sodium in his lapsometer. Now, however, Tom does not want to erase a patient's anxieties but to listen to them. He makes this new philosophy even clearer a short time later when, in the process of apologizing for his down-at-the-heels condition (his practice faltered long ago because no one has the time or patience anymore for the long, arduous process of analysis), he explains his core beliefs:

> Old-fashioned shrinks are out of style and generally out of work. We, who like our mentor Dr. Freud believe there is psyche, that it is born to trouble as the sparks fly up, that one gets at it, the root of the trouble, the soul's own secret, by venturing into the heart of darkness, which is to say, by talking and listening, mostly listening, to another troubled human for months, years—we have been mostly superseded by brain engineers, neuropharmacologists, chemists of the synapses. And why not? If one can prescribe a chemical and overnight turn a haunted little soul into a bustling little body, why take on such a quixotic quest as pursuing the secret of one's very self? (13)

It can be argued, of course, that the change in perspective indicated by this ironic yet quietly impassioned statement of belief is too radical, too abrupt a step in Tom More's evolution from one novel to another. In *Pilgrim in the Ruins,* Tolson writes, "Signs of slippage... abound in *The Thanatos Syndrome.*" Citing "numerous errors and inconsistencies of chronology and geography," first identified by John Edward Hardy in *The Fiction of Walker Percy,* Tolson argues that the delicate balance "between the moralist and the artist in Percy" was upset by the explicit moral concerns of *The Thanatos Syndrome* (452–53). No doubt there is something to this contention. Tom More's beliefs as a psychiatrist clearly have changed because Percy needed them to change to convey certain ethical and philosophical convictions. Tom's newfound orientation is not a consequence of his prison stay, because the unpopularity of traditional analysis first drove him to sell drugs. Nor is there anything at the end of *Love in the Ruins* to hint at the direction Tom's medical ethos will take when Percy returns to the character approximately fifteen years later. All Tom can think about, when he considers his professional future at the end of the earlier novel, is perfecting his lapsometer. "Some day a man will walk into my office as ghost or beast or ghost-beast and walk out as a man," Tom predicts in the epilogue to *Love in the Ruins,* and though he defines a man in religious terms, as a "sovereign wanderer, lordly exile, worker and waiter and watcher" (*LR* 383), it is clear that this miraculous transformation will not come about as the result of rigorous analysis or a sudden embrace of Christian faith but rather through the swift and effective intervention of Tom's finally perfected lapsometer.

Yet even if Tom's transformation from—in his terms—one of the "brain engineers" to an "old-fashioned shrink" is forced, fairness demands that we also acknowledge how effectively Percy conveys the deeply humane quality of Tom's orientation in *The Thanatos Syndrome*. There is a winning humility to Tom's description of the psychoanalytic process in the passage quoted above, a quiet optimism about human nature that borders on religiosity (though its nascent spiritual quality is cloaked—loosely—in the rubric of science). Most of all, perhaps, Tom's affirmation of the psychoanalytic process is convincing because his convictions are thoroughly consistent with the most abiding values of Percy's fiction. When Tom explains his belief that "one gets at it, the root of the trouble, the soul's own secret, by venturing into the heart of darkness, which is to say, by talking and listening, mostly listening, to another troubled human for months, years," he also maps the tortuous journey that all of Percy's protagonists make. For it is through a kind of dialogue that is often structured like a psychoanalytic encounter— one thinks, for example, of Will's colloquies with Sutter in *The Last Gentleman* or Percival's quiet interrogation of Lancelot—that Percy's characters discover their souls' own secrets. For this reason, perhaps, we are willing to accept Tom's intellectual metamorphosis in *The Thanatos Syndrome*. His belief in the healing power of dialogue seems like nothing more than an overt articulation of the principles that have animated his creator's fiction for more than a quarter of a century.

That belief, though, is the legacy of many of Tom's teachers in *The Thanatos Syndrome*. In contrast to *Love in the Ruins,* where Tom's grand desire to close the spiritual fault line that underlay the whole of Western civilization rendered him deaf to any voices but the demons of his own ambition, here Tom's convictions are the product of many influences: his self-proclaimed "mentor" Freud; to a lesser degree, Freud's one-time disciple Carl Jung (whom Tom says "turned out to be something of a nut, the source of all manner of occult nonsense"); and, most of all, the great American psychiatrist Harry Stack Sullivan (13, 67). Unlike Freud and Jung, whom Tom could only encounter secondhand, through their writings, Sullivan was a personal acquaintance who directed Tom's residency in psychiatry at Columbia. Or, at least, so Tom claims. By tracing the ostensible chronology of *Love in the Ruins* and *The Thanatos Syndrome,* Hardy (227–28) concludes that Tom's probable birth date of 1938 would make it impossible for him to have done his residency under Sullivan, who died in 1949. No doubt this inconsistency is another example of how the moralist in Percy ignored such niceties in pursuit of his themes, for Percy clearly wanted Sullivan's humanistic approach, which Tom describes as the source of his "psychiatric faith" (16), to overshadow the more austere rigor of Freud's science. As a result, Tom, who alludes to Freud's and Jung's ideas in a general way, quotes Sullivan directly when he recalls the simple yet fervently held belief that Sullivan repeated often to his residents: "Each patient this side of psychosis, and even some psychotics, has the means of obtaining what he needs, she needs, with a little help from you" (16). To Tom, this idea is tantamount to a spiritual truth; he calls it "the pearl of great price, the treasure buried in a field" (16). And by allowing Sullivan's voice to still echo in Tom's consciousness, Percy implicitly privileges Sullivan's perspective in the intellectual microdialogue that shapes Tom's professional orientation in *The Thanatos Syndrome*.

Of course, Percy does so precisely because he means for the vaguely religious quality of Sullivan's views to resonate with Tom. It is no accident that Tom credits his "psychiatric faith" to Sullivan or that Tom uses a specifically religious metaphor, "the pearl of great price," to describe Sullivan's core belief. Such expressions tacitly acknowledge that the sense of human possibility that Sullivan insists on is itself consonant with the Judeo-Christian view of humanity as "wayfarers." And though Tom claims that "I haven't given religion two thoughts . . . for years," it is clear from these references and other remarks that appear intermittently in his narrative that his consciousness has been shaped, in some measure at least, by the Catholic faith that he seemed on the verge of reaffirming at the conclusion of *Love in the Ruins* (46). Indeed, in *The Thanatos Syndrome,* Tom again uses religious and metaphysical terms in connection with this vocation—though now that language is not undercut by any misplaced faith in the power of technology. When, for example, he casually explains that the German word Freud used to connote the psyche, *seele,* can be translated as "soul," Tom's subsequent remark that Freud also "spent his life pretending there was no such thing" as the soul is inadvertently revealing (16). In much the same way, when Tom refers to himself—repeatedly—as a physician or doctor "of the soul" (16, 88), we cannot ignore the implications of the terms that he chooses to describe his work. Tom clearly possesses a lingering faith that Sullivan's influence nurtured, that is a residue of Tom's experiences in *Love in the Ruins,* and that, later in the novel, his interaction with Father Simon Rinaldo Smith will bring to fruition. For in the larger moral drama of *The Thanatos Syndrome,* Percy explicitly counterposes this tentative faith against the brutally pragmatic aims of the men who are behind the strange goings-on in Feliciana Parish. If their work, as we will see, methodically tramples on the most fundamental rights of the individual, then Tom's faith—psychiatric and otherwise—will champion the ability of individuals to achieve their own redemption (with perhaps a little help from one's analyst or priest).

The bulk of *The Thanatos Syndrome* details Tom's efforts to discover the cause of the strange behavior that he sees in those around him. He is aided in his quest by several people, particularly Lucy Lipscomb. With her help, he ultimately discovers a complex, quasi-legal conspiracy to bring about a massive form of social engineering by contaminating the local water supply with heavy sodium from a nearby nuclear reactor. The heavy sodium affects the cortex of the human brain and eliminates such all-too-human traits as "anxiety, depression, stress, insomnia, suicidal tendencies, chemical dependence" (180). As Tom explains to Lucy, "Think of it as a regression from a stressful human existence to a peaceable animal existence" (180). And as a result of this regression, Tom's old patients have lost their familiar terrors and, on a larger scale, many social ills in Feliciana Parish are all but eliminated. Violent crime, suicide, drug abuse, even teenage pregnancy are drastically reduced.

But the almost utopian results of this experiment, which is named Project Blue Boy by its authors, are shadowed by a darker side. For some of Blue Boy's subjects go wild when they demonstrate a more extreme form of the behavioral pattern that Tom in *Love in the Ruins* called "angelism-bestialism." Because exposure to heavy sodium dissipates the anxiety that restricts human behavior, its victims may act on their whims without restraint. As Tom tells Lucy, "Theoretically, the pharmacological effect of Na-24 [heavy sodium] on some cortices should produce cases of pure angelism-bestialism; that is, people who either consider themselves above conscience and the law or don't care" (180). This is why Mickey LaFaye shot several of her prize thoroughbreds. It may also be connected to hints of child abuse at a private school run by John Van Dorn, the enigmatic millionaire genius who is the guiding force behind Blue Boy.

These disturbing side effects do not ultimately motivate Tom's resistance to Blue Boy (though his efforts to expose the pedophiles at Van Dorn's academy are the most dramatic part of the novel). Rather, Tom objects to Blue Boy on philosophical grounds. Because he believes in this novel that his patients' anxieties are not just disorders to be cured but signs of some deeper, more fundamental conflict, he is disturbed by the blank, serene demeanor of the victims of the heavy sodium. We see this phenomenon early in the novel, before he even knows exactly what is going on, as he reviews his first hand-

ful of cases and struggles to articulate his inchoate uneasiness with what he
has observed:

> What's going on? What do they have in common? Are they better or
> worse? Well, better in the sense that they do not have the old symptoms,
> as we shrinks called them, the ancient anxiety, guilt, obsessions, rage
> repressed, sex suppressed. Happy is better than unhappy, right? But—But
> what? They're somehow—diminished. Diminished how?
>
> Well, in language, for one thing. They sound like Gardner's chimps in
> Oklahoma: Mickey like— Donna want— Touch me— Ask them
> anything out of context as you would ask chimp Washoe or chimp Lana:
> Where's stick? and they'll tell you, get it, point it out. Then: Tickle me,
> hug me. Okay, Doc?
>
> Then there's the loss of something. What? A certain sort of self-
> awareness? the old ache of self? (85)

The core idea here is the concept that without their guilts and terrors his
patients are, to use Tom's own cautious language, "diminished." Though he
tries halfheartedly to adhere to simple truths like "Happy is better than unhappy," Tom cannot hide his conviction, even though it is never explicitly
stated, that his patients are somehow better off with their anxieties than
without them. Of course, Tom cannot outwardly admit it—so he expresses
his thoughts here in a broken, halting manner—because to do so would
make a mockery of the healing function of his profession. In a 1988 interview, Percy referred to this idea as "the paradox, the scandal of the book"
(*More Con.* 195). But for Tom, it seems, our anxieties are the condition of
our humanity, and we are "diminished" without them, more like clever animals than humans. Possibly they are even a sign of our spiritual existence;
when Tom first described his orientation as an "old-fashioned shrink," he
distinguished between "a haunted little soul," afflicted with all the fears and
guilts of life, and the "bustling little body" that remains when those anxieties
are artificially eliminated (13). Most important, perhaps, for Tom the particular terrors that beset each of us are also a large part of what makes us individuals. Surely as a result, he refers to one's sense of self as an "ache" in the
passage above; we feel our individuality most strongly, Tom implies, in the
painful struggle that each of us wages to overcome his or her own set of
fears and to reconcile the conflicts that inevitably arise from the distinctive
complexity of our individual pasts. Thus, when Tom's patients no longer feel
this ache, they are diminished again, for they have lost the quality that makes
each of them unique.

For all of Tom's objections to Blue Boy, however, he cannot openly confront the men behind it: Van Dorn, who supplies the project with heavy sodium and acts as a liaison to the Nuclear Regulatory Commission, and Bob Comeaux, who oversees Blue Boy for the National Institute of Health. At the most fundamental level, Tom's dealings with Comeaux are shaped by his power over More, for Comeaux, the director of the Quality of Life Division at Fedville, the government research complex first described in *Love in the Ruins,* has been appointed to supervise Tom's parole. Tom's ability to stay out of prison and to practice depends on Comeaux's approval, and Comeaux himself is none too subtle in reminding More of this situation when Tom's inquiries bring him steadily closer to exposing Blue Boy. But Tom's dealings with Van Dorn are shaped by something even more delicate and troubling: sexual jealousy. An international bridge champion in his spare time, Van Dorn has taken as his partner Tom's wife, Ellen, and Tom has reason to believe that the two played other games together while he was in prison. Indeed, Lucy later offers proof of Ellen's infidelity, telling More that Ellen tested positive for herpes six weeks before his parole.

The instability of Tom's personal life has its greatest effect in his dealings with Comeaux and Van Dorn. Apprehensive of losing his freedom and his livelihood, gnawed at by jealousy, Tom is hesitant and guarded around the other men. Moreover, Comeaux and Van Dorn seem to sense Tom's weakness, the cracks in his resolve, and they try to win him over by appealing to what they must imagine is his certain pride of authorship. For as Comeaux reveals—in an ironic twist that subtly complicates the moral calculus of the novel—Tom's research in *Love in the Ruins* provided the theoretical basis for Blue Boy. Tom's use of heavy sodium in his lapsometer pointed the way for Comeaux and Van Dorn. "You broke the ground," Comeaux tells Tom (189). Or as Van Dorn puts it, Tom will go "down in history as the father of isotope brain pharmacology" (200). (To which Comeaux adds, "So for better or worse, Doctor, it appears you're one of us" [200]. It cannot be an accident, though, that Comeaux's phrasing echoes Ed Barrett's claim in *The Second Coming* only moments before he tried to kill both himself and Will. To be "one of us" in both novels is clearly to embrace Thanatos.) Because of this intellectual debt, both Van Dorn and Comeaux seem to believe that Tom can eventually be recruited for the Blue Boy team. So when Comeaux is confronted by Tom with what he knows a little more than halfway through the novel, Comeaux responds by offering Tom another deal with the devil. He invites Tom to join Project Blue Boy "as senior consultant on the Nuclear Regulatory Commission's Advisory Committee for the Medical

Use of Isotopes" (189). Tom will not only bring the scientific expertise that
first developed the lapsometer but also conduct a sort of group therapy for
the Blue Boy team and help them work through the ethical conundrums
created by their work. As Comeaux explains, suddenly adopting the language of a pop psychology text, "Both my colleagues and I need some dia-
loguing on the subject and we think you could contribute a very creative
input" (194).

Comeaux's invitation is ironic, however, because the way it is couched
only points out the impossibility of any real dialogue between himself and
Tom, despite Comeaux's repeated appeals—both in words and actions—to a
vague sense of professional fellowship. Comeaux's use of language, his self-
conscious appropriation of psychological jargon, is characteristic, for he is
something of an actor himself. As Tom observes at the beginning of the
book, "There is a space between what he is and what he is doing. He is
graceful and conscious of his gracefulness, like an actor" (26). Indeed, Comeaux has reinvented himself entirely over the course of his life, remaking
Robert D'Angelo Como of Long Island into Dr. Robert Comeaux, a Louisiana native of "old-line Delaware Huguenot stock" (99). But because of this
persistent artifice, and because Comeaux fears it will be discovered (as it has
been, by Tom), Comeaux is incapable of sharing his thoughts and feelings
with another in a true dialogue of heart and mind. In a way, Comeaux is a
bit like Binx Bolling at his most artificial (though Comeaux is nowhere near
as inventive and cunning a performer as Binx). Like Binx, Comeaux slips
easily into borrowed words and gestures, whether he is "striving for a standard medical heartiness" to conceal his threat to revoke Tom's medical license or whether, in an effort to ameliorate Tom's opposition to Blue Boy,
Comeaux lapses into a phony idealism (25). "I'm assuming, Tom . . . that we
live by the same lights, share certain basic assumptions and goals," he says,
adopting the lofty, patrician tone of a southern aristocrat like Emily Cutrer
in an effort, no doubt, to appeal to some inherited sense of noblesse oblige
in Tom: "Healing the sick, ministering to the suffering, improving the quality of life for the individual regardless of race, creed, or national origin"
(190).

Of course, Comeaux and Tom do not share "the same lights," and the
ideological divide between them is another obstacle to real dialogue. Even
the words they use mean different things to each of them. When Comeaux,
for example, speaks of "quality of life," Tom thinks of the brutal reality that
that seemingly well-meaning phrase obscures. "Are you still disposing of in-

fants and old people in your Qualitarian Centers?" he asks pointedly when Comeaux tries to recruit him for Blue Boy (199). (Comeaux responds with mock offense, protesting that he is only following recent Supreme Court decisions allowing euthanasia for the elderly and the disabled and designating babies as "neonates" who will acquire legal rights at eighteen months, around the same time they acquire language [199]. This set of decisions is one of the few reminders in *The Thanatos Syndrome* of the broad political satire in *Love in the Ruins*.) At bottom, though, Comeaux and Tom differ most radically on the value of the individual. Where Tom is concerned above all with the individual struggles and dignity of his patients, Comeaux and Van Dorn think only of the general good. In their quest to stamp out the little anxieties of everyday life and the larger social pathologies that infect American culture, they steadfastly refuse to measure their results in anything but faceless statistics, and so they have no concern with individual rights or anything as tenuous and ephemeral as a sense of self. As a result, Comeaux brushes off Tom's accusation—which itself is offered in a decidedly cautious manner as, in Tom's words, a "technicality"—of "assaulting the cortex of the individual without the knowledge or consent of the individual" (193). Instead of responding, Comeaux boasts of a drop in the crime rate and then speaks in sweeping, abstract terms about the need to redirect the course of human evolution. "The hypothesis, Tom," he explains, "is that at least a segment of the human neocortex and of consciousness itself is not only an aberration of evolution but it is also the scourge and curse of life on this earth, the source of wars, insanities, perversions—in short, those very pathologies which are peculiar to *Homo Sapiens*" (195). But, of course, the individual is long since forgotten here, subsumed entirely into the species, as Comeaux retraces the steps of so many of Percy's characters who ascend the ladder of abstraction, raising themselves high above the day-to-day world to which Tom clings so tightly.

In his own way, Van Dorn too invites Tom to "dialogue" with him, beginning early in the book, when he and Tom go fishing together. Van Dorn—who is both subtler and more dangerous than Comeaux—appeals to a kind of fellow feeling based on what he claims is a shared Louisiana heritage. "I'll make you a little confession," he tells Tom. "I think at long last I'm back where I belong. Among my own people. And a way of life" (59). Implicit in this "confession" is the notion that Van Dorn's "own people" include Tom himself. They are two of a kind, Van Dorn seems to say, scientists and technicians who are still rooted in a simpler "way of life." The trouble with this view, however, is that Tom suspects Van Dorn's representation of himself as a southerner. Not only does Van Dorn's accent sound "curiously unplaced"— "like Marlon Brando talking Southern," Tom thinks (57), but Van Dorn also seems hopelessly unaware of the sort of calculated silences that are part of the verbal and gestural language used and understood by More in his exchanges with authentic southerners like Leroy Ledbetter in both *Love in the Ruins* and *The Thanatos Syndrome*. As Tom observes in response to Van Dorn's "confession, "Louisiana fishermen would not dream of speaking of such things, of my own people, of a way of life. If there is such a thing as a Southern way of life, part of it has to do with not speaking of it" (159–60).

Indeed, both Van Dorn and Comeaux come off as latter-day carpetbaggers who attempt to hijack and corrupt southern traditions that they do not really understand. So Van Dorn purchases and restores Belle Ame, an old plantation house, and converts it to an elite private school. But behind the antebellum facade he engages in a very modern horror: the sexual abuse of his students. In a similar way, Comeaux—or Como—exults over the sight of black convicts, stoned on heavy sodium, contentedly picking cotton and singing spirituals like slaves in some Hollywood version of history. Yet this ersatz plantation is as bogus as the borrowed language that Comeaux uses to introduce it to Tom: "There is still grace, style, beauty, manners, civility left in the world. It's not all gone with the wind" (265). Comeaux refuses to acknowledge that the "civility" he celebrates is a product of modern pharmacology, not shared values or even a slave economy. Indeed, as François Pitavy has argued, "Comeaux's vision is in fact ahistorical. He does not dream so much of the antebellum society proper as of the escapist regressive images propounded by revisionist historians in the 1920s and 1930s and, above all (judging by his culture as a self-adopted southerner), of the never-never land of the southern plantation novel, in which the plantation has become the paradigm of that golden age—of paradise lost" (181).

As in so many of Percy's other novels, the struggle to define the southern past, to see it clearly, is an important subtheme of *The Thanatos Syndrome*. Tom is keenly aware of the falsity with which Comeaux and Van Dorn invoke the southern past—Tom calls Belle Ame "as much now the creature of Texaco [which initially funded its restoration] and Hollywood [which filmed several movies there] as King Cotton then" (213)—yet he must also resist a different aspect of southern history when he goes to visit Lucy Lipscomb at her estate, an old plantation called Pantherburn. While he and Lucy drink a considerable amount of bourbon and collect data on Blue Boy at her computer (which is itself an ironic intrusion in the old plantation house), he is pulled ever more into what John F. Desmond calls "the doom-ridden mythos of the old South" (66). For as he learns of both the scope of the heavy sodium contamination and Ellen's infidelity, he is overcome by memories of the sort of "poetic pessimism" that Percy describes as characteristic of the southern aristocracy in "Stoicism in the South" (*SSL* 85).

> I used to come here as a child for Christmas parties and blackberry hunts and later for the dove shoots at the opening of the season every November. It was a famous dove hunt.
>
> The tinkle of spoon against glass was the occasion of a certain kind of talk. The talk was of bad news, even of approaching disaster—what Roosevelt was doing at Yalta, what Truman was doing at Potsdam, what Kennedy was doing at Oxford (Mississippi)—but there was a conviviality and a certain pleasure to be taken in the doom talk. As a child I associated the pleasure of doom with the tinkle of silver against crystal. (160)

Of course, considering the personal and professional chaos in Tom's life at this point in the novel, the attractions of such "doom talk" are easily understood. But Tom also knows that assimilating such "doom talk" in his own microdialogue would lead to the same sort of destruction that befell his ancestor who supported the British in the Revolutionary War. "They, the English Lipscombs, must have spoken exactly the same way, with the same doomed conviviality and the same steady tinkle of silver against crystal, when the Americans came down the river two hundred years ago in 1796," he notes (161).

The "doom talk" that echoes in Tom's head mitigates against action, of course. Those voices tell him that Ellen is lost, that there is nothing he can do to stem the rise of the heavy sodium tide, that he might just as well go jump in a river and drown himself like his ancestor did—or at least drown himself in a bottle of good bourbon. (In this same spirit, when Tom asks Lucy to help him identify the Thanatos syndrome, he says, "you're going to have to tell me whether I'm as crazy as our ancestor" [139].) How is Tom to resist this "doom talk?" In essence, he follows the same path as his creator, who, in the midst of the battles over civil rights that rocked the South many years earlier, rejected the "poetic pessimism" of his stoic heritage that mitigated against action, that insisted that "the day has been lost and lost for good" (*SSL* 85–86), in favor of an empowering faith. And so, Tom too gradually turns to faith—in this case, in the form of his old friend, Father Simon Rinaldo Smith.

At the beginning of *The Thanatos Syndrome,* Tom is called on to treat Father Smith after the priest has secluded himself in a fire tower for three weeks, apparently because of depression.[5] But Tom's treatment of his old friend gradually becomes a kind of therapy for both of them, for their interaction is—alone among all of the various relationships in the novel's tangled plot—dialogic. In contrast to Tom's other exchanges, which are stunted by the effects of heavy sodium on the other or tainted by the bad faith that underlies Comeaux's or Van Dorn's words, only Tom's interaction with Father Smith constitutes a genuine dialogue. Here, each man's words echo in the consciousness of the other, which has a powerful effect on both of them. As Martha Montello writes in "The Diagnostic 'I': Presenting the Case in *The Thanatos Syndrome,*" "In his eight-by-eight foot cell at the top of the fire tower, the priest has stopped eating, sleeping, and talking for want of a real listener, a co-knower of the truth he has to tell. Tom brings him back to the world of others through the act of listening to what is troubling him" (35). Similarly, Father Smith's words make Tom aware of the true nature of the evil that he faces. If Tom identifies the symptoms of the Thanatos syndrome, Father Smith ultimately explains its pathology. And, in the end, the example of the priest's faith subtly gives Tom the strength and conviction to act on what he knows.

Tom is inclined to trust Father Smith, to let the priest's voice resonate in his heart and mind in a way that other voices do not, for several reasons. At the simplest level, Tom empathizes with Father Smith because Tom too has only recently returned to the community after a period of forced withdrawal. While Tom was in prison in Alabama, Father Smith was "almost next door on the Gulf Coast at a place named Hope Haven for impaired priests, mostly drunks" (115). Tom recognizes his own weaknesses in the priest, as does Father Smith in More, and this recognition creates a bond between them that is the ground of a deeper understanding. In the midst of what is called his "confession," when Father Smith most desires Tom's understanding and sympathy, the priest addresses the other as "one alcoholic to another" (243). Tom is also inclined to attend to Father Smith's words because the almost lunatic intensity of his voice contrasts sharply with the glib, self-conscious quality of Comeaux's and Van Dorn's words. Tom repeatedly evokes the force and the singleness of purpose with which Father Smith speaks. At various times, the priest is described as "concentrating terrifically on each word he speaks" (117); as talking "in a low intense voice, pausing between each word" (125); as speaking "in a rapid, dry monotone such as one might use giving a legal deposition, not having much time" (239). In contrast to the skepticism with which Tom receives Comeaux's and Van Dorn's words, he never doubts the conviction that lies behind Father Smith's, no matter how much he may wonder—at first at least—about the priest's sanity.

Tom only gradually begins to perceive the essential truth of what Father Smith relates. Tom's initial instinct, in the first of two long exchanges in the fire tower, is to see the priest's strange behavior as a sign of depression. Indeed, when Father Smith explains his complex theories about how words have been deprived of meaning by some malefic force and how the Jews "are a sign of God's presence which cannot be evacuated," Tom reacts with the same polite skepticism that his colleague and sometime doctor Max Gottlieb had offered to Tom's own theories about the strange behavior of his patients (123). Our only sign that Father Smith's ideas have registered at all in Tom's consciousness is when Tom literally appropriates a memory that the priest had shared with him of a boyhood trip to Germany in the 1930s. After a long night of drinking and computer-aided detective work that culminates in a confused, drunken tryst with Lucy Lipscomb, Tom dreams of hearing the same "high-pitched crystalline sound" (162) of church bells that Father Smith had heard as a boy in Germany. And though Tom does not acknowledge that this sound was first described for him by Father Smith—he only remarks, "I have never been to Germany" (166)—it is obvious that he has listened more closely to the priest's words than he will admit.

In his conversations with Tom, Father Smith ultimately limns the contours of what is for Percy the century of Thanatos, of Freud's death instinct run amok. Through hints, through questions, through obscure allusions, Father Smith warns how the spirit of abstraction that possesses Comeaux and Van Dorn—and that once gripped Tom—leads inevitably "to the gas chamber" (128). After all, Father Smith suggests, if an abstract idea like "quality of life" can be used to justify the deaths of "millions of old useless people, unborn children, born malformed children" in the Qualitarian centers of Fedville and other institutions, then it is only a small step, in his words, to "killing Jews" (127, 128).

Later in the novel, in the second of his conversations with Tom in the fire tower, Father Smith illustrates this idea when he talks about his 1930s trip to Germany, during which he stayed with a distant cousin, Dr. Hans Jäger, a professor of psychiatry at the University of Tübingen. For Father Smith, Dr. Jäger was an admirable and distinguished man. "When I think of him," Father Smith tells Tom, "I think of him as the 'good German' as portrayed in

Hollywood, say, by Maximilian Schell or earlier by Paul Lukas in *Watch on the Rhine*—you know, sensitive, lover of freedom, hater of tyranny, and so on, certainly the courageous foe of the Nazis" (240). Equally admirable were Dr. Jäger's colleagues, who attended a conference at Tübingen during Father Smith's visit. But though the name of the conference has an ominous significance in retrospect—"the Reich Commission for the Scientific Registration of Hereditary and Constitutional Disorders" (245)—Father Smith's impression at the time was of the humane qualities of these psychiatrists. One planned to work with Albert Schweitzer, one was the director of a mental hospital "which had been famous for its humane care of the insane going back to the sixteenth century" (245–46), one was noted "for his work on the social difficulties of children" (246), and so on. In short, these men appeared to be the flower of Western civilization: cultivated, rational, humane. And yet, as Father Smith relates, their passion for ideas, their good intentions for humanity in general, led to murderous results. Though none of them were Nazis, their enthusiasm for a book published before Hitler came to prominence, *The Release of the Destruction of Life Devoid of Value*—which argued for euthanasia for "the genetically unfit [and] the hopelessly ill" (247)—helped create an intellectual climate in which Nazism could flourish. And, ultimately, it also drove them to personally participate in the slaughter of mental patients, retarded children, and others deemed unfit to live. Even kindly Dr. Jäger directed a hospital where mentally ill children were put to death.

For Father Smith, these men are the exemplars of the century of Thanatos. He makes this view clear in a third conversation with Tom after the mystery has been resolved, relating a message that was supposedly conveyed by a vision of the Virgin Mary to a group of children in Yugoslavia.

"Do you know why this century has seen such terrible events happen? The Turks killing two million Armenians, the Holocaust, Hitler killing most of the Jews in Europe, Stalin killing fifteen million Ukrainians, nuclear destruction unleashed, the final war apparently inevitable? It is because God agreed to let the Great Prince Satan have his way with men for a hundred years—this one hundred years, the twentieth century. And he has. How did he do it? No great evil scenes, no demons—he's too smart for that. All he had to do was leave us alone. We did it. Reason warred with faith. Science triumphed. The upshot? One hundred million dead." (365)

This passage, which is surely the novel's most sweeping and explicit statement of Percy's moral theme, announces its challenge to modern values and beliefs like a manifesto nailed to the door of the cathedral of Western rationalism. Indeed, in his last interviews, Percy was only too happy to second Father Smith's words and to emphasize personal differences with the scientific community. In 1986, for example, Percy spoke in scathing terms of "the bad faith of some scientists." "The nihilism of some scientists in the name of ideology or sentimentality and the consequent devaluation of individual human life leads straight to the gas chamber," he declared (*More Con.* 155), echoing his own character and confirming—if there was any doubt—that Father Smith embodies the moralist's voice in *The Thanatos Syndrome*.

But what is the effect on Tom of Father Smith's words, particularly the long story about his trip to Germany that is labeled in the novel as "Father Smith's Confession"? It is difficult to say, for Tom rigorously hides his reactions behind a veil of medical professionalism. He seems to interpret all of Father Smith's words and actions as symptoms of psychological disorder, and even when Tom appeals to the priest for advice on how to respond to Comeaux's offer of a job (and his muted threat to have Tom returned to prison) Tom explains that this is a therapeutic tactic. "Long ago I discovered that the best way to get in touch with withdrawn patients is to ask their help. It is even better if you actually need their help" (233). Indeed, even after Father Smith responds to Tom's uncertainty by telling him of Dr. Jäger and his colleagues—whose murderous devotion to "quality of life" all too closely resembles Comeaux and Van Dorn's—More seems inattentive. His main reaction to Father Smith's story is to wonder if the strange vividness of the priest's memory is a sign of epilepsy or a brain tumor.

Yet Tom cannot help but be affected by the other's words because the most personal aspects of Father Smith's confession loosely parallel Tom's own situation, and, consequently, they reaffirm the channel of understanding between the two men, the dialogic link that enables Tom to dream the priest's memories. To cite the terms that Bakhtin uses when he describes similar moments in Dostoevsky's fiction, Father Smith's tale results in "a deep essential bond or partial coincidence between the borrowed words of one hero and the internal and secret discourse of another hero" (*Dostoevsky* 254). When Father Smith describes his friendship with Dr. Jäger's eighteen-year-old son, Helmut, who had just been admitted to the SS's officer training program, the *Junkerschule,* and who possessed "a serious and absolute dedication" (247) that the young Smith had never seen before; when the priest confesses to Tom that he was so consumed with admiration for Helmut's patriotism that, in Father Smith's words, "If I had been German not American, I would have joined him" (248) we know—and Tom too must realize at some level— that Father Smith has also come to the place where Tom is now, an obscure region where the line between good and evil is blurred. For the temptation that Father Smith experienced as a teenager in Germany echoes Tom's predicament as he considers Comeaux's offer to join the Blue Boy team. Like the boy in Germany decades earlier who could not see the evils of nationalism that lay behind Helmut Jäger's romantic willingness to die for his country, Tom risks losing sight of the fundamental evil of Blue Boy when he weighs what he calls "Bob Comeaux's impressive evidence of social betterment through the action of the additive heavy sodium" (234). Then, too, Tom has practical reasons to accept Comeaux's offer that the young American did not when he yearned to join Helmut Jäger's cherished *Schutzstaffel*. Comeaux's proposal not only guarantees Tom's freedom and his ability to practice but also offers financial security to the perennially impoverished analyst and—with that security—perhaps an opportunity to reclaim his family.

But if Tom stands on the brink of being pulled into an enterprise that violates some of his deepest principles, then the conclusion to Father Smith's story, in which he tells of returning to Germany and liberating the hospital outside of Munich where Dr. Jäger put to death psychologically disturbed children, must be instructive. For it was only then, Father Smith implies, that he began to perceive the reality that lay behind the glamour of Helmut's death's-head insignia and his sword etched with the words *Blut und Ehre*. Only in the fullness of time could the priest appreciate the horror of Dr. Jäger's actions—and, by extension, the whole Nazi regime—for as Father Smith tells More at the end of his confession, "We've got it wrong about horror. It doesn't come naturally but takes some effort" (254).

Of course, Father Smith's story is intended to goad Tom's own sense of horror, yet we cannot be sure of its precise effect because Tom's reactions are so closely guarded. Perhaps he recognizes in the priest's confession of his youthful infatuation with Helmut Jäger's zeal and purposefulness a personal liability to the abstraction and the godlike power of modern science. Perhaps the children who died in Dr. Jäger's hospital as a result of the theories propounded in a scientific text become for Tom reminders of the children at Belle Ame who are victims of Van Dorn's theories of sexual liberation. We cannot say precisely what motivates Tom, but it is clear that something in what the priest says echoes in his consciousness and moves him to action. For after hearing Father Smith's story, More abandons any consideration of Comeaux's offer. If Comeaux's voice and ethos had previously echoed in Tom's mind, if Tom admitted any possibility at all of identifying his own ambitions with Comeaux and Van Dorn's grand dreams of social engineering, it is all over now. For in a limited way, Tom achieves a kind of ideological becoming when he embraces something at least of Father Smith's beliefs and in so doing commits himself irrevocably to opposing Blue Boy. In short order, after Tom leaves the fire tower, he confronts the ring of child molesters and then forces Comeaux to shut down Blue Boy by threatening to reveal its illegal contamination of the water supply and its more disturbing side effects, including the child abuse at Van Dorn's school.

The dialogic encounter between More and Father Smith is clearly the moral center of the novel. But before we turn away from this crucial element in Percy's narrative scheme, we should note one more possible explanation for Tom's subsequent actions: that it is not only what Father Smith says to Tom that moves him but also what he does and what he is. For in spite of Tom's insistence throughout the novel that he has turned his back on religion, his behavior in his interaction with Father Smith reveals an almost unconscious curiosity about the source and endurance of the priest's beliefs. We see this phenomenon first in their initial conversation in the fire tower. As Father Smith goes on about the semiotic meaning of the Jews, Tom suddenly interrupts the priest's discourse, ostensibly in an effort to pry him away from his half-mad obsessions, to ask why he is still a priest (125). In itself, the question seems insignificant, another therapeutic technique perhaps to engage a patient in self-revelation. But when Tom resumes this line of inquiry at the end of their second conversation and asks Father Smith "Why did you become a priest?" it seems less calculated (257). Tom does not suggest any psychiatric purpose to his asking this question, and he even notes that only Father Smith's repeated attempts to provoke the doctor made him "feel free to ask" what he calls "a somewhat personal question" (257). Yet this seemingly unconscious repetition in Tom's behavior is, according to the principles of his own vocation, deeply suggestive. Why does he repeatedly demonstrate a need to ask about the priest's faith? Does Tom's curiosity bespeak a desire in this lapsed Catholic, this determinedly unreligious scientist, to believe? All we know is that after Tom asks this question and hears Father Smith's response—"In the end one must choose [between] [l]ife and death" (257)—Tom acts. Just as Father Smith's faith is embodied in the action of his

performing the sacrament of the Mass—because, as the priest himself suggests, the words of the Mass no longer signify—Tom's truest self finds expression in what he does rather than what he says. And perhaps because he
is empowered in part by a faith that insists on the sanctity of the individual,
Tom responds to Father Smith's belief in the language in which it is most
eloquently expressed, by acting on what Tom knows about the evil that he
faces.

This action occurs most dramatically in a confrontation at Van Dorn's
academy that masterfully and seamlessly shifts from suspense to satire. Aided
by Lucy Lipscomb's Uncle Hugh, a good old boy whose sometimes oafish
demeanor belies his deadly ability with his Colt rifle, and by Vergil Bon, a
quadroon prodigy who is as comfortable in the Louisiana bayous as the
chemical engineering laboratories of LSU (and who, as Hardy has noted, is
surely also the literary descendant of Faulkner's Charles Bon [230]), Tom
rounds up Van Dorn and his cohorts and forces them to drink undiluted
heavy sodium, which causes them to regress to an apelike state. In a short
time, the former pedophiles are seen contentedly grooming one another,
while Van Dorn struts and rages to show his dominance over his tribe. Indeed, in an ironic footnote to the plot, Van Dorn is temporarily confined at
the Tulane Primate Center in the company of a sign language–using gorilla
named Eve. Ever the master manipulator, though, Van Dorn converts punishment to prosperity when he writes a best-selling book about his experiences after he recovers from the heavy sodium and is transferred to a prison.

Yet the intensity of *The Thanatos Syndrome,* which Percy had sustained for
more than three hundred pages, rapidly dissipates after Blue Boy has been
shut down. Though the novel slogs on for another forty pages or so, its conclusion is tired and anticlimactic. In a series of brief, fragmentary chapters,
we see Tom try to reconstruct his broken family. But because neither Ellen
nor his children have been developed much at all over the course of the
novel, it is hard to care about Tom's domestic problems. At best, Percy ren-
ders Tom's home life in a pleasant, workmanlike fashion, but the author saves
his passion for Tom's professional life. And as a consequence, the whole subplot that involves Tom's romantic entanglement with Lucy and his efforts to
win back Ellen fails utterly because neither is a complex or compelling character. At the beginning of the novel, Ellen is a cipher, her personality dulled
by the heavy sodium. Yet this is almost preferable to the way her character is
presented after she has recovered from its effects. At the end of the novel,
Ellen has become a born-again devotee of televangelists, almost fanatical in

her belief and intolerant of Tom's friendship with Father Smith. When Tom occasionally helps the priest perform the Mass—another sign, as Percy remarked, "that Father Smith has gotten to him" (personal communication)— he must hide what he is doing from Ellen.[6] But because Tom's relationship with Father Smith is the most intense and truthful part of his life (certainly in contrast to his marriage), Ellen's opposition to it makes Tom's professed love for her almost baffling. How can he feel so strongly for a woman who understands him so little? At best, Ellen comes off as a kind of dim-witted sex toy—Tom describes her as "a little holy spirit hooked up to a lusty body" (353)—but that characterization does not justify the ostensible depth of his feelings for her. It is no accident, perhaps, that this novel, unlike *Love in the Ruins,* ends in Tom's office rather than his bedroom.

Nor does Lucy come off much better than Ellen. Though she has an important role to play in helping More expose the conspiracy, Percy insists on portraying her as a fundamentally needy woman, endlessly pining after Tom. Throughout the novel, she continually reminds Tom of her desire for him and her wish that he leave Ellen. And when she does finally bed a drunken and virtually helpless Tom, he sees her as "a sweet heavy incubus" (163) whose desirability is also demoniac. As Hardy writes, "The truth is that once Lucy has done her stuff with the computer networks, and examined the children at Belle Ame to determine that some of them have been sexually abused, she has about exhausted her usefulness to Tom, and is quietly retired to the background of his consciousness and of the action" (238).

Judged solely on novelistic terms, *The Thanatos Syndrome* must be regarded as a flawed work. The microdialogue that dominated the language and structure of Percy's earlier works is at best muted, so that the most distinctive quality of Percy's best work is barely in evidence in his last novel. Moreover, the inconsistency in Tom's character development from *Love in the Ruins,* the chronological missteps, and the shallow presentations of many of the secondary characters pull at the fabric of believability and intensity that must envelop a successful narrative. Yet his final novel is, on its own terms, a better book than some of its critics have suggested. At the most basic level, we cannot help but admire the complexity of its plot and Percy's deft use of the conventions of the thriller. Always a master of detail and nuance, he coolly allows the darkness to gather in *The Thanatos Syndrome* through an accumulation of small, seemingly insignificant details. Over the course of the novel, such "small things" as a track of discolored willows, an under-and-over shotgun mounted on the rack of a pickup truck, and Comeaux's subtle violations of certain unspoken rules of medical courtesy all take on an ominous cast. Then, too, Percy allows his mystery to be unraveled in a logical, consistent way. The scene in which Tom and Lucy tap into the mainframe computer at Fedville and trace the geographical distribution of heavy sodium contamination—it hovers over Feliciana Parish like a storm front—is a triumph of narrative ingenuity.

But, ultimately, if we are going to take *The Thanatos Syndrome* for what it most abundantly is, a work of satire and polemic, its achievement is best measured by the acuity of its moral vision. For in the wake of revelations seven years after the publication of *The Thanatos Syndrome* that the U.S. government conducted secret experiments throughout the cold war, exposing countless Americans (primarily from minorities and the working class) to radiation without their consent or knowledge, Percy's depiction of Project Blue Boy seems astonishingly prescient. This historical parallel suggests that *The Thanatos Syndrome* is best appreciated as an artfully disguised jeremiad. And taken on those terms, as a vivid and compelling denunciation of the hubris and dehumanization of modern science, Percy's final novel largely succeeds. Only when Percy abandons his moral theme to chart the half-imagined terrain of Tom's personal life does the novel founder.

The final scene of the novel returns to the situation that initiated the mystery, a consultation between Tom and Mickey LaFaye. At the beginning of the novel, the changes in Mickey—whom Tom had not seen since he went to prison—were his first hint that something was wrong in Feliciana Parish. Once a woman who suffered from a strange, unfocused terror, Mickey was now serene, unreflective; even the recurrent dream that haunted her was forgotten, erased by the heavy sodium in her drinking water. But when she returns to Tom's office at the end of the novel, Mickey's terror has returned. No longer intoxicated by the heavy sodium, she suffers her old anxieties again. And yet, as noted earlier, for Tom such anxiety is not an aberration but the condition of humanity. Moreover, as Tom and Mickey take up their work again on the novel's last pages, once more trying to understand the dream that has troubled her for years, Percy again affirms the simple value of talking and listening, of dialogue. If there is hope for the human community, he seems to suggest, it is only in the interaction between one troubled human and another.

This quiet optimism is a fitting conclusion to the novel. Like all of Percy's other fiction, *The Thanatos Syndrome* ends by suggesting that human life finds its greatest value within an intersubjective relationship. And in many ways, the intimation of a long and potentially transforming dialogue is a fitting conclusion to Percy's fiction as well. For as I have suggested throughout this study, dialogue is both the message and method of his art. At moments like this, Percy's novels tell us again that the only earthly paradise is to be found in the interaction between one troubled soul and another. Yet his artistic representation of dialogue as it is woven into the very fabric of consciousness— more often than not—saves Percy from the simple, monologic didacticism to which a moralist can so easily fall prey. The anguished, anxious quality of his prose, brimming with echoes of voices struggling with one another in a contest for dominance, is his greatest strength. It makes his characters' struggle for faith and meaning in life vivid and concrete. And, at his best, it grounds that struggle in a more complex and ambiguous world than the moralist can represent.

Indeed, it is even possible to see *The Thanatos Syndrome,* like *Lancelot* and *The Second Coming,* as a self-referential depiction of Percy's conflicting allegiances to his moral concerns and his art. For when the all-too-human complexity of his characters is sheared away by the heavy sodium, the resulting husks of human beings—efficient, practical, direct—seem like metaphors for the sort of deliberately two-dimensional characters who are used as representative figures in the moralist's scheme. Ironically, too, Tom's celebration of the soul's own terrors that return when his patients' humanity is restored to them reminds us that a vision rooted in the Judeo-Christian tradition of human beings as wayfarers—a vision that is always the moral center of Percy's work—demands that we see human beings in exactly the sort of way that the satirist cannot represent them: as creatures who are fundamentally unfinished, undetermined, in search of something, and always capable of change.

This fundamentally religious vision is, at bottom, the essential core of Percy's work, and it is embodied in novels that at their best resound with an artful dissonance of many different and vivid voices. Percy's ability to give himself over to the voices of his imagination, trusting his characters to speak for themselves and trusting also that the truth—or at least his truth—will out, is the key to his achievement as a novelist. Like all great writers, of course, his ability to work at such levels is inconsistent; Percy continually struggled throughout the body of his fiction to resist the dominance of the moralist's voice. Yet Percy more often than not won that struggle. For at his best the form of his fiction achieves the freedom and the possibility on which the hard-won faith of both author and characters insists. And at such moments, ironically, when his work speaks in a polyphony of voices, Percy's faith and his art are as one.

Notes

ONE. A QUALITY OF CONSCIOUSNESS: WALKER PERCY'S DIALOGIC ART

1. I am not the first critic to recognize the potential of Bakhtin's ideas to help us understand the distinctive qualities of Percy's fiction. Robert H. Brinkmeyer Jr.'s 1987 article, "Walker Percy's *Lancelot:* Discovery through Dialogue," was the first explicitly Bakhtinian reading of Percy's fiction. However, many other critics have noted the dialogic qualities of Percy's fiction, even if they have not used Bakhtinian terms to describe those qualities. As early as 1969, for instance, in Lewis A. Lawson's seminal essay "Walker Percy's Indirect Communications," Lawson's description of the bond between Binx Bolling and Kate Cutrer at the end of *The Moviegoer*—"they literally depend upon the recognition of themselves they see in each other's eyes for their feeling of authenticity"—strongly suggests the kind of interaction that is essential to Bakhtin's concept of dialogue (Lawson, *Following* 22–23). Indeed, given the parallels between Bakhtin's ideas and Gabriel Marcel's concept of intersubjectivity, many critics, writing about intersubjectivity, have pointed toward the Bakhtinian qualities of Percy's fiction. When Gary Ciuba, for example, writes in *Walker Percy: Books of Revelation* that "consciousness, for Percy, depends on a knowing with, a dialogue of heart, mind, and soul" (135), his assertion explicitly acknowledges the dialogic quality of Percy's fiction.

2. In *Lost in the Cosmos,* Percy modifies this terminology. Citing what he calls "an almost intractable confusion about the terms *sign* and *symbol,*" Percy chooses in this work "to use the word *signal* for the former and, following Saussure, the word *sign* for the latter" (87). However, to maintain consistency in this book with Percy's earlier nonfiction and with the quotations I have selected from those works, I will retain Percy's earlier terminology.

3. Percy's interpretation and use of the word *consciousness* is strikingly similar to a crucial word in Bakhtin's critical vocabulary: the Russian word *sobytie* (event). In describing the dialogic quality of Dostoevsky's fiction, Bakhtin describes Dostoevsky's evocation of "a *plurality of consciousnesses, with equal rights and each with its own world,* [that] combine but are not merged in the unity of the event" (*Dostoevsky* 6).

As Caryl Emerson explains, though, in a footnote to her translation of Bakhtin's *Problems of Dostoevsky's Poetics,* the root of *sobytie* is *bytie* (existence or being). Thus, Emerson reasons, *sobytie* in Bakhtin's work "can be read both in its ordinary meaning of 'event,' and in a more literal rendering as 'co-existing, co-being, shared existence or being *with* another.' An event can occur only among interacting consciousnesses; there can be no isolated or solipsistic events" (6).

4. See Howland for a fuller discussion of Percy's debt to Marcel.

5. This reading of Bakhtin, particularly its emphasis on the intellectual continuity of his work, relies in a large measure on the understanding of Bakhtin's life and achievement that is offered by Clark and Holquist in their biography of Bakhtin. To be sure, however, there are alternate interpretations of Bakhtin that offer different visions of his career and his achievements. Most notably, Gary Saul Morson and Caryl Emerson's comprehensive work, *Mikhail Bakhtin: Creation of a Prosaics,* argues that Bakhtin's "intellectual development displays a diversity of insights that cannot be easily integrated or accurately described in terms of a single overriding concern" (1). In place of Clark and Holquist's emphasis on the struggle between centripetal and centrifugal forces as the overarching subject of all Bakhtin's work, Morson and Emerson suggest that Bakhtin's various interests can be organized loosely around three "global concepts" (10): "prosaics," a term of their own that connotes both Bakhtin's interest in the art of prose and his convictions regarding the deep significance of "the everyday, the ordinary, the 'prosaic' ";"unfinalizability," Bakhtin's insistence on the fundamental openness and freedom of life; and "dialogue," that constant state of interaction with others and the world around us that for Bakhtin defines the condition of our existence (15).

Ultimately, however, while there are important distinctions between Clark and Holquist's and Morson and Emerson's approaches to Bakhtin, there are also fundamental areas of agreement, particularly in each book's emphasis on the centrality of dialogue and a kind of essential open-endedness in Bakhtin's ideas. Perhaps only the narrative obligations of Clark and Holquist's intellectual biography require an understanding of Bakhtin that emphasizes the continuity and development of his life and thought. In any case, it seems fitting that Bakhtin, the great apostle of unfinalizability, should in the end escape the totalizing vision of any particular scholar's interpretation.

6. In *Walker Percy: Books of Revelation,* Ciuba's study of the apocalyptic theme in Percy's fiction, these intersubjective relationships are themselves the signs of renewal—and renewed vision—on which apocalyptic literature insists. As Ciuba writes, "The newly discovered communion amounts to a change in consciousness so that the cosmos is seen anew in its perpetual freshness" (20).

7. In writing of the distinctions between Percy and Sartre in her essay "*Lancelot* and Walker Percy's Dispute with Sartre over Ontology," Kathleen Scullin notes, "For Sartre, the self, alone and empty, can sustain itself only by seizing the freedom to create a self out of its own nothingness. Other persons constitute a threat to that

self-creation. For Percy, the self is rooted in connectedness with others and sustained in celebrating that connectedness" (110).

TWO. OUT OF THE EVENING LAND: *THE MOVIEGOER*

1. Perhaps the best single discussion of Binx's—and Percy's—stoic legacy can be found in Lawson's essay "*The Moviegoer* and the Stoic Heritage," included in his collection *Following Percy*.

2. The suicide of the father is a constant specter in his fiction. As William Rodney Allen argues in *Walker Percy: A Southern Wayfarer*, all of Percy's protagonists have "a secret, psychic wound: a weak, even suicidal father" (5). Though I disagree with Allen's contention that this theme is "the *sine qua non* of all Percy's novels" (131), its recurrence indicates its profound importance in the psychological landscape of Percy's fiction.

3. In *The Sovereign Wayfarer*, Martin Luschei defines "everydayness" as "a generalized loss of awareness that walls a person off from his surroundings and diminishes his vitality. It is connected with routine and the anonymity of people in the mass, and it results in numbness and anxiety" (21).

4. Edward Dupuy suggests that this state of being between possibilities is a fundamental characteristic of all Percy's work and thought—as well as one of the motivating factors in the deliberate repetition of autobiographical writing. As Dupuy writes in *Autobiography in Walker Percy*, "the gap between the signifier and the signified must remain so that the self will not flee the dread of its unformulability and objectify itself. The only name that can place the self in this age—*homo viator*—places it paradoxically 'nowhere,' between the transcendence of art and science and the immanence of consumerism. From this interesting place, the signless *autos* retrieves possibilities in the hope of beginning again in the openness of repetition, in the space of the sign itself" (63–64).

5. As Percy suggests in a prefatory statement to the novel, Binx reacts here not to Holden the man but to Holden's persona: "When movie stars are mentioned it is not the person of the actor which is meant but the character he projects upon the screen" (9).

6. Percy often comments throughout his writings on the way that the stylized presentation of people and events in movies and television seems so much smoother and more accomplished than in reality. As Tom More observes in *The Thanatos Syndrome*, "Failure is what people do ninety-nine percent of the time. Even in the movies: ninety-nine outtakes for one print. But in the movies they don't show the failures. What you see are the takes that work. So it looks as if every action, even going crazy, is carried off in a proper, rounded-off way" (75).

7. Luschei's reference to Kate as "a cripple" (110) is fairly typical of the way she is seen in much of the criticism of *The Moviegoer*.

8. Much has been written about Percy's use of existentialist ideas. For a further

discussion of Percy's use of these terms from Kierkegaard, see the work of Luschei, Lawson—notably "Walker Percy's Indirect Communications," in *Following Percy*—and Coles.

9. In *Still Following Percy,* Lawson argues that "maternal loss"—as it is expressed in a scene like this—is one of the central themes of Percy's life and work (xi).

10. In *Walker Percy: A Southern Wayfarer* (36–37), Allen identifies Sam as the first in a series of figures modeled on Hemingway in Percy's fiction. According to Allen, all these figures are designed to illustrate the failure of Hemingway's particular brand of stoicism.

11. As Lawson explains in a note to "Moviegoing in *The Moviegoer,*" Rory Calhoun was alleged to have committed adultery with seventy-nine different women by the time his wife, actress Lita Baron, divorced him (42).

THREE. WHITE MAN'S BURDEN: *THE LAST GENTLEMAN*

1. Various accounts of this episode can be found in Lewis Baker's *The Percys of Mississippi;* in Jay Tolson's biography, *Pilgrim in the Ruins;* and, most comprehensively, in Bertram Wyatt-Brown's *The House of Percy.* As Wyatt-Brown demonstrates, LeRoy Percy's defeat was sweeping and total. Vardaman not only "carried all but five of Mississippi's seventy-nine counties," but his followers "were swept into all the other state offices too" (190).

2. Will is referred to at various times as the "engineer," the "boy" (in flashbacks), and the "young man," often in combination with different adjectives or even strings of adjectives—such as the "courteous and puissant engineer" (106).

3. In a brief prefatory note to the novel, Percy explains that many of the locations in the book "have been deliberately scrambled" (2). Thus, though the university in the novel is set in Alabama, it is patterned after Ole Miss, as the riot itself is based on the turmoil surrounding Meredith's arrival.

4. By contrast, Kieran Quinlan in *Walker Percy: The Last Catholic Novelist* sees this scene as ineffective: "If Percy's intention was to show power of the Christian proclamation to the unconverted, then it is doubtful that the final scene of Jamie's death succeeds in this: the uncommitted onlooker is likely to be suspicious of a conversion that has been dubiously effected at the last moment from a person who showed little previous aspiration toward such a belief. . . . In other words, the Catholic theology that is required to undergird this scene demands a prior belief in its efficacy, and the fiction thus fails for those who still remain 'outside'" (116).

5. In a 1971 interview, Percy says, "although he is a skeptic, in a way an unbeliever, Sutter was aware of exactly what was going on [in the baptism scene]. He was aware of the importance of it. And Will Barrett was not. All Will Barrett was aware of was that Sutter was aware of the importance of it" (*Con.* 42).

6. In "Narrative Triangulation in *The Last Gentleman,*" Simone Vauthier sees the

novel as "the story of [Will's] acceptance of himself as a subject through the free use of his name" (80).

7. Perhaps the most explicit formulation of this idea occurs in Percy's early essay "The Man on the Train," when he notes that the man on the train reading a novel about alienation is less alienated than the man sitting next to him reading a detective novel or nothing at all. As Percy explains, "the reading commuter rejoices in the speakability of his alienation and in the new triple alliance of himself, the alienated character, and the author" (*MB* 83).

FOUR. THE MORALIST'S VOICE: *LOVE IN THE RUINS* AND *LANCELOT*

1. In "On the Porch with Marcus Aurelius: Walker Percy's Stoicism," Jan Nordby Gretlund argues for a more balanced view of southern stoicism in Percy's fiction: "What Percy shows us about his ethical Stoic heritage is not that there is something wrong with it but that Stoicism is not enough. He does not reject his inherited Stoicism, but he warns of its limits" (83).

2. In "The Double Bondage of Racism in Walker Percy's Fiction," Michael Pearson takes a different view. He argues that throughout Percy's fiction, "the racial issue and the spiritual dilemma are very much linked" (481). In *Love in the Ruins* and other works, "Percy, like Flannery O'Connor, sees social, political, and spiritual issues as inextricably linked. In the white world, it is men like Tom More or Will Barrett, striving to reappropriate self, who will serve the cause of racial equality. It is only in finding self that one can recognize the individuality and importance of the other" (Pearson 494–95). This is no doubt an accurate reading of Percy's hopes and intentions, and yet, for all of Tom More's claims of healing his friends' and neighbors' broken selves, the only time in *Love in the Ruins* that Tom actively considers an explicit link between spiritual pathology and racial injustice is, as we will see, in a brief scene with his friend Leroy Ledbetter.

3. Both John Zeugner in "Walker Percy and Gabriel Marcel: The Castaway and the Wayfarer" and Ciuba in *Walker Percy: Books of Revelation* single out this scene as being particularly effective. As Ciuba writes, "Percy finds more dramatic significance in the social implications of Tom's stepping an ambiguous foot too far into the Little Napoleon with Victor Charles than in all the exact and abundant details of Tom's many journeys by foot, his stealthy attempt to surprise the sniper in the pro shop of the clubhouse, or his ingenious escape from Saint Michael's" (135).

4. Zeugner makes a similar claim when he asserts, "The really written parts of *Love in the Ruins,* as versus the merely recited parts, all concern the clash of manners" (205).

5. Percy originally conceived Lancelot's listener as actively responding to all that he heard. As Percy explained in a 1977 interview, "I wrote the book in several versions, and none of them worked. I had two complete characters, long conversations between

them. But as soon as the priest opened his mouth it was no damn good. Maybe it's because religious language is shot, just *defunct,* you know. The trick was to make the priest real without saying anything, to make his silence operable" (*Con.* 156).

6. Several of Percy's critics have commented on the way that Lancelot and his visitor parallel each other. Vauthier, for example, describes Lancelot's visitor as his "alter ego" ("Story" 42). Howland writes that "each man provides a mirror in which the other may come to see himself" (87). In "Walker Percy's *Lancelot*," Brinkmeyer sees Percival as a reflection of "that inner part of [Lancelot] that does not coincide with [the] hardened self-image" that dominates Lancelot's monologue (39).

7. Of course, the name *Percival* suggests an autobiographical link between character and author, and indeed Percival's faith clearly parallels Percy's own deeply felt Catholicism. But as Lawson makes clear in "The Fall of the House of Lamar," both Percival and Lancelot can be seen as versions of their creator (243). That phenomenon is suggested early in the novel, when Lancelot describes their respective families: "The men in my family (until my father) were gregarious, politically active (anti-Long), and violent. The men in your family tended toward depression and early suicide" (15). These comments echo the Percys' prominence in Mississippi politics, the heroism of Percy's great-grandfather in the Civil War, and the suicides of Percy's grandfather and father.

8. Of course, Robert Merlin's name adds one more layer to the structure of Arthurian allusions that underpins the novel. Robert Merlin is as much a sorcerer as his namesake, creating illusions through the magic of film. But where Lancelot's insistence on calling his listener *Percival* stems from his need to impose a particular interpretation on his actions, Robert Merlin's name derives from Percy's desire to create a structure of mythic allusions. In contrast to the reasons within the text for calling Lancelot's listener *Percival,* Merlin's name is either an extraordinary coincidence or a self-consciously literary device.

9. The willfully mundane quality of Percival's intentions parallels what Morson and Emerson see as Bakhtin's celebration of "the everyday, the ordinary, the 'prosaic'" (15). Indeed, throughout Percy's fiction, his characters often choose similar courses of action, from Binx's decision at the end of *The Moviegoer* to "listen to people, see how they stick themselves into the world, hand them along a ways in their dark journey and be handed along," to Father Smith's advice to Tom in *Love in the Ruins* to focus on "doing our jobs, you being a better doctor, I being a better priest, showing a bit of ordinary kindness to people" (*MG* 233; *LR* 399). The ethical component in these choices echoes what Morson and Emerson suggest is Bakhtin's vision of "a moral wisdom derived from living rightly moment to moment and attending carefully to the irreducible particularities of each case" (25).

10. In "Walker Percy: The Novelist as Moralist," Ashley Brown makes a similar point. In *Lancelot,* he argues, "Walker Percy the satirist has arrived at another stage with this book—the satirist himself (Lancelot) is satirized" (175).

FIVE. BRAVE NEW WORLD: *THE SECOND COMING*
AND *THE THANOTOS SYNDROME*

1. For variations on this theme, see the interviews with Ashley Brown, Carlton Cremeens, Charles T. Bunting, John C. Carr, and Barbara King in Lawson and Victor Kramer, eds., *Conversations with Walker Percy.*

2. It was in the same interview that Percy uncharacteristically acknowledged Faulkner's work as "the backdrop" of Percy's own, claiming Binx Bolling as his version of "Quentin Compson who didn't commit suicide" (*Con.* 300).

3. As Doreen Fowler suggests, however, in "Answers and Ambiguity in *The Second Coming,*" Percy's happy ending is not necessarily as clear-cut as it seems: "He advocates commitment to society, but the society he pictures is an inferno of sordid passions and discontent. Of all the characters in *The Second Coming* only the two main ones and Father Weatherbee, who is tacked on like an afterthought at the end, are spared from caricature. All the rest, the society members with whom Will and Allison mean to live and work, are lampooned.... Can Will and Allison 'achieve their lives' attending PTA meetings with people like these? One is strongly disposed to think not" (118).

4. Like *Love in the Ruins, The Thanatos Syndrome* is set in the near future. In *The Fiction of Walker Percy,* Hardy estimates the time of *The Thanatos Syndrome* to be the "middle to late 1990s," though he notes that many of the futuristic qualities of *Love in the Ruins* are missing here (226). "One of the curiosities of this novel as 'futuristic fiction,'" Hardy writes, "is that the culture it represents, both in social and technological and scientific developments, seems in some respects less rather than more advanced than the one in *Love in the Ruins*" (228). Tom More's world is less fragmented politically, as Hardy points out; gone too are the sleek bubble-top cars of *Love in the Ruins* and the vines that sprouted ominously through the masonry. One possible explanation of this inconsistency is that, as Percy told Kim Heron of the *New York Times* in an interview following the publication of the novel, "I made a point of not rereading *Love in the Ruins* while I was writing *The Thanatos Syndrome*" (22).

5. In a 1988 interview, Percy compared Father Smith to St. Simon Stylites, who sat on top of a column for twenty years as "an act of penance to escape the sinful world,... which admittedly is a little odd" (*More Con.* 196).

6. Indeed, there are many signs in the final pages of the novel that Father Smith's influence on More is growing. Not only does More help perform the Mass, but he finds himself echoing the priest's ideas on the devaluation of language. "Why am I beginning to think like Father Smith?" More wonders (339).

Bibliography

Allen, William Rodney. *Walker Percy: A Southern Wayfarer.* Jackson: UP of Mississippi, 1986.

Baker, Lewis. *The Percys of Mississippi: Politics and Literature in the New South.* Baton Rouge: Louisiana State UP, 1983.

Bakhtin, M. M. "Discourse in the Novel." *The Dialogic Imagination.* Trans. Caryl Emerson and Michael Holquist. Ed. Michael Holquist. Austin: U of Texas P, 1981. 259–422.

———. *Problems of Dostoevsky's Poetics.* Trans. and ed. Caryl Emerson. Minneapolis: U of Minnesota P, 1984.

Blair, John. "To Attend to One's Own Soul: Walker Percy and the Southern Cultural Tradition." *Mississippi Quarterly* 46.1 (1992–93): 77–89.

Bloom, Harold, ed. Introduction. Bloom, *Walker Percy* 1–7.

———. *Walker Percy.* New York: Chelsea House, 1986.

Bosworth, Sheila. "Women in the Fiction of Walker Percy." *Louisiana Literature* 10.2 (1993): 76–85.

Brinkmeyer, Robert H., Jr. "Walker Percy's *Lancelot:* Discovery through Dialogue." *Renascence* 40.1 (1987): 30–42.

Brooks, Cleanth. "The Southernness of Walker Percy." *South Carolina Review* 13.2 (1981): 34–38.

Broughton, Panthea Reid, ed. *The Art of Walker Percy: Stratagems for Being.* Baton Rouge: Louisiana State UP, 1979.

———. "Gentlemen and Fornicators: *The Last Gentleman* and a Bisected Reality." Broughton, *Art of Walker Percy* 96–114.

Brown, Ashley. "Walker Percy: The Novelist as Moralist." Gretlund and Westarp 169–76.

Ciuba, Gary M. *Walker Percy: Books of Revelations.* Athens: U of Georgia P, 1991.

Clark, Katerina, and Michael Holquist. *Mikhail Bakhtin.* Cambridge: Belknap-Harvard UP, 1984.

Coles, Robert. *Walker Percy: An American Search.* Boston: Little, Brown, 1978.

Crowley, J. Donald, and Sue Mitchell Crowley, eds. *Critical Essays on Walker Percy.* Boston: G. K. Hall, 1989.

Desmond, John F. "Disjunctions of Time: Myth and History in *The Thanatos Syndrome.*" *New Orleans Review* 16.4 (1989): 63–71.

Dowie, William J. "*Lancelot* and the Search for Sin." Broughton, *Art of Walker Percy* 245–59.

————. "Walker Percy: Sensualist-Thinker." *Novel* 6 (1972): 52–65.

Dupuy, Edward J. *Autobiography in Walker Percy: Repetition, Recovery, and Redemption.* Baton Rouge: Louisiana State UP, 1996.

Fowler, Doreen. "Answers and Ambiguity in Percy's *The Second Coming.* Bloom, *Walker Percy* 115–24.

Godshalk, William Leigh. "*Love in the Ruins:* Thomas More's Distorted Vision." Broughton, *Art of Walker Percy* 137–56.

Gretlund, Jan Nordby. "On the Porch with Marcus Aurelius: Walker Percy's Stoicism." Gretlund and Westarp 74–83.

Gretlund, Jan Nordby, and Karl-Heinz Westarp, eds. *Walker Percy: Novelist and Philosopher.* Jackson: UP of Mississippi, 1991.

Gwynn, Frederick L., and Joseph L. Blotner, eds. *Faulkner in the University.* New York: Vintage, 1959.

Hardy, John Edward. *The Fiction of Walker Percy.* Urbana: U of Illinois P, 1987.

Heron, Kim. "Technological Hubris." *New York Times Book Review* 5 April 1987: 22.

Holquist, Michael. Introduction. *The Dialogic Imagination.* By M. M. Bakhtin. Austin: U of Texas P, 1981. xv–xxxiv.

Howland, Mary Deems. *The Gift of the Other: Gabriel Marcel's Concept of Intersubjectivity in Walker Percy's Novels.* Pittsburgh: Duquesne UP, 1990.

James, Henry. "The Art of Fiction." *The Future of the Novel.* Ed. Leon Edel. New York: Vintage, 1956. 3–27.

Kazin, Alfred. "The Pilgrimage of Walker Percy." *Harper's Magazine* June 1971: 81–86.

Kennedy, J. Gerald. "The Semiotics of Memory: Suicide in *The Second Coming.*" Crowley and Crowley 208–25.

Lawson, Lewis A. "The Fall of the House of Lamar." Broughton, *Art of Walker Percy* 219–44.

————. *Following Percy: Essays on Walker Percy's Work.* Troy: Whitston, 1988.

————. *Still Following Percy.* Jackson: UP of Mississippi, 1996.

Lawson, Lewis A., and Victor Kramer, eds. *Conversations with Walker Percy.* Jackson: UP of Mississippi, 1985.

————. *More Conversations with Walker Percy.* Jackson: UP of Mississippi, 1993.

LeClair, Thomas. "Walker Percy's Devil." Broughton, *Art of Walker Percy* 158–69.

Luschei, Martin. *The Sovereign Wayfarer: Walker Percy's Diagnosis of the Malaise.* Baton Rouge: Louisiana State UP, 1972.

Montello, Martha. "The Diagnostic 'I': Presenting the Case in *The Thanatos Syndrome*." *New Orleans Review* 16.4 (1989): 32–36.

Morson, Gary Saul, and Caryl Emerson. *Mikhail Bakhtin: Creation of a Prosaics*. Stanford: Stanford UP, 1990.

Oates, Joyce Carol. "*Lancelot*." Bloom, *Walker Percy* 63–68.

Pearson, Michael. "The Double Bondage of Racism in Walker Percy's Fiction." *Mississippi Quarterly* 41.4 (1988): 479–95.

Percy, Walker. *Lancelot*. New York: Farrar, Straus, and Giroux, 1977.

———. *The Last Gentleman*. New York: Farrar, Straus, and Giroux, 1966.

———. *Lost in the Cosmos: The Last Self-Help Book*. New York: Farrar, Straus, and Giroux, 1983.

———. *Love in the Ruins: The Adventures of a Bad Catholic at a Time Near the End of the World*. New York: Farrar, Straus, and Giroux, 1971.

———. *The Message in the Bottle: How Queer Man Is, How Queer Language Is, and What One Has to Do with the Other*. 1975. New York: Farrar, Straus, and Giroux, 1980.

———. *The Moviegoer*. New York: Knopf, 1961.

———. *The Second Coming*. New York: Farrar, Straus, and Giroux, 1980.

———. *Signposts in a Strange Land*. Ed. Patrick Samway. New York: Farrar, Straus, and Giroux, 1991.

———. *The Thanatos Syndrome*. New York: Farrar, Straus, and Giroux, 1987.

Percy, William Alexander. *Lanterns on the Levee*. New York: Knopf, 1941.

Pindell, Richard. "Basking in the Eye of the Storm: The Esthetics of Loss in Walker Percy's *The Moviegoer*." Crowley and Crowley 103–14.

Pitavy, François. "Walker Percy's Brave New World: *The Thanatos Syndrome*." Gretlund and Westarp 177–88.

Quinlan, Kieran. *Walker Percy: The Last Catholic Novelist*. Baton Rouge: Louisiana State UP, 1996.

Samway, Patrick, S.J. *Walker Percy: A Life*. New York: Farrar, Straus, and Giroux, 1997.

Scullin, Kathleen. "*Lancelot* and Walker Percy's Dispute with Sartre over Ontology." Gretlund and Westarp 110–18.

Telotte, J. P. "A Symbolic Structure for Walker Percy's Fiction." Crowley and Crowley 171–84.

Tolson, Jay, ed. *The Correspondence of Shelby Foote and Walker Percy*. New York: Norton, 1997.

———. *Pilgrim in the Ruins: A Life of Walker Percy*. New York: Simon and Schuster, 1992.

Van Cleave, Jim. "Versions of Percy." *Southern Review* 6 (1970): 990–1010.

Vauthier, Simone. "Narrative Triangulation in *The Last Gentleman*." Broughton, *Art of Walker Percy* 69–95.

———. "Story, Story-Teller and Listener: Notes on *Lancelot*." *South Carolina Review* 13.2 (1981): 39–54.

Wyatt-Brown, Bertram. *The House of Percy: Honor, Melancholy, and Imagination in a Southern Family.* New York: Oxford UP, 1994.

———. *Southern Honor: Ethics and Behavior in the Old South.* New York: Oxford UP, 1982.

Zeugner, John F. "Walker Percy and Gabriel Marcel: The Castaway and the Wayfarer." *Mississippi Quarterly* 28 (1974–75): 21–53.

Index

DATE DUE
